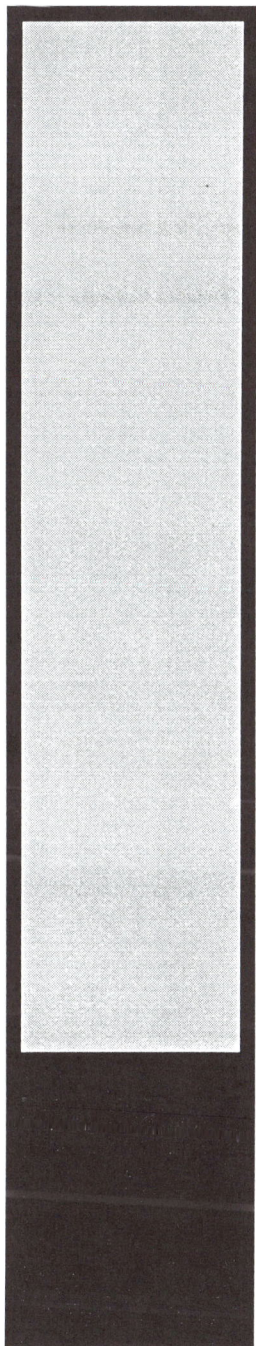

How to Automate Your Computer Center:

Achieving Unattended

Operations

How to Automate Your Computer Center:

Achieving Unattended Operations

Howard W. Miller

QED Information Sciences, Inc.
Wellesley, Massachusetts

© 1990 by QED Information Sciences, Inc.
P.O. Box 82-181
Wellesley, MA 02181

Library of Congress Catalog Number: 89-24229
International Standard Book Number: 0-89435-318-7

Printed in the United States of America
90 91 92 10 9 8 7 6 5 4 3 2 1

Library of Congress Cataloging-in-Publication Data

Miller, Howard W. (Howard Wilbert), 1943-
  How to automate your computer center: achieving unattended operations.

  Includes bibliographical references.
  1. Electronic data processing departments — Automation.
I. Title.
QA76.M554   1990   004'.0285   89-24229
ISBN 0-89435-318-7

Table of Contents

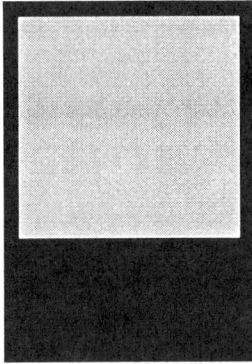

Preface

Over the last decade, I have automated two different computer centers. The first automation project was for a food service company. Using different techniques, I accelerated the development of on-line database software applications while simultaneously reducing maintenance support but was finding it difficult to maintain momentum with additional staff.

If each new application system required only 10% of the original investment in labor to support and maintain, and assuming level staffing, all my staff would be consumed by software support before I increased my application software 8-fold. The problem was simple. As new systems were installed, I was expanding the amount of software that needed to be maintained. Since additional staffing was not available, it was becoming increasingly difficult to keep labor dedicated to development.

Food service companies are notorious for controlling expenses on head count and one day I realized that by automating the computer center, I had a ready pool of labor. I could redirect manpower that was eliminated through computer center automation back into software development. When the automation was complete, the retailer had a

15 MIPS class IBM mainframe computer, operating twenty-four hours a day, seven days a week with a staff of eight. The center operated with one operator per twelve hour shift or five operators. It had two people on the day shift, a scheduler and a utility person, and one management person. A total of eight people to operate a 15 MIPS class computer center. Had the computer center been able to eliminate tape processing, it could have operated without operators, or *unattended computer center operation*. Furthermore, my service levels had improved and the number of program ABENDS decreased.

Computer centers are just beginning to recognize that unattended computer center operation is achievable. The *dark room* or *peopleless* computer center is still the rare exception but the direction is clear, to provide a self-service, utility type environment for computer users. Business is dependent on computer centers; brown outs, interruptions and manual intervention are unacceptable methods of operation. Yet, computer centers have allowed themselves to lag behind in the process of automation; they have not insisted on automating themselves. This is changing — unattended operation has arrived.

Computer centers have been automating for a long time. What this automation process has lacked is a target. Recently, the industry has established a target: *dark room* operation, *lights-out* operation, computer center automation or unattended computer center operation.

The objective of unattended computer center operation is quality. One of the significant obstacles to the expansion of information technology is a lack of confidence on the part of computer center users, organizational management and even computer center staff, that the technology can work. They do not believe that the computer center will be available when it is needed or that response time will be adequate to complete the work. What has developed is a fundamental lack of confidence that information technology in general, and that computer centers specifically, can meet their expectations. Computer centers have a quality problem.

Computer centers are so complex that it is not possible to inspect quality into the services provided. The solution to is to build quality into the center by systematically identifying and then permanently eliminating the fault points. Elimination of fault points is the definition of unattended computer center operation.

Achieving unattended computer center operation is accomplished by marketing the quality concept to management, staff and end user alike. Unattended computer center operation is achieved by systematically removing obstacles, by designing new application systems to accommodate this direction, and by putting pressure on hardware and software vendors to create designs for unattended operation.

The obstacles to achieving unattended computer center operation are both human and technical. The human obstacles are the most diabolical because they are difficult to detect and even harder to correct. Many computer centers do not recognize that unattended computer center operation is both possible and desirable. Where the recognition of possibility is absent, so is opportunity. Second, there are those computer center professionals who do not believe that it is possible or desirable to achieve unattended computer center operation. This, of course, is a self-fulfilling prophecy.

Computer vendors who offer mid-range or departmental computers provide a computer environment that runs unattended. As a result, management is beginning to realize that unattended computer operation is possible. It is the mid-range or departmental computer that is the computer center's real competition.

The second obstacle is technical. Although it appears more formidable on the surface, it is actually far less severe. The most significant technical obstacle is tape usage. Although there is no simple, inexpensive replacement alternative to tape, there are ways to significantly reduce the use of tape, to automate the manual handling of tape cartridges and to eventually eliminate its use.

Solutions for other technical obstacles, such as computer scheduling, operator interaction with the computer, and hard-copy report distribution are available. In some cases, they do not provide a complete solution, but the inadequacies can be solved or skirted. This article focuses on the only real technical obstacle — the elimination of tape.

The benefits of unattended operation are immense; improved quality of service, increased flexibility, increased productivity and improved quality of life. Although quality and service are the objective of unattended computer center operation, they also have the additional benefit of translating into improved cost efficiency.

This book serves as a practical guide to implementing unattended computer center operation. It is based on the experience of a practitioner who believes unattended computer operation is achievable with the tools that are available. It identifies requirements, prerequisites and vendors. The book is divided into four sections: The Unattended Direction, Eliminating Manual Functions, Automating The Computer Center and Obstacles To Achieving Unattended Computer Center Operation.

The first four chapters are dedicated to defining the direction (planning, strategy, and implementation). The first chapter is a primer on unattended computer center operation. It defines the concept of unattended computer operation and identifies an implementation strategy based on value added data handling, self-service computing and computer center automation techniques. The chapter identifies the obstacles that must be overcome and the benefits that are derived from success.

Chapter two emphasizes that the single biggest obstacle inhibiting the rapid expansion of information technology is poor quality. Information technology professionals are not able to provide high-quality low cost computing in support of application systems. The problems associated with computer center quality, the eight dimensions of quality and the the fourteen steps to implementing computer center quality are discussed. This is a background chapter that sets the stage for the concept of quality in an unattended computer center.

The third chapter outlines the methods for implementing unattended computer center operation. This chapter features quality as the objective of unattended computer center operation and goes on to outline strategies for implementing quality. It identifies where to build quality and what to look for in computer center automation products. Finally, it lists the steps that are necessary to make it happen.

In chapter four, the author discusses the human side of unattended computer center operation. Computer center automation is central to unattended operation and this book discusses the human element at great length. Successful implementation depends heavily on the human aspect of unattended operation. The computer center staff needs to have a sense of security; they need to feel that they will benefit from the process. The computer center user needs to understand that quality and service will improve and that they are the benefactor. Management must see it as a self-funding project which enhances the ability to implement technology. These are some of the human challenges discussed in this chapter.

The next six chapters cover the elimination of manual computer center functions. Chapter five starts with the manual side of unattended computer center operation. Embedded in the day-to-day operation of the computer center are many manual activities. Some, like data entry and input/output control, are traditional to the computer center, while others, such as help desks, are relatively new functions. In order to achieve full unattended operation, these manual activities need to either be eliminated or automated. Chapter five lists the manual computer functions and discusses how to eliminate, modify or automate each.

Chapter six reviews some of the prerequisites for unattended computer center operation; the functions which need to be in place prior to even starting unattended operation. This chapter discusses data security, physical security, computer center disaster contingency planning and continuous operation. The value of a data security and a physical security exceed the protection value of individual programs or devices. The sense of security that is derived from a fully tested computer center disaster recovery contingency plan is worth the investment of time and monies, and continuous processing furthers the computer center objective of self-service. All of these are worthwhile business objectives and at the same time they are crucial prerequisites to achieving unattended computer center operation.

One of the prerequisites for unattended computer operation is physical and data security. Chapter seven is a detailed approach to assessing a security risk index. This index indicates a numerical scale to measure the areas of computer center security liability. The security assessment isolates high-risk items. The high-risk items are listed out in check-list fashion: the highest risk items are listed first and proceeds down to the lowest risk listed last. Furthermore, the assessment gives the computer center the opportunity to take a fresh look at security precautions and to continually tighten security as the computer user and potential abuser become more familiar with computing practices.

Chapter eight discusses how to eliminate dependency on tape as a data storage media. It uses quality as a bridge into the topic of tape as a labor-intense and error-prone activity. Trends in computer storage and direct access storage are analyzed and a new class of storage is identified: A storage class that provides on-line access with a longer response time. This new class of storage is the logical replacement for the tape media.

Chapter nine accompanies Chapter eight: it discusses electronic vaulting. The requirements for adequate, controlled, off-site storage of critical information is apparent to most every computer center director. Despite the critical nature of this responsibility, little has been done to automate this labor-intense error-prone activity. Chapter nine discusses the options for electronic off-site vaulting of critical information.

Most computer center management only have the opportunity to design a computer center from scratch once or twice in their entire career. Should this opportunity arise, computer center management has the opportunity to create a computer center that best supports the underlying principles of unattended operation. It is an opportunity to introduce automatic hardware and software monitoring equipment, to isolate equipment that does not require human intervention and to recapture space to handle equipment expansion without increasing the size of the computer center.

The next six chapters discuss the high profile aspect of unattended computer center operation — computer center automation. The first chapter of this section is a transition chapter. Unattended computer center operation requires the selection of three primary software packages, four secondary software packages and eight or more support software packages. Since software selection is central to computer center operation, Chapter eleven discusses a method for quantitatively evaluating and selecting purchased software. This chapter discusses the purchased software dilemma and the benefits derived from purchased software. It then goes on to describe a methodology for evaluating and selecting software.

Chapter twelve is an overview of the software automation tools while chapters thirteen through sixteen are an indepth analysis of the three primary computer center automation tools. This chapter emphasizes the secondary software such as data security systems, automated computer system monitor, automated rerun/recovery and automated problem notification. The chapter further addresses the eight support software systems such as on-line data entry, report balancing and control, disk space abend and security and environment monitoring.

Chapter thirteen presents the latest thought on an automated computer job scheduling system. As one of the three primary unattended computer center operation software packages, the computer job scheduler is one of the oldest computer automation tools. It addresses a delinquency in the OS operating system that dates back to 1967. Chapter thirteen discusses benefits and expectations for an automated computer job scheduling system and goes on to define how to establish these expectations. When used in conjunction with Chapter eleven it significantly reduces the labor required to select or reinstall a computer job scheduling system.

Chapter fourteen is titled The Tie That Binds and it discusses automatic console response systems. The title of this chapter is significant. Although the automated console response system is a relatively new product when compared to the scheduler, it has the potential for tieing together many different products which previously required human intervention. In the same way, as Chapter thirteen, this chapter discusses attribute, benefits and expectations and goes on to define how to establish these expectations. Again, when used in conjunction with Chapter eleven it significantly reduces the labor required to select an automatic console response system.

The automated operator does not reduce a lot of human intervention in the computer center but it is a unique opportunity to pull together a number of different automation techniques into an automated computer center management package. It performs the reactive functions of a console operator while creating an opportunity to do the active management functions that were never performed or performed poorly. Chapter fifteen describes how to go beyond automating the console, it describes how to exploit the console automation software.

Chapter sixteen explores the concept of electronic report distribution. Electronic report distribution is a bridge to have computer users think in terms of information rather than reports. By presenting reports electronically, the problems related to the timely production and distribution of reports are overcome. More importantly, it accustoms computer users to viewing information electronically and moves the computer user toward data query and away from large hard-copy reports. This chapter discusses requirements, selection, justification and benefits. When used in conjunction with Chapter eleven it significantly reduces the labor required to select an electronic report distribution system.

The last three chapters put unattended computer center operation into perspective. They discuss how to overcome the obstacles to unattended computer center operation by addressing many of the common questions, by giving tips on how to proceed and by clarifying the direction that the technology is moving.

The concept of unattended computer center operation is fraught with many misunderstandings. The seventeenth chapter addresses these misunderstandings by giving a concise, frank reply to the 50 most frequently asked questions about unattended computer center operation. The discussion centers on understanding the concept and objectives of unattended computer center operation and answers such questions as why computer centers are moving in this direction and what will happen if they don't. It responds to questions about computer center staffing, such as unions and staff displacement, the impact of unattended operation on computer center users and the perceived obstacles to achieving unattended computer center operation.

If there is any message that this book conveys to the reader, it is that unattended computer center operation is achievable today with the tools that are available today. This book is not an academic exercise, it is based on more than a decade of experience implementing the techniques that are presented. Chapter eighteen follows the idea that: "you can learn things the easy way or you can learn things the hard way: you can learn from other people's mistakes or you make the mistakes yourself." It gives the reader twenty practical tips for achieving unattended computer center operation.

What happens when the computer center is fully automated and all the fault points have been eliminated? Does computer center management turn out the lights and go home or go on to the next computer center? Is the job done? Chapter nineteen addresses the trends in computing and identifies the next frontier for unattended computer center operation as the network of computers. As more and more computers are installed, the total amount of computing is being fragmented across many different computers, both big and small. All the problems associated with operating a mainframe computer are present in the smallest computer. The challenge of the future is to automate the operation of this network of computers in a way that does not compromise the advantages that are gained from installing them. When the computer center is automated the job is not done. A new and exciting challenge starts.

The history of computer center automation is characterized by projects which achieved results that did not meet expectation. Many of the problems can be attributed to a lack of planning and direction. The following statements were published in an article titled, "Maximizing Return On EDP Investments" in the September, 1972 issue of The Journal Of Systems Management. The statements summarize what can all too often happen in computer center automation planning.

> "The process of conceiving, designing, installing, and operating any major data processing system is inherently a difficult, time consuming and frustrating task."

> "A carelessly planned project will take three times longer to complete than expected. A carefully planned project will only take twice as long."

"If anything can go wrong it will . . . if nothing can possibly go wrong it will anyway."

"When things are going well, something will go wrong."

"When things appear to be going better, you have overlooked something."

"Projects progress quickly until they are 90% complete, and then they remain 90% complete forever."

"The system installed will be installed late and won't do what it is supposed to."

"The benefits will be smaller than initially estimated, if estimates were made at all."

"No major computer project is ever installed on time, within budget, with the same staff that started it, nor does the project do what it is supposed to . . . it is highly unlikely that yours is going to be the first."

Although these comments are intended to be humorous, they do reflect what happens all too often in a computer center automation project. They are presented here to emphasize the need to establish direction and for careful planning. I am confident that you will find this book beneficial. Good luck and good planning.

The
Unattended
Direction

Planning for Unattended Computer Center Operation

Chapter 1

INTRODUCTION

The onslaught of new technology, both hardware and software, is making the computer center more complex. Furthermore, this technology is outstripping the computer center's ability to manage using traditional manual techniques. As a result, it is becoming increasingly difficult to provide the quality and service expected by computer center users.

In early computer centers, the manual processes were acceptable. Computer systems were less complex, manual backup procedures were available for computer systems, and computer users were less demanding. However, as the dependence on computer centers increased, so did the demands placed on them. This forced technology to accelerate and, as it did, the manual computer center processes did not keep pace.

Economic variables accentuate the situation. The cost per unit of computer processing is decreasing while the cost of manpower is increasing. There are no industry standards for computer operation and each computer center has it own standards. It is, therefore, difficult to find qualified replacement staff. An experienced operator has limited value when he comes to the door; he usually needs extensive retraining, unlike other professions.

In addition, the available labor force is shrinking and, despite the popularity of computing, fewer high school graduates are expressing an interest in computer operation as a career and not many college graduates enter the profession. The computer center is no longer an avenue into programming and systems careers. Organizations are constantly looking for college graduates to assume these positions. Finally, there is an increasing awareness that each point of human intervention in computer operation is a potential point of failure, a fault point that needs to be eliminated.

The early years of data processing were plagued by a barrage of computer operation problems: Equipment failures, missed schedules, quality problems, lost media and similar problems. The problems were accentuated by the rapid acceptance of computers and the corresponding change in the technology. However, there was no precedence for managing a computer center and, therefore, no model for a solution.

Data processing and general management both recognized that the work produced on the computer is analogous to the production of a manufacturer. The routine processing and output of a computer center took on the name of *production*. The solution to data processing production problems was to structure the department similar to a manufacturing operation. Production and support departments (computer operations, data entry, production schedulers, media library and network management) evolved to operate the computer.

The organization structure succeeded and support functions improved. However, the architecture of data processing did not remain the same. It shifted from central processing to RJE (remote job entry), to on-line processing and it continues to evolve with the introduction of microcomputers, microcomputer networks, small business systems and, most recently, cooperative processing. Data center management techniques have also evolved. Operating systems were improved. Computer center management software, such as tape management systems, production schedulers, restart software, software library management systems, on-line system monitors and change and problem management systems, were introduced.

The complexity of the technology is outstripping the computer center's ability to manage using traditional manual techniques. As a result, there is a movement to reduce and eliminate the human intervention required to operate computer centers; the movement is sometimes referred to as dark room operation, lights-out operation, computer center automation, dim-room operation or as unattended computer center operation. This book consistently uses the term unattended operation for reasons that are defined in more detail later.

Regardless of the name, unattended computer center operation is growing in momentum. For example, SHARE sponsored two conferences held by the Guide International project on Unattended Data Center Operations. The attendance at these Guide sessions on unattended operation, one in July, 1987 in Boston, and the other the two day session in Denver, exceeded 600. AFCOM has sponsored two conferences on computer center automation. Gartner Group is following the progress and there are a number of consulting firms dedicated to assisting companies devise and implement unattended data center operation strategies.

DEFINITION OF UNATTENDED OPERATION

A computer center is defined in the very broadest sense as a computer processing center regardless of computer size or computer vendor. Unattended operation is the total automation of all computer center functions; a dark room environment in which computers run without human intervention.

Unattended operation requires the elimination of traditional and seemingly essential computer center operation functions such as computer operators, data entry, input/output control and media distribution. Furthermore, it calls for the elimination of relatively new functions such as librarians, production coordinators and help desks. Computer professionals already view some of these functions as being on the decline, as is data entry. Other functions are viewed as being on the rise, such as the help desk concept. The concept of unattended operation requires looking beyond solutions for today's problems, to looking at the future requirements of the computer center as capacity expands, availability requirements increase and on-line processing becomes the only mode of processing. In all cases, the objective of unattended computer center operation is improved quality and service.

The computer center needs to take a lesson from the the auto industry. The objective of Detroit was to produce cars at the lowest possible price. They assumed that they had a captive market and as a result sacrificed quality and service. When someone offered improved quality and service at equal or less cost they lost their market. Alternatives, such as personal and the departmental computers, can either expand the computer market or capture the market of the computer center.

Achieving unattended computer center operation requires modification to hardware, operating system software, physical security software, environmental monitoring, processing control, application software, manual functions and even the physical computer center layout. Many, if not all, of these modifications are currently available:

- **Hardware** that operates in an unattended mode.
- **Operating system software** that manages the processing environment in an unattended mode.
- **Physical and data security software** that features interactive problem resolution and notification functions.
- **Environmental monitoring** that features interactive computer center monitoring, problem resolution and reporting.
- **Processing control facilities** that permit processing both batch and on-line work in an unattended mode.
- **Application software systems** that are written for operation in an unattended mode.
- **Supportive manual functions** that are either eliminated or automated.

IMPLEMENTATION STRATEGIES

Implementation of unattended computer center operation is achieved through a five step process. First, define the areas of human intervention. Second, define the directions that are necessary to eliminate them. Third, agree on a method for incorporating the directions into new application software and into all changes to existing application software. Fourth, isolate the directions that are easy to implement, organize into projects and implement. Last, organize a project to complete the process when unattended operation is within easy striking distance.

This five-step strategy targets on immediate return and guarantees the long term compliance with the spirit of unattended operation. Implementation of these strategies requires that both manual and automated aspects of computer center operation be reviewed. Manual functions should be eliminated whenever possible. Automation is required wherever elimination is not achievable. The focal point of all automation is system management software, which replaces the manual intervention of computer center operations personnel.

1. **Manual Functions**

    Any point of human intervention in the computer center operation is a fault point and is subject to scrutiny. The concept of fault points is discussed in great length in later chapters but here it is sufficient to note that some of these fault points are integral to the traditional computer center (computer operators, tape drives, data entry, and report distribution). Other fault points, such as service interruptions to change from on-line to batch processing and vice versa, installing terminal devices and installing software changes, are merely accepted features of computer operations.

    *   *Reduce and Eliminate Operator Intervention*

        Identify all computer center procedures that require computer operator intervention. Divide the results of this evaluation into a) those procedures which are easy to eliminate and b) those which are difficult to eliminate. Further divide the difficult procedures into 1) those which can be resolved with installed software and 2) those which require new software.

        Establish a plan which defers the difficult changes and implement the easy changes. The easy changes provide ample opportunities for reducing operator intervention and, once accomplished, establish a presence and a foundation for proceeding.

Next, determine what new software is required. New software requires a long lead time for selection, installation and implementation; this process needs to be started early. Proper utilization of existing software is also a factor.

Farber/LaChance Consultants have found that in many cases software has been purchased and installed but is neither properly nor fully utilized. With these two plans in place, it is much easier to go back and address the more difficult changes.

Unattended operation is being legitimized by the major hardware and software vendors and new products are being announced. In 1987, Boole and Babbage announced AutoOperator based on a previous offering called System Manager. AutoOperator is designed to detect and correct routine system errors which leaves operators free to handle other activities. IBM is also targeting its NetView offering at this market as is Computer Associates with its CA-OPERA™, and Impact Software with its WTO-MANAGER™. Appendix A lists twenty-one different products just for console automation.

- *Reduce and Eliminate Tape Processing*

  There are a few alternatives for tape today. These include mass storage devices, automatic tape libraries, disk and optical disk. The most promising immediate solutions are the mass storage device and disk. Automatic tape libraries are difficult to cost-justify, and optical disk has yet to receive widespread acceptance.

  However, in recognizing that tape is an obstacle to unattended operation, methods are becoming available to manage and reduce the use of tape prior to installing hardware solutions. Substitute disk media for tape media when and where possible. Evaluate routine disk back-up cycles to determine if it provides the necessary data retention. Eliminate excessive back-ups and ridiculously long retention periods. Remember, there is no such thing as permanent retention. Even though disk back-ups are placed on tape, tape utilization can be improved by placing more data on a single volume of tape. Store tape data on disk and back-up the disk data.

- *Eliminate Data Entry*

  Data entry has become an accepted computer center function but it is more of an end user task. Each person that handles data reduces its reliability and increases its cost. The ideal is to collect data at its source via point of collection machines (electronic cash registers, automated tellers and the like), data collection devices and on-line data entry. Design new computer applications to use these approaches and convert existing applications to these approaches or to user friendly data entry systems that interface directly to computer based systems. Removal of card entry equipment and tape handling is a prerequisite to this process.

  In all cases, dismantle the data entry function and integrate data entry into the skill set of the user staff. A word of caution is in order: the operative word is *integrate*. If the creator of the information continues to transcribe it and passes it to a data entry person, the function is only being relocated; therefore, productivity and reliability gains will not be realized.

- *Continuous Operation*

  Continuous operation accompanies unattended computer center operation. Automatic teller machines, voice response systems and similar devices require continuous operation to be effective. Computer centers need to provide 24 hour on-line system availability. Organizations need to design application software that supports concurrent on-line and batch processing while eliminating cross system dependencies. Computer center management needs to bring pressure to bear on vendors for concurrent processing and database backup, terminal implementation and operating software changes without interrupting computer processing and fault tolerant computer architecture. This technology is both available and technically feasible and can become universally available with sufficient pressure from commercial computer users.

- *Eliminate Print*

Over the last decade, all new computers have been designed for on-line processing. However, computer users have been taught to think of information in report form. This is contrary to the way that data is used and to the direction of the technology. Applications should be designed to provide information on-line. When hard copy is requested, printing should be discouraged, output should be viewed on-line as either a query or a hard copy stored on disk and redirected to a video display terminal. A number of very good report distribution systems are available on the market. Eleven different report distribution packages are listed in Appendix A.

A common guideline for eliminating print is to limit print to exception reports, reports of 10 pages or less. Reports longer than 10 pages are reference documents. Reference documents are documents that cannot be digested by the recipient and are referenced as pieces of information as required. The information contained in reference documents should be viewed on-line. If hard copy is required, encourage printing individual pages via remote printers. The objective is to get out of the print production and distribution business. Remember, it is difficult for a clerk to lose an electronic document.

2. **Automated Functions**

    Achieving unattended operation requires that the power of the computer be used to manage itself. For more than two decades, information technology experts have been applying their skills to managing the business. It is time to do the same for the computer center. This is a classic case of the cobbler's children going without shoes. There are many areas where automation can be applied; the following are some suggested areas.

    • *Automatic Batch Job Scheduler*

        Install a batch job scheduler to manage the routine daily processing schedule. Extend the features of this software to the computer center users providing them with the ability to change the routine schedule or process ad hoc work without computer center intervention. If you are purchasing a small business computer or a turnkey system, make sure this is an integral feature of the operating software.

    • *Operator Response Automation*

        Install software that eliminates all routine computer operator interaction with the computer. Impress upon hardware and software suppliers that console responses are unacceptable. They are labor intensive and error prone. Some such activities have become so ingrained in software that suppliers do not even realize they are designing or perpetuating this kind of activity. Let them know!

    • *Report Distribution*

        Report management and distribution software is available. This software directs reports in an output queue to a disk device rather than to a printer. Once on disk, it can be retained for a predefined period, viewed, and if necessary, printed under the control of the computer user. This is not a substitute for an on-line query but it is an outstanding intermediate step.

* *Security and Environmental Monitoring*

  Security and environmental monitoring devices are available to monitor the vital aspects of the computer center in the absence of computer room staff. Such equipment can recognize failing equipment or intrusions and phone designated staff on an exception basis using voice synthesizers. Furthermore, the devices can be queried by cautious or inquisitive management.

* *Automated Job Restart*

  Automated batch job and on-line transaction restart is crucial to unattended operation. In the automated computer center batch job scheduling and on-line transactions are within the control of end users; reliance on computer center staff for clean-up and restart is unacceptable. Software is available to handle these conditions and new applications should be designed with this as a requirement.

* *Automated System Monitors*

  Interactive computer system monitors provide the computer operator with the ability to interactively monitor the performance of the computer system. Within the software, thresholds are set for computer performance and when exceeded, corrective actions can be taken. This software, when used with an automated console response system, can automatically correct a system imbalance before it impacts on the computer user.

* *Automated Problem Notification*

  Security and environmental monitoring devices are available to monitor the vital aspects of the computer center in the absence of computer room staff. A similar device is available for the computer. Messages are passed to a microcomputer where they are logged and filtered. Messages which require no action are ignored, while those that cannot be satisfied initiate a phone call to on-call support personnel.

* *Disk Space Management*

   One of the alternatives that is becoming more cost-effective as a trade off for tape processing is to substitute disk or Direct Access Storage Devices (DASD) for tape as permanent or temporary storage. As a result of these and other uses, the data stored on disk media is growing at a rate of 30% or more a year. This growth pattern has resulted in the increased use of disk management software to ensure that sufficient disk space is available, that it is used efficiently and that its use is not dependent on human intervention.

* *Tape Management System*

   Unattended operation requires the elimination of tape since this is the most rudimentary of manual functions. Realistically, however, tape will be with us for a long time and tape management software helps to improve reliability and reduce the direct labor associated with the use of this media. Remember, tape management systems make tape labeling or, unnecessary labor, a thing of the past.

* *Tape Dataset Stacking*

   Tape dataset stacking software should be used in concert with tape management software. Many tapes are back-ups used only in exception processing. Furthermore, many of these back-ups use only a fraction of a tape volume. By stacking these kinds of tape datasets, the computer center can reduce the physical handling of tapes, reduce the volume of tape inventories, decrease off site storage costs and improve cost containment. Purchased utilities are available to do tape dataset stacking; an example is TDSU (Tape Data Stacking Utility) from U. S. West, Denver, Colorado.

• *Automate Report Balancing*

Automate the report balancing process. Banks, insurance companies and other companies which process much report balancing and have large staffs to accomplish it are moving in this direction. For the most part, this has been accomplished through in-house developed software but there is at least one purchased software package on the market to accomplish automated report balancing, U/ACR from UNITEC Systems, Inc., Oak Brook, Illinois.

Many different software packages can be used to assist the conversion to unattended computer center operation. Some automate the computer center and some assist the conversion. Other software that can facilitate the conversion to unattended computer center operation includes JCL Scan Utilities, Application Software Library Management Software, Electronic Mail and On-line Data Entry Software. Based on the specific computer center technical environment there can be many such software packages. These packages do not actually automate the computer center; they assist in the conversion to unattended computer center operation.

BENEFITS OF UNATTENDED COMPUTER OPERATION

The primary benefit of unattended computer center operation is consistent, high quality service. Unattended operation eliminates human error by removing human intervention from routine computer center operation. It eliminates recurring error producing situations and improves the reliability of the entire physical plant. Computer service centers are in the service business, and their users expect consistent quality. This is what unattended computer center operation delivers.

However, benefits are not just limited to quality. There is increased flexibility. By standardizing and automating manual functions, unattended operation provides the ability to rapidly adjust to changing business needs. It also improves the ability of the computer center to absorb additional workload with minimal environmental change.

Unattended operation improves productivity by eliminating manual, repetitive functions and by allowing the computer center to emphasize the primary functions of the business, not just in the computer center but also in the user area. Remember, we are doing source data entry and source control, therefore eliminating paperwork, follow-up, control logs and endless meetings. In many cases, the productivity gains in user areas are greater than in the computer center. It is an education medium. It increases the knowledge level of the non-technical staff and, where required, prepares them for an assignment in areas of information technology outside the computer center. Finally, it provides a less stressful and chaotic work environment for the remaining information technology professionals, computer center users and management.

Unattended computer center operation improves cost effectiveness. It reduces personnel expense through head count reduction, through the reduction of benefit expenses and through the elimination of premium pay (overtime, off-shift & holidays). Further, it optimizes the use of the computer hardware by allowing the computer center to use the computer hardware up to its MIPS rating and therefore maximizing resource utilization. Finally, it avoids expenses through improved reliability. Unattended computer center operation focuses on the removal of fault points and therefore reduces software maintenance expense. It eliminates rerun expenses.

Specifically, the benefits can be detailed as follow:

1. **Consistent Quality Service**

    • Improves hardware reliability by using fault tolerant hardware.

    • Eliminates human errors by removing human intervention from routine computer operation functions.

    • Eliminates error producing situations.

2. **Increased Flexibility**

    - Provides the ability to rapidly adjust to changing business needs.

    - Improves the ability of the business to absorb additional workload with minimal environmental change.

3. **Improved Productivity**

    - Eliminates manual repetitive functions.

    - Emphasizes primary functions of the business.

    - Increases technical knowledge.

    - Provides a less stressful and chaotic work environment.

4. **Improved Quality Of Life For Employees**

    - Eliminates the need for off-shift staffing.

    - Permits holidays at home.

    - Eliminates shift rotation.

    - Results in normal business working hours.

5. **Increased Cost Effectiveness**

    - Reduces personnel cost.

    - Eliminates premium pay for:
      - Overtime
      - Off-shift
      - Holidays

    - Optimizes the use of computer hardware by allowing the computer center to use the equipment up to its MIPS rating.

    - Avoids cost through improved reliability.

    - Reduces maintenance expense.

Computer centers are in the service business and unattended operation promotes improved service. The benefits of unattended operation are improved service, flexibility, productivity and quality of life, which translate into dollar saving. Farber/LaChance quote savings from 10% to 20% of operational budget depending on the magnitude of the project.

SUMMARY

Unattended computer center operation is achievable with the technology that is available *today*. It can be achieved by teaching management, computer center staff and computer end users alike that it is possible, by 1) systematically removing obstacles, 2) designing new application systems to accommodate unattended operation and 3) putting pressure on hardware and software vendors to design for unattended operation.

The benefits of unattended operation are immense: Improved quality of service, increased flexibility, increased productivity and improved quality of life. All these benefits are worthwhile in and of themselves but, interestingly enough, they have the additional benefit of translating into improved cost efficiency.

Organizations are just beginning to move toward unattended computer center operation. The *dark room* or *peopleless* data center is the rare exception. The direction of the technology is to provide a utility type operation for computer users. Business is becoming dependent on computer centers; brown outs, interruptions and manual intervention are unacceptable methods of operation. Computer centers have allowed themselves to lag behind in the process of automation; they have not insisted on automating themselves. This is changing — unattended operation has arrived.

Quality and Unattended Computer Center Operation

INTRODUCTION

One of the questions asked most frequently about unattended computer center operation is, Why do we want to remove the people from the data center? This is a very significant question. It communicates a fundamental misunderstanding about the objective of unattended computer operation.

Computer center professionals are being pressured by their management to reduce operating cost and they are focusing on the expense reduction opportunities of unattended computer center operation. From this perspective, staffing is not a large portion of the expense of operating a computer center. Furthermore, the staffing component, as a percentage of the total expense of operating a computer center, is becoming smaller, while conversely, the hardware and software components are becoming an increasingly larger percentage.

The computer professionals who ask, "Why remove the people?" are correct. In most computer centers, the expense of the staff component is in the range of 30%, while the hardware, software and supply components are in the 70% range (see Figure 2.1). Furthermore, when the capacity of the computer center doubles, the number of people required to operate the center does not double. As a result, the cost of hardware and software is increasing at a faster rate than the need for staff to operate the computer centers.

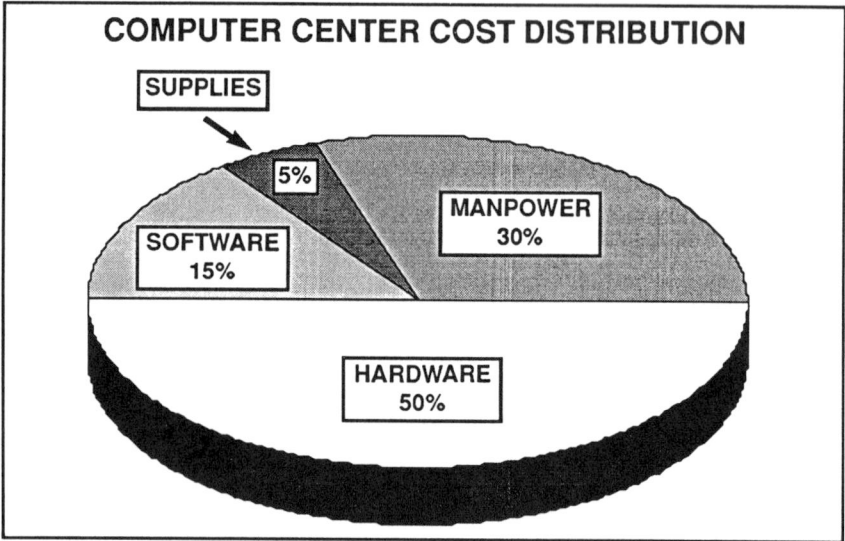

COMPUTER CENTER COST DISTRIBUTION

SUPPLIES
5%
SOFTWARE
15%
MANPOWER
30%
HARDWARE
50%

Figure 2.1. Manpower is only 30% of the total cost while hardware, software, and supplies is 70%. The amount spent on hardware, software, and supplies inreasing at a faster rate than manpower.

However, the objective of unattended computer center operation is not expense reduction. The objective is quality. One of the significant obstacles to the expansion of information technology as a whole, is a lack of confidence on the part of computer center users, organizational management and even the computer center staff who are not convinced that the technology can work. They do not believe that the computer center will be available when it is needed or that response time will be adequate to complete the work. Computer center users have been conditioned to believe in poor computer center quality from years of unacceptable quality, thereby creating a fundamental lack of confidence on the part of key staff that information technology in general, and that computer centers specifically, can meet their expectations.

QUALITY

There are two ways to deliver quality in a product or service. Quality can either be *inspected* into the product or service or quality can be *built* into the product or service. In the first case, the product is produced, and then it is inspected for errors. When errors are detected, the product is reworked to correct the error or errors. If it is not repairable, it is destroyed, and a replacement is produced.

However, when quality is built into the product, the process takes on a different perspective. Here, the product is produced, but the effort is directed at identifying the source of the error. When the source of the error is located, it is permanently corrected. This sounds so basic, but often problems are identified and fixed without any effort expended to isolate the source.

Computer centers are inspecting quality into their products and services. The computer center has been segmented into groups such as help desks, change coordinators, quality control, schedulers, operators, input/output control, production coordinators and even Job Control Language (JCL) specialists. These groups are all acting as inspectors. They are a human bridge, interfacing between the computer center user and the computer. This bridge is either at the front end of the process or at the back end. These groups are either looking for errors when the data is submitted or when the product is produced. Furthermore, they have little or no opportunity to locate and resolve the source of the problem.

Meanwhile, computer centers have become very complex, and there is every reason to believe that they will continue to become increasingly complex. It is not uncommon for a computer center to have a thousand or more terminals, hundreds of concurrent simultaneous users, dozens of concurrent jobs, millions of on-line transactions, billions of bytes of on-line storage, thousands of tapes in its library and millions of lines of print.

The result of this complexity is that there are billions of points of human interface between the user of the computer center and the computer. This translates into billions of potential errors or billions of fault points. Worse yet, these are recurring fault points.

The fact that computer center personnel did one of these manual tasks correct today is no assurance that they will tomorrow. In fact, the computer center can assume that their very best staff will make mistakes.

Therefore, the problem is that computer centers are so complex that it is not possible to inspect quality into the services provided. The solution to this problem is to build quality into the center (see Figure 2.2) by systematically identifying and permanently eliminating the fault points. Elimination of fault points is the very definition of unattended computer center operation.

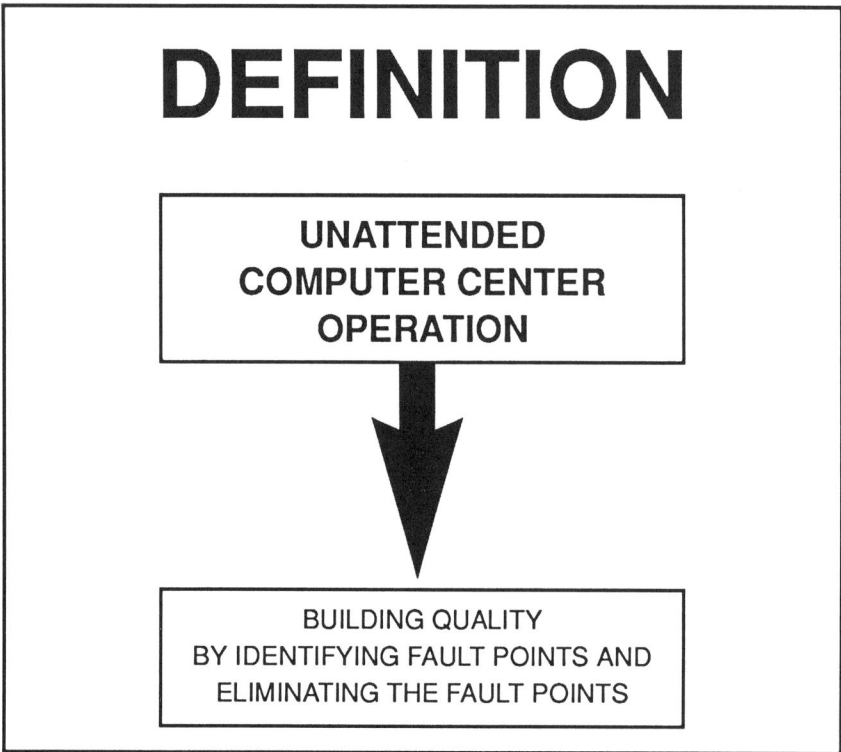

DEFINITION

UNATTENDED
COMPUTER CENTER
OPERATION

BUILDING QUALITY
BY IDENTIFYING FAULT POINTS AND
ELIMINATING THE FAULT POINTS

Figure 2.2. The definition of unattended comptuer center operation is building quality.

IMPLEMENTING QUALITY

There are two ways to implement unattended computer center operation, *lights-out*, and what is call *problems-out*. Lights-out is the process of isolating equipment that does not require intervention and moving it into a dark room or unattended environment. Such equipment would include the central processor, disk drives, communication controller and like equipment. This is not a new concept, large computer centers have been doing this for a long time.

A second approach to lights-out is clustering noncritical computer processing into an unattended lights-out period. In this approach, noncritical processing is clustered into periods such as weekends, holidays or the graveyard shift. During this period, the computer center is then operated without staff. If the computer processing fails, it is left until morning or Monday, and it is corrected and rerun at that time.

Problems-out, on the other hand, is the process of implementing tools and techniques that eliminate or reduce the dependency on human intervention. Its objective is not to black out space or time periods but to implement tools and techniques to reduce the the fault points — the points of human intervention. As the points of human intervention are reduced, the amount of staffing is reduced. Lights-out and problems-out are addressing the same issue in different ways.

Boston University, for example, is implementing a problems-out approach to unattended computer center operation (see Figure 2.3). Since the beginning of 1987, it has implemented tools and techniques that automate or eliminate the manual functions of the Administrative Computing Center. During this period, the capacity of the computing center has doubled: The amount of DASD has increased by 60%, the number of programs executed has increased by 40%, there has been an improvement in service of 50%, the amount of staffing has decreased by more than 60% and the actual cost of running the computer center decreased by 10%. The stated objective of the University is to increase the amount and the service level of work processed while simultaneously decreasing the staffing level to zero.

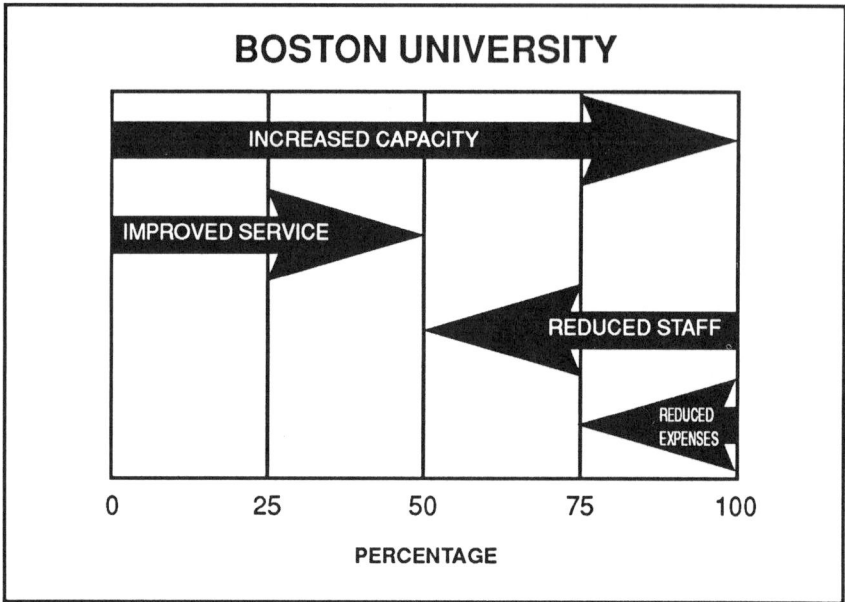

Figure 2.3. Boston University increased capacity, improved service, and simultaneously reduced staff and expenses through unattended operation.

WHAT IS THE PROBLEM?

Operating a computer center is a detailed, intricate and labor-intense activity. The complexity and intricacy is compounded by the conscious effort to improve quality and service through inspection. The effort required to operate a moderate size computer center is equivalent to the effort and meticulous detail expected of monks during the Middle Ages when the Bible and other precious documents were transcribed by hand. The solution to their problem was automation in the form of the printing press, and the solution to the computer center problem is also automation.

Unattended computer center operation requires an understanding of business methods and procedures, and of available technological solutions. The implementer must have analytical, reasoning and interpersonal skills. In addition, implementation requires a high level of precision. If that is not enough, the task is further complicated by several external factors.

Introduction of new functions and procedures. Unattended computer center operation does not automate existing procedures; unattended computer center operation requires the design of new procedures. For example, an on-line batch job scheduling system changes the way in which batch computer jobs are scheduled. It eliminates the need to develop hand written transmittal forms, reduces the labor-intense process of manually checking the status of job, and it provides organizations with a more positive control over its computer processing. It provides departmental management with control information that was previously not obtainable. The automated schedule replaces procedures that were developed and tested over many years of operation, yet the new automated procedures must be developed quickly and work properly the first time.

Involvement of many functional areas. Sophisticated computer centers are almost never developed for a single user. Several departments and sometimes several companies are involved, each with their own requirements and perspective of how those requirements can best be satisfied. A large part of the computer center resources are spent resolving conflicts and negotiating compromises. Getting a group to agree to a new set of procedures is never an easy task, but when it involves sophisticated computer based software, it is a major obstacle.

Computer center size and complexity. There is a dichotomy between the size and complexity of a computer center and the way it impacts the future of an organization. Most organizations operate one or sometimes two very complex computer centers that have evolved to their current status over a long time span. These complex computer centers influence the way in which the organization operates its business, and frequently the direction of the organization changes during the elapsed period of evolution.

Conversely, the computer center evolves through countless small changes, limited in scope and frequently not in concert with the overall direction of the organization. The result is, at any one time, significant portions of the computer center's products and services are not in synchronization with the technical direction of information technology or with organizational objectives.

The size and complexity of the computer center often exceeds the estimates of management and the expectations of the end user. Further, most organizations have already installed the obvious automation tools and all that remains are the large, complex tools that require new and advanced technology.

Changing environment. Computer center automation takes time. A computer center can take from three to five years to automate. During this time, the project is impacted by countless changes: The organizational goals, product development cycles, competitive impact, governmental regulations, as well as computer users being able to see the results of their specifications or gaining insight into the problem. Any of these conditions can alter automation priorities and requirements.

Changes in information technology can make tools obsolete and suppliers to either go out of business, merge or be bought out. The high demand for information technology professionals makes turnover for this type of personnel very likely. Automating the computer center in an environment of shifting requirements, changing economic conditions, changing personnel, and constant improvment in information technology tools is akin to playing Russian roulette with a loaded automatic gun.

Lack of understanding. Because unattended computer center operation is a new concept, it is frequently misunderstood. Management does not understand the impact of designing new procedures for this kind of computer center, the complexity of the implementation process or the changing computer center environment. Computer users do not understand the role of computer center professionals or how to communicate and work with these people. Computer center professionals tend to concentrate on the technology and do not understand the business. In addition, this whole process is exacerbated by the apparent ease with which personal computers, personal computing and departmental computers seem to satisfy user needs.

The Eight Dimensions of Quality

For the last twenty years the information technology industry has focused on techniques for improving productivity of the computer center staff. The result was the introduction of a plethora of tools including schedulers, software libraries, tape management systems, disk management systems, automatic rerun/recovery systems and automatic problem notification systems. Despite these tools, the complexity of the computer center increases and quality and service continues to be elusive.

Compensating for this lack of quality, specialized groups, such as help desks, quality assurance groups, computer center acceptance test groups, data control and distribution functions, were created to inspect quality into the product. The amount of labor dedicated to management and support functions in most information services groups now represents 40 to 60 percent of all information technology staff. As a result, the consensus among information technology professionals is that quality continues to be elusive and computer centers continue to be as difficult to operate as ever.

The solution to the computer center dilemma is to concentrate on quality rather than productivity. The easiest way to improve the productivity is to remove the error from the operation of the computer center. If the software is developed correctly the first time, there is no need for quality assurance functions, and the software support effort goes away.

A November/December, 1987, *Harvard Business Review* article titled Competing on the Eight Dimensions of Quality, by David A. Garvin, discusses the eight dimensions of quality. Understanding and applying the dimensions of quality is essential to improving the quality of the computer center.

Performance. Performance is the primary operating characteristic of a computer center. It covers the diverse aspects of a computer center as the expected response time for on-line systems, the turnaround time for batch-oriented systems, the ability to operate the batch and on-line portions of a system simultaneously, the amount of computer capacity to satisfy peak workload, the ability to meet delivery schedules for critical reporting and the availability of databases for ad hoc type processing.

Some performance standards are based on subjective standards, while other standards are based on the measurable aspects of technology and are, therefore, objective. The importance of performance is in understanding the computer user's expectation. The ability to meet the computer user's expectation for performance is one of the most important aspects of quality. In addition, it tends to be an aspect of computer center operation that continues to be completely ignored and is, therefore, a basic contributor to poor quality.

Features. Similar in nature and closely related to performance are features. Features are the *bells and whistles* of the computer center; they are the functions that are added to the computer center after the basic requirements of operating the computer center are satisfied. They could include ad hoc data query, labor saving functions for low volume activities and the ability to select out information for inclusion into other technologies such as word processing or graphics.

To many users of the computer center, superior quality is not just the ability to meet the day-to-day needs of a software system, but rather, it is the ability of the computer center to satisfy features that were not anticipated or that are the logical extension of the basic requirements of a computer center. Such a feature might be the ability to access the computer center from home during off-shift hours using a personal computer. This feature is not likely to be specified as a requirement for a computer center but could be perceived as a value added feature when the requirement arises.

Employing flexibility, ease of use and other such features in a computer center are aspects of quality and service that tend to grow in importance after the computer center satisfies the day-to-day requirements of the organization.

Reliability. This dimension of the computer center reflects the probability that the computer center will work correctly when required, that response time will be adequate and that the content of the data is correct. The most common measure of reliability for the hardware component of software systems is meantime to failure. Typically, reliability is only a critical aspect of the computer center during the early days of hardware or software installation. During this period, the measure of reliability is the frequency of failure. Frequent failure is a relative measure that tends to create a negative aura that can stay with a computer center long after problems are resolved.

Another measure of reliability is the capability of the computer center to perform during periods of peak demand or after it is subject to enhancement or modification. Failure at these times does not seem to have the lasting impact that it has during the period of initial installation. However, frequent change does seem to be interpreted as a measure of an unreliable computer center, driving computer users to desire a replacement solution to the perceived unreliability. Reliability becomes more important to computer center users when it impacts the organization's ability to meet routine business schedules.

Conformance. Conformance is the most commonly recognized dimension of quality. It is the degree to which the computer center conforms to the requirements of the users. In manufacturing, conformance typically is defined as the ability of the product to satisfy the requirements of the design, while in the computer center, it is conformance to the stated requirements of the computer user.

The subtle difference between stated requirements and design is significant. Requirements for a computer center can be satisfied in many different ways. Some computer centers satisfy the requirements in a less labor-intense manner, with more options for flexibility, or in a manner more responsive to computer user demands than others. The perception of conformance is higher for some computer centers than others although each may meet the specified requirements.

An important aspect of computer center conformance is the question, How does it conform? It is important that computer centers conform not only to the requirements of the computer user, but also that they conform in an acceptable fashion.

Durability. As a measure of the life expectancy for a computer center, durability has not been a particularly important measure of computer center quality. The history of computer centers is short; few systems have lasted for more than five to ten years, and those which have existed have been subject to major technological conversions. The result is that not much importance is attached to durability.

However, as the complexity of the computer center increases and as the cost of solutions such as personal computers and departmental computers decreases, there is increased emphasis on improving the quality, flexibility and serviceability of the computer center. There is a shift to an evolutionary mentality where user requirements are better satisfied by extending the technological life of the computer center through automation. In this environment, durability takes on a new dimension of importance.

Serviceability. As a dimension of quality, serviceability is the ease with which a computer center can be repaired or modified. With manufactured products, consumers are only concerned with serviceability if they perceive a high likelihood that it will require repair. Computer centers are perceived differently. Computer centers are typically perceived as being both unreliable and subject to change by external and internal requirements. Banks need to be able to use Automatic Teller Machines, Electronic Funds Transfer and on-line banking systems. They need to be able to service their environment quickly to maintain their competitive edge.

Serviceability is an ever increasingly significant dimension of computer center quality as new technologies are introduced. Moreover, as the computer center evolves, this aspect of quality takes on more importance. The computer center that is not moving forward is falling behind.

Aesthetics. The last two dimensions of quality, aesthetics and perceived quality, are the most subjective dimensions of computer center quality. Aesthetics is the appearance of the computer center. It means something different to users, management and technicians. To the user, aesthetics is almost always the appearance of display screens or reports, their ease of use, their readability or the continuity of format from one screen/report to the next. To the technician, a beautiful computer center is one that is easy to maintain and does not consume excessive resources.

In computer centers, aesthetics is closely related to serviceability. Since appearance is highly subjective, it is likely to take on or lose significance based on changes in staff. The ability to easily service the computer center can increase or decrease the importance of aesthetics.

Perceived Quality. The complexity of computer centers acts as a barrier to users having an in depth understanding of the performance, features, reliability, conformance, durability and serviceability of the computer center. Over time, computer users develop a perception of the computer center; unfortunately in many cases, it is a negative perception.

If discussed at all, the majority of discussion about a computer center is almost always negative. The discussion addresses the failure of the computer center to satisfy one or more of the dimensions of quality. However, as technicians, users and management alike discuss business with their peers outside the organizations, there is a propensity for the same people to discuss the positive aspects of their computer center operation. If the features discussed by another organization are missing, the negative perception of the organization's computer center is further reinforced.

Perceived quality is a strong driving factor in computer centers. It is not uncommon for organizations to replace hardware, change vendors or disband computer centers because the general perception is that the computer center no longer meets the needs of the organization when it might easily have been modified to satisfy the shortfall. Perceived quality is a diabolical aspect of computer center quality. All of the aspects that make computer center operation difficult also make it easy to develop negative perceptions.

Improving Computer Center Quality

Like most business activities, the effort required to improve computer center quality follows the "80-20" rule, 80% of the improvement comes from 20% of the effort. Therefore, the natural

1.   Create constancy of purpose for improvement of product and service.
2.   Adopt the new philosophy.
3.   Eliminate dependence on inspection to achieve quality.
4.   End the practice of awarding business on the basis of price tag alone. Instead, minimize total cost by working with a single supplier.
5.   Improve constantly and forever every process for planning, production, and service.
6.   Institute training on the job.
7.   Adopt and institute leadership.
8.   Drive out fear.
9.   Break down barriers between staff areas.
10. Eliminate slogans, exhortations, and targets for the work force.
11. Eliminate numerical quotas for the work force and numerical goals for management.
12. Remove barriers that rob people of pride of workmanship. Eliminate the annual rating or merit system.
13. Institute a vigorous program of education and self-improvement for everyone.
14. Put everyone in the company to work to accomplish the transformation.

Figure 2.4. The fourteen points that are Deming's way *out of the crisis.*

question to ask is, Where should the effort be concentrated to maximize the results of quality improvement effort?

The answer to this question is found in an adaptation of the same practices which apply to manufacturing. W. Edwards Deming's fourteen points for improving quality to the computer center is a good starting point (see Figure 2.4).

1. *Establish a constancy of purpose toward computer center quality.* Define to computer center users exactly what you mean by quality in operational terms. Specify standards for computer

center quality to technical support and application development groups for the next year and for the five year period thereafter. Define the computer user whom you are seeking to satisfy. Put resources into hardware and software tools to automate the computer center. Focus on tools that automate the process, and eliminate error creation opportunities.

2. *Adopt the new philosophy.* Computer Center error has become an accepted part of information technology. Software that does not fit the job, hardware that does not perform as specified, technicians that do not know their job, technicians that are resistant to the introduction of new technology, staff that are afraid to suggest new alternatives, and incompetent management that correct and excuse mistakes instead of correcting the cause are not acceptable in the computer center. Computer center management must put resources into this new philosophy, with commitment to ongoing training.

3. *Eliminate dependence on inspection to achieve quality.* Require evidence of quality software regardless of whether it is purchased or manufactured. Inspection does not produce quality. Inspection is too late and is unreliable. When needed, require immediate and permanent corrective action for all software and hardware problems. Institute a rigid program of feedback from computer users with regard to their satisfaction with software on the eight dimensions of quality. Identify the quality evaluation criteria, and communicate it to computer users, staff and suppliers alike.

4. *End the practice of awarding business on the basis of price alone.* Instead, minimize total cost by working with a single supplier or a reduced number of suppliers. Suitable measures of quality require a reduced number of suppliers. The problem is to find a supplier or suppliers that can furnish statistical evidence of quality. Work with suppliers so that they understand the procedures required to achieve the expected level of quality. Take a clear stand that price has no meaning without adequate measure of quality. Without rigorous measures of

quality, organizations drift to the lowest bidder, and low quality and high cost are the inevitable result.

5. *Constantly improve the quality of computer center operation.* Quality improvement is a never ending process. There is no acceptable level of quality; continue to improve quality forever. When evaluating this improvement, look at current and potential competition, and then determine what needs to be done to widen the gap.

6. *Institute training on the job.* Restructure training to rely heavily on in-service training. Rely heavily on the use of tutors. The process of in-service training using tutors reinforces both the tutor's understanding of the expected level of quality in the computer center and defines the responsibilities of the trainee in terms of job expectation. Define all jobs in terms of expectation.

7. *Adopt and institute leadership.* Supervisors need time to help people on the job, and they need to find ways to translate the constancy of purpose to the individual employee. Supervisors should find the source of error. They need information that shows when to take action, not just figures which describe the level of production and the level of errors in the past. Supervisors need to commit time to people who are not meeting expected levels of quality and not on those who are low performers. If the members of a group are meeting quality expectations, there will be some who are low performers and some who are high performers. Teach supervisors how to use the results of surveys of computer users.

8. *Drive out fear.* Break down the distinctions between types of staff within the organization — technical and operations, database and analyst. Discontinue finger pointing. Stop blaming employees for problems of the computer center. Management should be held responsible for faults of the computer center. People need to feel secure to make suggestions. Management must follow through on suggestions. People on

the job cannot work effectively if they dare not offer suggestions for simplification and improvement of the way the computer center operates.

9. *Break down barriers between staff departments.* Start with internal data processing departments, that is, system development, technical services, data base administration, computer center operations and the information center. Learn about the problems in the various departments. One way would be to encourage switches of personnel in related departments.

10. *Eliminate numerical goals, slogans, and posters imploring people to do better.* Instead, display the accomplishments of the management to assist employees to improve their performance. People need to understand what management is doing to make these fourteen points happen.

11. *Eliminate numerical quotas for the work force and numerical goals for management.* Work standards must produce quality, not mere quantity. It is better to take aim at removing errors and defects and to focus on ways to help people do a better job. It is necessary for people to understand the mission of the organization and how their jobs relate to achieving that mission.

12. *Remove barriers that rob people of pride of workmanship.* Eliminate the annual rating or merit system. Institute a feedback system; therefore people will know when they have done well and are assisted when results do not meet expectations.

13. *Institute a vigorous program of education and self-improvement for everyone.* People must be secure about their jobs in the future and must know that acquisition of new skills will facilitate security.

14. *Put everybody in the information technology area to work to accomplish the transformation.* Create a structure in top management that will push the above thirteen points every day. Information technology management may organize a task

force with the authority and obligation to act. This task force will require guidance from an experienced consultant, but the consultant cannot take on obligations that only the management can carry out.

These fourteen points for improving quality are not a solution, but rather they are a formula for hard work. They are a skeleton that needs to be fleshed out with automated tools and techniques, management commitment and in-service training.

SUMMARY

The single biggest obstacle inhibiting the rapid expansion of the computer center and information technology as a whole continues to be the inability to provide quality products and services which meet the expectations of the computer user and which operate flawlessly without human intervention. The obstacles to computer center quality are complex and legitimate and, as a result, little has been done to correct the situation. Therefore, computer centers continue to be manually operated — inspecting quality into their products and services. However, the return on an investment in quality is immense.

The solution requires a belief that quality is achievable, and a commitment to make it happen. If the computer center professional does not accept that flawless computer operation can happen, it will never happen. Furthermore, everyone must understand why quality has to happen. The first step is to address the human side, belief and commitment. It is only through a commitment to quality that productivity can be improved. Make sure that the computer end user, organizational management and, most importantly, the computer center professionals understand why it must happen and that they buy into the process. If necessary, err in favor of over communicating.

Look for the source of error and correct it. Automate as many aspects of the computer center as possible. Transfer as much responsibility as possible for the operation of the software to the user. Every automated tool that reduces human intervention in the computer center eliminates a fault point and improves quality, and every action that reduces the need to communicate specifications from users to computer center professionals, improves quality.

Reinvest the dollars that you save from improved quality back into the hardware and software required to automate the computer center. Reinvest the labor saved back into the process of improving quality. The whole process of improving quality is easier to sell to all involved when it is self-funding. Further, the whole process is an opportunity for in-service training, to develop new techniques and, more importantly, new attitudes. Financial return in terms of improved revenues or decreased expenses will follow.

The whole future of the computer center is bound to the ability of computer center professionals to provide high quality, low cost products and services that meet and exceed the expectations of the computer user. There is nothing mysterious about achieving this goal; it requires a perpetual commitment to identifying and correcting the source of error. The result is a continuous and measurable improvement in quality and productivity.

Implementing Unattended Computer Center Operation

INTRODUCTION

Chapter Two introduced the concepts of *lights-out* and *problems-out* unattended computer center operation. Lights-out is the process of isolating equipment that does not require intervention and moving it into a dark room or unattended environment. In lights-out operation, in Figure 3.1, the computer center can be envisioned as a pie where sections, such as the graveyard shift, weekends and holidays, are darkened by removing slices. Hopefully, when *all* the pieces of the pie are removed, full unattended operation is achieved. Very large data centers have been doing this for a long time.

Problems-out, conversely, is the process of implementing tools and techniques which eliminate or reduce the dependency on human intervention. Its objective is not to black out time periods but to implement tools and techniques to reduce the fault points due to human intervention. As the points of human intervention are reduced, the amount of staffing is reduced. In this case, the computer center can be envisioned as a pie, and rather than removing slices, the size of the pie is reduced in diameter (see Figure 3.2). The emphasis of this chapter is on problems-out.

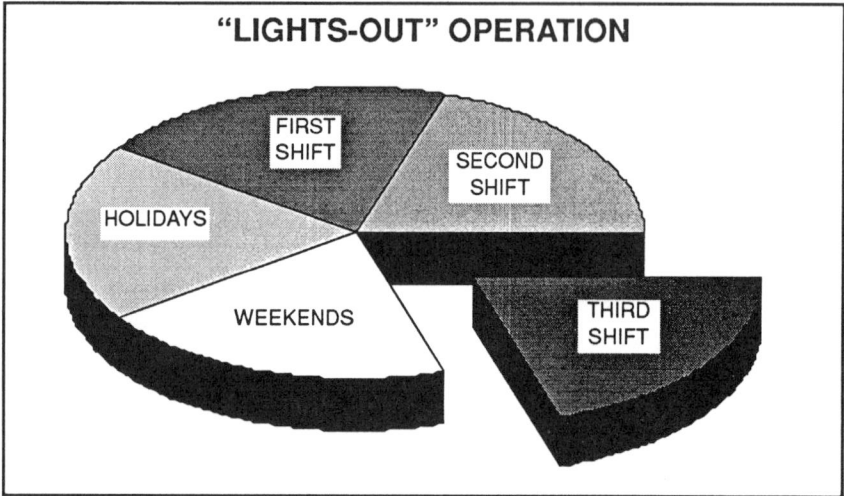

Figure 3.1.   Remove a slice and *darken* the computer room. Unattended operation is achieved when the pie is gone.

Figure 3.2.   Unattended operation is achieved by reducing the size of the pie to nothing, rather than by removing slices.

STRATEGIES FOR ACHIEVING UNATTENDED COMPUTER CENTER OPERATION

The strategies for implementing an unattended computer call for the elimination of the points of human intervention. These strategies include value added data handling, automating all manual data center functions and providing a utility type computing environment.

Value Added Data Handling. Eliminate all the procedural steps which do not add value to the data entered into the computer or produced by the computer. Wherever possible, eliminate the paperwork and bureaucracy associated with computer center interfacing. In most cases, the people that intervene between the data entered into the computer center and produced by the computer center add NO value to the data. They are actually reducing the quality and timeliness of the product.

Automate All Manual Computer Center Functions. Install automated computer center management tools to eliminate the fault points which are created by human intervention between the computer center and its users. Some amount of dialog is required between the computer center and its users for scheduling, report distribution changes, control parameters and similar activities. There is no need for these to be manual.

Provide a Self-Service Environment. Provide a computing environment where users can enter their own data, schedule their processing and control the distribution of their output and so on. Provide an environment where the user has complete control over his or her data from start to finish.

Implementing Unattended Computer Center Strategies

There are many opportunities for implementing these strategies and some of the more significant ones are addressed here. There is no particular relevance to the sequence since the positive impact of accomplishing one versus another differs greatly from one computer center to another. These opportunities are intended as thought provokers and are by no means a comprehensive list.

The first area to look at is automated computer center management tools that automate manual functions and eliminate failures due to human error. These software tools include the following type of software (See Appendix A):

- Electronic report distribution
- Automated console response system
- Automated computer job scheduler
- Automatic report balancing
- Tape management system
- Automated rerun/recovery system
- Security system

For instance, security software is very important. The computer center is returning control of computing priorities to the users, and the computing center needs to have a high level of assurance that they can access their data without impacting someone else. The computer center further needs a high level of assurance that someone is not intentionally accessing information they should not access.

Many of these software tools required to achieve unattended computer center operation are already installed in computer centers. However, the challenge is to change the administration of these products from the computer center to the computer center user. The computer center needs to seek software that can be administered by the computer center while avoiding software that requires dependence upon central computer center administration. These software packages and their attributes are discussed further in future chapters.

Second, introduce quality into the computer center by implementing a physical plant monitoring system: Equipment that recognizes failing computer or ancillary equipment, interruptions to application processing or security breaches and initiates automatic notification of service support staff when automatic recovery is not possible. Some aspects of a physical monitoring system are inexpensive while others are very expensive. Regardless, such monitoring is available, and it is important to assume that it is necessary.

Identify recurring computer center problems, and set up a work plan to eliminate the source of the problem, not the latest occurrence of the problem. Remember, the computer center is establishing creditability, and it needs to focus on the source of error.

Provide an automatic computer job scheduling system — a software system that provides the ability for all users to directly schedule their own work. This includes the ability to schedule ad hoc work and to alter the schedule for routine work. Again, the objective is to remove human intervention between the end user and the computer.

Eliminate control statements from batch jobs, but if elimination is not possible, automate the process for computer user creation and submission. When control statements are required, an edit facility is essential to ensure that the process works correctly the first time. For those computer center users who operate out of remote sites, this may be matter of course, but for others, this could be a monumental task.

Introduce a JCL scan product to ensure that the computer job is correct before it is submitted into the computing environment. It is important to remember that the computer center is establishing its creditability, and if users have the ability to submit jobs, the computer center needs to increase the likelihood of success on the first try.

Eliminate *centralized* data entry functions. It is an obsolete concept, and it makes the transition to real on-line processing more difficult. However, during the interim, make *distributed* data entry the transition to real on-line processing. Provide facilities for direct data entry via an on-line data entry package or by distributing the terminals of a key entry system. On-line processing establishes a dialog with the computer and even greater opportunities for a positive return.

Many computer centers still have a requirement for the batch report balancing. Automate the report balancing and control procedures, and return this function to the user department. User control of report balancing increases the chances of correcting the source of out-of-balance conditions. Automated report balancing improves reliability, eliminates manual procedures and expedites distribution of information.

Tape processing is a major fault point, and although there are replacement media available, such as tape cartridge handling systems and optical disk, tape is likely to be part of computer centers for a long time. Elimination of tape may be difficult to justify at this time, but the dependence on it can be mitigated by reducing the use of tape processing. Computer centers can identify that tape is an obsolete medium, that it is a roadblock to unattended computer center operation, and then consciously reduce its use. When it is used, it will be a conscious deviation from this strategy, and the computer center will be cognizant of the consequences. Seek to reduce this media.

Reduce the need for hard-copy printing at the computing center. Encourage exception printing, remote printers and electronic report distribution systems. These techniques are not an end in themselves but are a bridge to real on-line processing.

Eliminate hard-copy computer operation instructions. It is probably incorrect and out of date. Automated computer center tools need to be self-documenting and manual documentation eliminated. Remember, the objective is not to have anyone in the computer room to read the hard-copy manual documentation.

Install electronic mail and electronic forms authorization. Neither of these tools is integral to the unattended computer operation process, but they do make the transition easier. Electronic communication makes communications easier and quicker during this transition to an automated computer center.

Automate the job turnover process. Installing new jobs into production status is a source of error in most computer centers. Moving programs into the correct libraries, changing JCL and so on are very labor intense and error prone processes.

In summary, the significance of any one idea for implementing unattended computer center operation will vary from computer center to computer center. This list is not intended to be comprehensive; however, the list does represent some very important areas to address.

What to Look for in Computer Center Automation Products

Figure 3.3 shows an analysis of the typical computer center. It reveals that about 25% of the labor required is for managing print, 25% is required for handling tape, 10% for console management and 40% for production control. In order to achieve an unattended computer, each of these needs to be automated. In many cases, automation tools for these areas already exist in the computer center, while in others they will need to be selected.

Where the software is already installed, it not uncommon to modify or replace it in order to achieve the features necessary for unattended computer center operation. For example, a scheduling system may not provide the ability for computer center users to

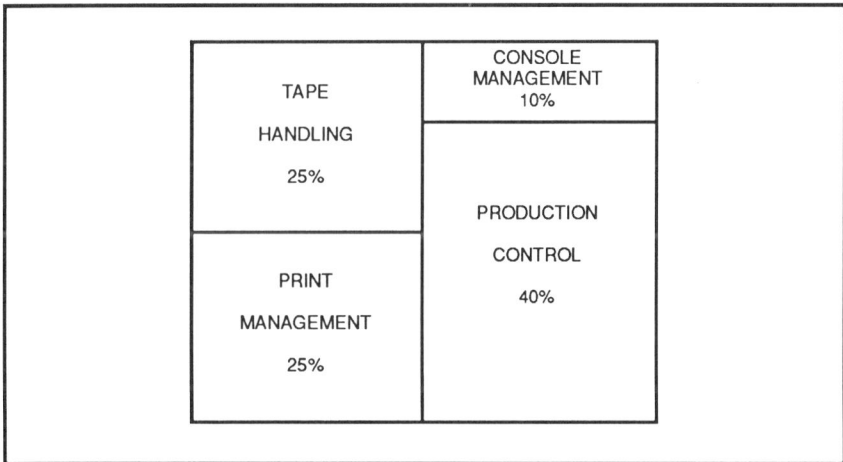

Figure 3.3. The labor in the computer center can be broken up into four categories, much of which can be displaced through automation.

schedule their own work. In this case, the features will need to be added or the package replaced in favor of one that can provide the function.

In other cases, the computer center must identify the requirements and select the software necessary to achieve unattended computer center operation. The following is a discussion of the kinds of software available and some of the criteria essential for unattended computer center operation.

Tape Handling. The elimination of tape essentially requires a hardware solution, and the hardware alternatives to tape are discussed in detail later. However, understanding how tape is used in the computer center and a commitment to reduce the use of tape as a storage medium are essential prerequisites to any tape elimination solution.

- *Tape Management Systems* reduce the labor associated with tape handling, improve the quality of retention process and assist in identifying ways to reduce tape usage. Furthermore, in some cases the tape management system retains its value for the tape replacement hardware. Tape is a data storage medium that is likely to be with us for a long time and the tape management system will retain its value.
- *Tape Dataset Stacking Utilities* reduce the number of physical tapes used, and eliminate the corresponding tape handling labor.

Print Management. Like tape, print requires a combination of hardware and software solutions. The proliferation of on-line systems has resulted in an installed base of computer terminals and distributed printers. Some organizations are even beginning to reach a computer terminal to staff ratio of one to one and it is becoming increasingly common to find departmental printers. As a result, it is now feasible for organizations to store and view reports on-line. The direction is to eliminate the print cycle and to produce exception reports on local printers when necessary.

The software solution in this instance is Electronic Report Distribution. Electronic report distribution is not a replacement for on-line processing, it is a bridge to on-line processing.

Electronic report distribution provides the following kinds of functions to the computer center.

- Enables the user to view reports on-line, to administer their own report distribution and to print exception reports locally or at the central computer site.
- Provides LOTUS like capabilities for formatting and reformatting reports. Most reports are not designed for an 80 column screen; therefore, some formatting capabilities are necessary to effectively view these reports.
- Offers retention and archival facilities for reports, thereby eliminating not only the need to print reports but also the need to rerun them when they are lost.

A very effective way to implement the report management and distribution system is by developing a *do as I do* attitude rather than a *do as I say* attitude. Start to implement this product in the computer center: Put all JCL, dumps and all internal reporting on the system. In many computer environments, the largest single user of hard-copy reports is the computing center.

Console Management. Although console management represents only 10% of the labor required to manage the computer center, its impact far exceeds its opportunity to reduce staff. Console management is an opportunity to integrate tape and print management, and production control automation. The automated console response system is an opportunity to improve the quality of the computer center by automating performance management. The Automated Console Response System should:

- Handle all routine console messages. Target to eliminate all system messages either through software or through system modifications.
- Trap any system console message and provide an automatic response. Put pressure on hardware and software suppliers (especially IBM) to eliminate these operating system activities. If the messages can be responded to automatically they can be eliminated. IBM is the worst offender, so let them know.

- Perform all computer or master console operator functions. The lights on the console are gone, the hard-copy console is gone, and now it is time to eliminate the console.
- Automatically cancel and reset terminal and similar devices when a system *hang* condition is detected.
- Automatically balance the system workload when system thresholds are exceeded or system standards are violated. Computer centers have expected operators to balance workloads for a long time but have not provided the criteria for balancing. If the criteria can be established, it can be done automatically.

Working very closely with the Automated Console response system is the Automated System Monitor. The monitor should:

- Provide the ability to define the measures of normal computer operation (response time, CPU utilization, resource utilization, elapsed time and so on).
- Identify abnormal processing, and provide on-line diagnostic functions to isolate problems.
- Provide statistics for historical analysis of abnormal processing conditions and their correction.
- Identify the status of all processing on the system with the flexibility to isolate and provide additional resources to specific highly sensitive work.

Working together, these software products can improve the quality of the computer center operation by reducing or eliminating the computer human interaction and by consistently managing system performance.

Production Control. Production control is a very labor-intense activity in the computer center. It includes functions such as Input/Output Control, the Help Desk, Production Scheduling, JCL Specialists and Data Entry. Central to the automation of these activities are the concepts of value added data handling and self-service.

Value Added Data Handling. Eliminate all the procedural steps that do not add value to the data entered into the computer or produced by the computer.

Provide a Self Service Environment. Provide an environment where users can enter their own data, schedule their processing and control the distribution of their output.

Production Control is automated using software such as the automated job scheduler, JCL Scan Utilities, automated report balancing and automated software library management. In many cases, these are in place but will need to be reinstalled or replaced to incorporate the concepts of value added and self-service.

For example the Automated Computer Job Scheduler should:

- Provide computer users with the ability to schedule their own workload. The objective is not to support the computer center but to support the computer center user.
- Eliminate the need to submit paper documents to schedule or reschedule routine or ad hoc work.
- Provide the facility to submit job control parameters directly into jobs without any knowledge of JCL or without assistance from computer center personnel.
- Provide computer users with the ability to know the run status of their own work. The user needs to know whether something ran or did not. The last thing a computer center wants is hundreds of calls asking the status of a job.
- Provide the ability to see other systems and scheduled work. This aids in scheduling work that has cross-system dependencies and ensures that jobs will not be submitted when capacity or availability is not there.
- Provide the ability to model the production schedule, allowing computer center users a high level of confidence that their desired schedule can be met.

Automated Report Balancing and Control software should provide the ability for computer users to define balancing rules and to change them as necessary. It should automatically check and balance reports where required.

Other Automated Computer Operation Software. There are many automation packages that can assist the conversion to unattended computer center operation. Most are oriented at improving the quality of computer center operation and therefore reducing the need to inspect quality into the computer center. Automated Rerun/Recovery software, for example, enables the automatic restart of on-line and batch jobs without technical support, database or computer center personnel assistance. Disk Space ABEND software eliminates DASD abends due to insufficient space problems. Security Systems enable users to access their data and software without interfering with the integrity of other users or without reliance on central administration.

OBSTACLES TO ACHIEVING UNATTENDED COMPUTER OPERATION

There are two obstacles to achieving unattended computer center operation: *Human* and *Technical.*

Human Obstacles. The human obstacles are diabolical. First, most computer centers have yet to recognize that unattended operation is achievable, and second, if they have recognized it, they do not consider it possible. The first obstacle is easily overcome through education. The second is the most diabolical obstacle because it becomes a self-fulfilling prophecy. Total unattended operation may not be immediately achievable but partial accomplishment is immediately achievable in most organizations. Movement toward the goal will result in immediate gains; it positions the organization to take advantage of new solutions to traditional obstacles.

Unattended operation can be threatening. By definition it involves, in part, reassigning and reeducating staff. The nature of information technology is such that there is always a greater demand for qualified staff than there is available staff. Attack unattended operation from a positive perspective, emphasize the desire to improve service, to return management control to end users and to develop qualified staff.

Lastly, computer center users are the benefactors of this process. The early years of data processing were characterized by departments relinquishing some of their management responsibilities to the computer centers. This was the only alternative available for realizing the benefit of the computer. The computer center assumed responsibility for data entry, computer processing, scheduling, report generation and report distribution. Unattended operation returns responsibility for the system to departmental management.

Computer center users need to understand that they are the benefactors. If they view this process as unloading undesirable tasks on them, they will resist the process. User involvement is essential. Emphasize productivity gains: Enormous amounts of time are expended in meetings and on memos addressing problems caused by human intervention. Emphasize morale improvements: Errors result in disruptions to work schedules, finger pointing and a reduction in the quality of work life. Promote an awareness that unattended operation resolves these problems.

Technical Obstacles. There are some technical obstacles to unattended operation. On the surface these look more significant, but when investigated, are far less severe. Tape usage is one of the more significant; there are viable alternatives available for the storage of large volumes of data for such things as back-ups. However, with the advent of cartridge tape systems, automated tape storage and retrieval systems are becoming both practical and available. Further, mass storage systems and optical disk technology is becoming more reliable and economically feasible and the per unit cost of disk is being reduced significantly. These types of technologies and others eliminate this obstacle.

Where true technical obstacles exist, treat them as temporary road blocks. Seek solutions that will minimize their use and identify them as obstacles to hardware and software suppliers. Sufficient marketing by a large enough base of users can eliminate these technical obstacles.

MAKING IT HAPPEN

So, if the benefits are great but the implementation is fraught with pitfalls, how does a computer center go about making unattended computer operation happen? The answer is the seven steps to unattended computer center operation.

First, believe that it can happen. If the computer center does not recognize that the technology has evolved to this point or it does not see the value in achieving the objective, then it never happens. The first step is to attack this human element.

Second, make sure that everyone understands why unattended computer center operation must happen. The objective of unattended operation is quality. It is only through quality that the creditability of the computer center can be established. Make sure that computer center users, organizational management and most importantly, the computer center staff, understand why it must happen and buy into the process. It is important to understand that the competition for the computer center is the departmental computers that already provide unattended operation. If necessary, err in favor of excessive communication.

Third, ensure that computer center staff does not lose its livelihood as a result of making unattended operation happen. Implementing unattended computer center operation has a built in requirement for training. The staff that is targeted for displacement needs to be trained for a position of equal or better pay than the position displaced.

Fourth, be opportunistic. Unless the organization is in a growth mode, it is difficult to achieve number three. As computer center turnover is experienced, treat it as an opportunity. Do not replace the position, look for an opportunity to change priorities and work on some aspect of the unattended computer center project that makes the position unnecessary. This approach makes number three easier.

Fifth, reinvest the dollars that you save back into the hardware and software needed to implement unattended computer center operation. The whole process of unattended computer center operation is much more palatable to management if they are convinced that it is a self-funding project.

Sixth, as computer center personnel become available, provide opportunities that will utilize their time by having them participate in the implementation of unattended computer center operation. Reinvest the manpower you save back into the process of making unattended computer center operation work. The staff loves it, and it is an opportunity to train them. Note the word opportunity again.

And finally, treat the process as a project with measurable goals and target dates. Projects that are planned tend to happen, and targets tend to be met.

SUMMARY

The objective of professional information technology management is to promote and expand the use of information technology to achieve the goals of their organization. Not once in the twenty odd years that I have worked with information technology has my management asked me to curtail the use of information technology. Management essentially believes in the goodness of information technology.

However, one of the major obstacles to achieving this objective is a lack of confidence on the part of users, management and even the computer center staff that the computer center can provide expected service, availability and response time, and that the computer center can provide a high quality service.

The problem is that computer centers have been attempting to inspect quality into their product. However, computer centers have become so complex that it is no longer possible to inspect quality into the computer center. The solution is to build quality into the computer *center* by identifying fault points and by eliminating the fault points.

The definition of unattended computer center operation is *the removal of fault points.*

The Human Side of Unattended Computer Center Operation

INTRODUCTION

There are many challenges to achieving unattended computer center operation, but the human side is the most important. First, the concept of unattended computer center operation is new and many computer centers are not aware of it. Second, when computer center management does recognize it, they do not consider it possible. This is being reinforced by many of the major hardware and software vendors. No single vendor has all the tools required to achieve unattended operation. To compensate, they contend that unattended computer center operation is not possible and that we should be satisfied with some lesser objective. Recently, a representative from IBM suggested that the objective should be reduced staffing, not unattended operation. They refer to it as dim room operation, clearly reinforcing the second challenge.

Do not let these human obstacles stand in the way. Unattended computer center operation is achievable with the technology that is available today. Do not let the nay-sayers deter your resolve. It takes management skill and time but unattended computer center operation is achievable.

The first challenge to unattended computer operation is easily overcome through education. The second is the more diabolical obstacle. It is a self-fulfilling prophecy. Partial accomplishment is immediately achievable in most organizations, and full unattended operation is achievable over a slightly longer time frame. Movement toward the unattended computer center operation results in immediate gains and positions the organization to take advantage of new solutions to traditional obstacles. The objective, however, remains total unattended computer operation.

Unattended operation is threatening. By definition, it involves reassigning staff, reeducating, redirecting career paths and eliminating vacant positions. The nature of information technology is such that there is always a greater demand for qualified staff than for available staff. Attack unattended operation from a positive perspective. Emphasize the desire to improve service, to return management control to end users and to develop qualified staff. The key to success is not the automation tools. Management of the human side of unattended computer center operation is the key to success.

Computer center users need to understand that they are the benefactors. If they view unattended computer center operation as unloading undesirable tasks on them, they will resist the process. User involvement is essential. Emphasize productivity gains (the elimination of the enormous amounts of time that are expended in meetings and on memos addressing problems caused by human intervention). Emphasize morale improvements (the elimination of the errors that result in disruptions to work schedules, finger pointing and a reduction in the quality of work life). Promote an awareness that unattended operation resolves these problems.

Remember that the objective of unattended computer center operation is not expense reduction. The objective is quality. One of the significant obstacles to the expansion of information technology as a whole is a lack of confidence on the part of computer center users, organizational management and even computer center staff that the technology can work. They do not believe that the computer center will be available when it is needed or that response time will be adequate to get work done. These groups of people have been conditioned to believe this from years of unacceptable quality. What has developed is a fundamental lack of confidence on the part of key groups of people that information technology in general and computer centers specifically can meet their expectations.

COMPUTER CENTER MANAGEMENT ISSUES

For computer center management, unattended computer center operation is a career decision. If the computer center does not improve quality, the computer center users will leave. Computer center users will justify departmental machines that already operate without human intervention. Alternatively, organizational management will recognize the need for unattended operation, and will bring in someone else to implement unattended computer center operation. There seems to be little choice for computer center management. Technology professionals are in a footrace with professional obsolescence, and if computer center management does not want to lose the race, management must move in the direction of unattended operation.

The beauty of unattended operation is that the resources required to implement unattended computer center operation are already in the computer center. If the computer center markets the concept to management by emphasizing quality and improved service, most organizations will commit to redirecting the monies saved back into the process. As the computer center experiences turnover, do not replace the positions. Use turnover as an opportunity to eliminate that function. Target to eliminate key functions, and use the staffing as implementers. This is an opportunity to train and implement at the same time. Make unattended computer center operation a self-funding, self-training project.

Computer center users will be suspicious, concerned and unbelieving. They will think the computer center is trying to unload its work onto them. The users will be concerned that they will be left to flounder about without any assistance, and they will not believe that unattended operation can be accomplished. You might be lucky and have computer center users that have a different perspective, but to be on the safe side, assume they will be skeptical. Put together a communication program that addresses these concerns and work with computer center users that are supportive to implement the direction. Talk is cheap . . . prove that your communications are correct.

Address unattended computer center operation from the quality perspective. Remember, these computer users have experienced up to twenty-five years of things not working quite right, of poor response time, of computer failures and incorrect reports. Emphasize that your objective and your only objective is to improve quality, and improved quality will make their life easier.

Computer center management needs to commit to making unattended operation happen. They need to teach organizational management, computer center staff and computer users that it can be achieved. They need to systematically identify and remove fault points, design new application systems to accommodate this direction and put pressure on hardware and software vendors (especially IBM) to design for unattended operation. There is no magic . . . just daily commitment, hard work and fun.

COMPUTER CENTER STAFF ISSUES

The computer center staff that is being displaced by unattended computer center operation acts as an intermediary between the computer user and the computer. These functions are data entry, operators, help desks, tape librarians, media handlers, quality control clerks, production coordinators and all the associated layers of management. The objective is to stop inspecting quality into the computer center and to start building quality. The objective is to automate the computer center and to give the computer user the ability to manage its own computing requirements.

Yes, there will be staff in the computer center, but it will service the computer center not the computer center user. Unattended computer operation removes the people that interface between the computer user and the computer; it does not displace the people responsible for servicing the computer. There will be computer operation analysts to analyze and install new hardware and communications as the computer grows, to analyze and replace obsolete hardware and software, and to manage the multimillion dollar resource. The new computer center is likely to include these people, as well as technical service and application service staff.

For some computer users, it will be difficult to stop working through someone else to get their job done. It is always pleasant to deal with someone nice and helpful. Self-service is the direction of many industries, whether it is pumping gas, an automatic teller machine, a voice recognition telephone system or a pregnancy test. The computer center is no exception.

Under no circumstance should the unattended computer center project put someone out of a job. Do not focus in on alternatives such as outplacement or assistance in finding another job. Outplacement and assistance are not a substitute for professional development, job enrichment and job security. Emphasis on these alternatives will cause you to lose the commitment of your staff.

To be successful with unattended operation, the computer center needs to enlist the assistance of the computer center personnel and the computer center user. These are the people that understand the computer center best. Over the last 25 years, there has been a chronic shortage of computing personnel, and there seems to be no solution to this shortage in the near future. If you want unattended operations to work, the computer center needs to enlist the assistance of the people that know it best. Computer center personnel need to be confident that their careers can benefit from the change to unattended operation.

Further, the valuable training that the displaced staff receive as they implement unattended computer center operation prepares the computer center staff for better positions in other areas of computing. Be prepared to make the commitment to training. The only people that will have any problem in this scenario are those that are not prepared to learn and grow, and these are not personality traits of computing people.

If the computer center is a union shop, there is no doubt that unattended computer center operation is eliminating bargaining unit positions. Unattended computer center operation is committed to improved quality, productivity and quality of work life. It offers staff the opportunity to expand their job knowledge, horizons and salaries. The alternative is the same as other industries that failed to automate . . . no job at all. Unions need to decide whether they are there to improve the quality of work life for their members or to protect the union itself. Unattended operation seems to clearly offer an opportunity to those that support it, and unions can play a vital role in ensuring that organizations do not subvert the intent of unattended operation by the desire for short term financial gains.

Introducing the topic of unattended computer center operation is sensitive. Do it as a group. Go through the concepts and cover as many questions as you can anticipate. Give the computer center staff the materials to review over at their leisure. Emphasize that unattended operation is vital to the success of the computer center and the organization, and ask them for suggestions. Schedule time to get back together and discuss suggestions and questions. It is often helpful to get the computer center users involved.

Spend time communicating. Do it one-on-one or in groups that include supportive staff. Share your plans. Make your time frames public knowledge, and provide a forum to communicate successes. Computer center staff naturally feel threatened by unattended computer operation. There will be some staff that are not supportive and may even instill doubts in others. This will not be a frequent occurrence. If it is frequent, assume you are doing something wrong and rethink your tactics. Remember, the success of unattended computer operation is based on the computer center staff.

The computer center is committed to retrain the staff for better positions in other areas of information technology. Make a commitment to promote all positions from within and hire from the bottom. Train the displaced staff to fill open positions in other areas of the information services group. Remember, there are still facilities management, technical services, database services, application services, the information center and computer user departments. Look around. There are all kinds of people using computers, and they are all looking for staff. Put the computer center staff to work implementing unattended computer operation. When the computer center staff achieves their objective, they are ready for more responsible positions.

If you encounter resistance, intensify the communications with the computer center staff. It is hard to picture someone that does not want a better position. If you do encounter someone like this, then as a very last resort, assist that person in finding something in another computer center. Ultimately, this person will have a problem that only he or she can solve. This is an uncommon situation.

If the organization is shrinking and there are no open positions to retrain staff into, you have a problem that exceeds the capacity of the computer center to solve. You can work this out with your human resources personnel. But, if it is a question of just not growing or growing very slowly, then it may be necessary to carry some extra staff for a while. Most organizations have a minimum of 5% to 10% turnover annually. If you commit to filling positions from within, the information technology group should be able to place the displaced people over time. Remember, the computer center is saving monies. If the center carries some people until a position opens, it is only deferring the savings. It is not adding cost. Talk to your human resources staff at the start, and get their support. Do not surprise them. It is my experience that human resource and management people are supportive if given a chance.

The opposite is more likely the case today. Turnover is high for computer center operation personnel, and you may have more open positions than you are prepared to eliminate. Try to avoid filling the positions. Consolidate job functions and use temporary personnel to fill the voids. Filling a position may result in hiring staff that you will want to displace. Displacing a new person is a much more difficult problem to solve than temporarily filling the void created by an open position.

Finally, tell the computer center staff what you are achieving and why it is important. Encourage them to ask questions and to participate in the process. Ensure that everyone has the opportunity for an equal or better position. Use the conversion to unattended operation as an on-the-job training exercise. It gets the staff involved, provides in-service training and actually improves morale.

COMPUTER CENTER USER ISSUES

Computer center users are the benefactors of unattended computer center operation. User departments relinquished some of their management responsibilities to the computer centers as a way of realizing the benefits of the computer. The computer center is returning this management responsibility. If computer center users view this process as unloading undesirable tasks on them, they will resist the process.

Remember, user involvement is essential, and to achieve it, you need to emphasize the productivity gains and morale improvements. Highlight the reductions in meetings, correspondence, work disruptions and finger-pointing. Emphasize the improvement to the quality of work life. Promote an awareness that unattended operation resolves these problems and improves morale.

Computer center users already schedule their own work, key their own data and administer their own report distribution. They are developing a schedule, writing it down, hand carrying it, following up, and attending meetings to discuss why it did not work today when it has for the last twenty days and so on. The computer user is doing the same for data entry and report distribution. What is more, the computer center is doing a similar set of activities. Everything gets done at least twice. If the computer center user does it directly, it takes less time, and it is done more effectively.

The computer center is reducing the effort of the computer user. There are no user budget increases. However, computer users are skeptical; therefore, implement using the path of least resistance. Find a computer center user prepared to be part of the implementation, and demonstrate that unattended computer operation does reduce the effort of the computer center user. Computer center users are doing their work in a more streamlined manner. They are better able to service their mission. Computer center users are being given the opportunity to demonstrate to their management how they can improve quality and improve productivity at a reduced cost.

Keypunch or batch data entry is an obsolete concept. It is much more effective for a computer user to enter data at the source and to edit and correct errors at the source. The information is available immediately. There are no transcription or transcription errors, and there is no lost paperwork. No batches are processed incorrectly, and there is no need for meetings to determine who created the error, etc. It is a more efficient process. It reduces data entry staff, and it reduces computer user staff. Direct data entry improves quality and saves more time.

SUMMARY

The success of unattended computer hinges on the human side of unattended computer center operation. The computer center management must believe that it can happen. If the computer center does not recognize that the technology has evolved to this point or it does not see the value in achieving the objective, then it will never happen.

Everyone has to understand why it must happen. The objective of unattended operation is quality. It is only through quality that the creditability of the computer center can be established. Make sure that computer center users, organizational management and, most importantly, the computer center staff understand the concepts of quality and unattended computer center operation.

The computer center staff cannot lose their livelihood as a result of making unattended operation work. The people being displaced are the people that are needed to implement unattended computer center operation. Conversely, the computer center cannot fill open positions. Look for an opportunity to change priorities and to work on some aspect of the unattended computer center project that makes the position unnecessary. This makes it easier to ensure that staff will not lose their livelihood.

As computer center personnel become available, train them to implement. Reinvest the manpower you save back into the process of making unattended computer center operation work. The staff loves it, and it is an opportunity to train them.

Remember, the key to successfully implementing unattended computer center operation is to emphasize the human side of unattended computer center operation.

Eliminating Manual Functions

The Manual Side of Unattended Computer Center Operation

INTRODUCTION

The common aspect throughout the three strategies (value added data handling, automation and self-service computing) required to achieve unattended computer center operation is the elimination of manual intervention between the computer user and the computer, and between computer center staff and the computer. Each point of human intervention is a fault point and each fault point is an opportunity for error.

Value added data handling eliminates all manual procedures from the computer center which do not add value to the data entered into the computer or produced by the computer. This strategy eliminates the paperwork associated with interfacing to the computer center. In most cases, the people who intervene between the data entered into the computer and produced by the computer add *NO* value to the data. They are actually reducing the quality and timeliness of the products and services.

Computer center automation is achieved by installing automated computer center management tools, thereby eliminating the fault points which are created by manual human intervention between the computer center and computer users. Some amount of dialog is required between the computer center and computer users in such areas as scheduling, report distribution changes, control parameters and console interaction. However, these activities and other computer center activities need not be manual.

A self-service computing environment permits computer users to enter their own data, schedule their processing and control the distribution of their output. Self-service provides a computing environment where the computer user has complete control over information from creation through processing.

Unattended computer center operation is achieved by isolating and analyzing the manual activities of the computer center. Once isolated and analyzed, these manual activities are either eliminated or automated.

MANUAL FUNCTIONS

Remember the quality scenario, any point of human intervention between the computer and the computer user is a fault point (a potential error) and every fault point is the subject of scrutiny. Some fault points are integral to the traditional computer center: computer operators, tape drives, data entry, production schedulers, input/output control desks and report distribution. Some fault points are relatively new innovations, such as change coordinators, help desks, quality control coordinators and JCL specialists. Other fault points, such as the operator intervention required to activate and deactivate the on-line system network, for installing terminal devices to perform database backups and to implement software changes are merely accepted features of computer operations. None of these points of human intervention are necessary, and each one needs to be systematically removed from the computing center.

Eliminate Centralized Batch Job Scheduling. Unattended computer center operation requires that computer center management rethink the way they provide service to computer center users. Unattended operation is giving the computer center users the facilities to manage their routine computer processing schedule and to process ad hoc work without computer center intervention. This strategy is normally achieved through an automated computer job scheduler.

To achieve unattended computer center operation, it is essential that the functions of the computer job scheduler be extended to computer center users. The computer job scheduler provides computer users with the ability to schedule their own information requirements. Computer center management needs to recognize that the scheduler is not automating the computer center but is improving the quality of service to the computer center user. One of the underlying strategies of unattended computer operation is to create a self-service mentality while eliminating the need for support groups. In this instance, the support group is centralized computer center schedulers.

The automated scheduler creates a self-service mentality by eliminating the need to submit paperwork to schedule or reschedule routine or ad hoc work. Ideally, the system provides the facility to submit job control parameters (dates, check numbers, batch control numbers and so forth) directly into batch jobs without any knowledge of JCL or without assistance from computer center personnel. Furthermore, computer users need to know whether the work has been processed correctly; therefore, they need to be able to query the status of computer processing. In a self-service environment, the last thing the computer center wants is the computer user calling to find out the status of computer jobs.

Finally, the computer user needs to be able to view other scheduled work. This assists the computer user to schedule work that has cross-system dependencies and ensures that jobs are not submitted when sufficient capacity is not available. It establishes a basis for modeling the production schedule and gives both the computer center and computer user a high level of confidence that their desired schedule can be met.

Reduce and Eliminate Operator Intervention. Identify and eliminate all computer center procedures which require computer operator intervention. However, this is not always easily achieved. Computer center procedures which require operator intervention need to be evaluated. Divide the results of this evaluation into a) those which are easy to eliminate and b) those which are difficult to eliminate. Further divide the difficult into 1) those which can be resolved with installed software and 2) those which require new software.

Remember, in many cases, the software required to reduce and eliminate human intervention in the computer center is already installed in the computer center. It is not being used to automate computer center services, it is being used to provide self-service to computer center users.

Implement the easy changes immediately and defer the difficult changes. Implementing the easy changes immediately reduces operator intervention, but more importantly, it establishes a track record of success and a firm foundation for addressing the more difficult changes. Next, determine if additional automation software is required. Software, such as the automated console response system can eliminate all routine interaction between the computer operator and the computer, and a tape dataset stacking utility can reduce tape mount messages.

It is important to impress upon hardware and software vendors that console traffic is unacceptable. It is both error-prone and labor-intense. Yet, these activities have become so ingrained in software and hardware that suppliers do not even realize they are designing or perpetuating this kind of activity. Suppliers continue to perpetuate console traffic because computer centers are not telling them to stop. Let software and hardware suppliers know their objective is to eliminate the console.

An automated console response system supports the objectives of unattended computer center operation; however, it does not do the complete job. In most cases, multiple software packages are required, and the console response system acts as an integrator for these software packages. The automated console response system is the tie that binds together the numerous software packages that are used to achieve unattended computer operation and is, therefore, the new quality assurance manager. It improves the service quality of the computer center by eliminating the human intervention between the application software systems and the computer, and between the computer operation software and the computer.

Eliminate Print. Computer users rarely desire large masses of information. When provided with large reports, they are typically using them as a reference document or as input into some other analysis process. Statistics show that the average person does not read a report from end to end if it is longer than ten pages. Over the last decade, virtually all new computers have been designed for on-line processing, thereby providing direct access to information without the intermediate report production stage. The objective of the computer center, therefore, should be to provide reference information on-line and reports of less than ten pages of paper.

End users, however, have been educated to associate computer based information with reports. This is contrary to the way in which information is used, and the direction of the technology. Application software needs to be designed to provide information on-line. This, however, is a long-term solution. In the interim, centralized printing of hard copy reports should be discouraged. Output can be viewed on-line as an electronic report. The report is stored on a direct access storage device and viewed on a terminal. Exception reports can be printed at low-cost, local printers. A number of very good electronic report distribution systems are now available (See Appendix A).

Electronic report distribution software directs reports to a direct access device rather than a printer. Once on direct access device, it can be retained for a predefined period, viewed and, if necessary, printed under the control of an end user. This is not a substitute for on-line access to information; it is a bridge process to move from reports to on-line processing. It causes the computer user to think in terms of the information rather than in terms of reports.

Therefore, a common guideline for eliminating print is to limit its use to exception reports, reports of ten pages or less. Reports longer than ten pages are reference documents. Reference documents are documents that cannot be digested by the recipient. They should be viewed on-line and referenced when pieces of information are required. The objective is to eliminate print production and distribution.

A very effective way to implement an electronic report distribution system is to adopt a *do as I do* attitude rather than a *do as I say* attitude. Start to implement this product in the computer center: Put all JCL, dumps and all internal reporting on the system. In many computer environments, the largest single user of hard-copy reports is the information technology group.

Get computer center users involved by migrating large volume reports, reference reports and reports that are periodically refreshed with up-to-date information (financial reports, lists of names and addresses, marketing information and so on). Start with users who are receptive to the technology, product and approach. Get these users involved early in the process. Take them on site visits before the software is purchased and installed.

Reduce report handling for the remaining reports by installing an electronic storage bin system. An electronic bin system significantly reduces the handling of reports. If computer users are coming to the computer center to pick up reports, the electronic bin system eliminates the need for computer center personnel to distribute reports. In addition to using the bin system as an output vehicle, use it as an input device. Assign specific bins to receive input documents and further reduce labor. Keep in mind, the more the computer center reduces manual handling, the more it improves the quality of service.

Reduce and Eliminate Tape Processing. Many computer centers are being overwhelmed by magnetic tapes. Every time a tape is read, written, cleaned, stored or archived, it requires manual handling. There are a number of alternatives for completely replacing tape. The most promising solutions are high density storage devices such as mass storage devices and optical disk. Mass storage devices such as the M960 from Masstor Systems in Santa Clara, California, can provide up to 1.6 terabytes of data in a box the size of an IBM 3390 disk drive. Optical disk is available but has yet to have widespread acceptance.

Recognizing that tape is a major obstacle to unattended operation, there are ways to manage and reduce its use prior to implementing less labor-intense hardware solutions. Substitute disk media for tape media when and where possible; disk is becoming less and less expensive and does not require manual intervention. Evaluate routine disk backup cycles to determine if they result in excessive data retention. Eliminate unnecessary back-ups and reduce ridiculously long retention periods. Remember, there is no such thing as permanent retention. Improve tape utilization by placing more data on a single volume of tape.

Many computer centers have installed IBM 3480 cartridge tape drives. One of the reasons computer centers chose this new technology was its increased reliability. The comparatively poor performance of the 3420's technology and the associated problems of reel tapes caused computer centers to increase the retention periods of their back-ups. Technology problems and other changes, such as personnel turnover, add to the increase in the number of back-ups. Examine the frequency and number of back-ups in light of this new technology, and reduce the number of tapes that are retained. In most cases, the number of tapes stored can be significantly reduced without putting the computer center at risk.

In addition to examining data retention, there are other alternatives to reduce tape handling. Automated tape library systems such as StorageTek and the newly announced Memorex-Telex automated tape library provide automatic retrieval and storage of cartridge tapes. In addition, automatic stackers for the IBM 3480 tape drive eliminate the need to manually load scratch tapes, and mass storage devices such as the M960 and M1000 from Masstor Systems have the potential for completely eliminating tape.

Eliminate Data Entry. Data entry is an obsolete function. It has become an accepted function of computer centers even though it is best performed at the source of the information. Each person who handles data reduces its reliability and increases its cost. The ideal situation is to collect data at its point of creation via point of collection machines (electronic cash registers, automated tellers, touch tone telephone interface and so forth), data collection devices and on-line data entry. Design new computer applications to use these approaches and convert existing applications to these approaches or to user friendly data entry systems which interface directly with computer based systems.

Dismantle the data entry function, and integrate data entry into the skill set of the computer user. A word of caution is in order: The key word here is integrate. If the originator of the information continues to transcribe information to a paper document and passes it to a dedicated data entry person, the function is only being relocated, and productivity and reliability gains will not be realized. Transcribing information to a document for processing by the computer center is a time-consuming, expensive and error-prone process.

Another word of caution: Distribute data entry to the source of the information. Do not decentralize data entry. Provide the originator of the information with the ability to communicate with the mainframe either on-line or in data collection mode without using input documents. This eliminates logs, coordination meetings, missing batches and peak volume problems. If data entry is simply decentralized none of these activities will be eliminated and no benefit will be derived.

Direct data entry provides the computer users with more time to get data into the system since no intervention is required. It also improves the quality of the input because the person who understands the information best is entering the data into the computer.

Eliminate The Input/Output Control Desk. It is not uncommon to find that computer centers are performing input/output control functions which are no longer required. For example, is the computer center still filling out control logs and transmittal forms? Is it really important for the computer center to know that computer users signed for a report which they never received or which was subsequently lost? Tracking every source document and every report in and out of the computer center is costly. It consumes computer center labor and results in delays for the computer user. Ultimately, the computer center reruns the lost report anyway.

Take a close look at these control activities and eliminate everything that is questionable. If the control function turns out to be necessary, it will be easy to reinstitute and the new procedures are usually better. Remember one of the strategies for achieving unattended computer center operation is to provide a self-service environment. Self-service eliminates the need for control functions. The computer center recaptures staffing which can be allocated to implementing other aspects of computer center automation and the computer user achieves a higher level of quality and service.

Substitute automation for inspection. Use automation tools such as automated report balancing and control, automatic job scheduling and electronic JCL review to build quality. Build quality into the computer center's product; do not delay the product or service by manually inspecting it after it has been produced.

Eliminate Change Coordinator. Unattended computer center operation is synonymous with self-service. Changes can be made through the automated computer job scheduler. Program library and support library management can be performed by programming and technical support staff under the protection of a security package. Programming and technical support staff can move modules into production libraries as part of the application development process. In a self-service environment, change coordinators are a thing of the past.

Remember that computer center librarians do not know what a new software module can do, only that the proper forms were provided and that they had proper authorization. Using the security system as a substitute for authorization, the computer center can allow programming and technical staff to maintain their own libraries. This eliminates labor in the computer center and expedites the task of the applications or technical person.

Eliminate Quality Control Coordinators. Do not attempt to inspect quality into the computer center: Build quality into the computer center by substituting automation tools for inspection. The quality control coordinator is delaying the computer center products or services by manually inspecting it after it has been produced.

For example, an automated console response system supports the objectives of building quality; it binds together such software packages as automatic restart and recovery and the performance monitor, thereby eliminating manual intervention. It improves the quality of the service of the computer center by eliminating the operator or technical service intervention with application software and the computer. Therefore, the automated console response system becomes the quality assurance manager.

Automate the report balancing and control process. Frequently, ten or more years of effort are expended on the efficient design of application systems, and little or no effort is spent on automating the balancing process. An entire processing stream can be halted for hours or even days waiting for computer users to review and balance their system. Report balancing software should provide the ability for computer users to define balancing rules and to change them as necessary. It should automatically check and balance reports where required.

Quality control coordinators are a thing of the past. The objective of unattended operation is to build quality throughout the computer center. Inspecting quality is an obsolete concept. Unattended operation seeks out the source of error and permanently corrects the error.

Alter the Concept of the Help Desk. The help desk is a relatively new concept. The theory is to provide a single point of contact to assist computer center users when they have problems. In theory, it is a good concept, but in actuality, it is often a source of frustration. The person at the help desk frequently cannot resolve the problem and ultimately refers the problem to another person. The person at the help desk has no assurance that the problem is referred to the correct person or that the person corrects the users' problem.

As a result, help desk staff feel helpless, and they attempt to provide the computer user with an explanation or a solution which they are not qualified to give. Frequently, upon further investigation, this explanation or solution turns out to be wrong. When dealing with repetitive problems such as slow response time, service interruptions or chronic software bugs, the computer user is given insignificant or inconsequential responses. From the computer users' perspective, the information is incorrect, and it appears that they are being shuffled around from one person to another while the problem goes unresolved. The computer user does not view the help desk as providing value but views it as a source of frustration.

The help desk is another IBM concept that adds staffing to the computer center and interjects human intervention between the computer and the computer user while adding little or no value. Have you ever called a service organization, such as a bank, with a question on an account or an auto loan and to had deal with a help desk? Banks do not have help desks to redirect your query to the correct person. Banks expect their customers to call the correct department. The computer center is a complex environment, and there are only two options to handle this complex environment:

reduce the complexity and educate the computer user to call the correct person.

Identify the correct person to call for response time problems, for terminal problems and when software is not giving correct results. Train the information technology staff to assume responsibility for the problem from the beginning through to the correction stage even when the computer user calls the wrong person. Have a knowledgeable phone operator available or a voice message system which directs computer users to the correct support person. Even in an unattended computer center, there will be software and hardware support staff.

Eliminate The JCL Specialist. JCL continues to be a very labor-intense and error-prone activity. JCL is the source of many computer center problems and interruptions, and as a result, many computer centers have established JCL specialists to improve quality and relieve the application programmer of this chore. This is another example of inspecting quality rather than building quality.

Scanning JCL for syntax errors and/or conformance with computer center standards should be part of building the computer center batch operation schedule, program library maintenance, and production and test job submission. Syntax checking is part of the operating system. Some automated job schedulers include it as an integral part of their software, and stand-alone software is available for scanning JCL.

Provide computer users with the facility to submit parameters into their system without knowing JCL. There is no reason why the computer user has to send the computer center a piece of paper. The computer center enters the parameters into the computer using an on-line facility; provide the same on-line facility to the computer user. Allow the computer users to enter parameter information into a simple application that can edit parameters and submit them into the JCL ready for job execution.

Avoid job parameters as much as possible. They are points of human intervention and, therefore, are fault points no matter who enters them. Also, remember that no matter how tough the edit controls are, there will be situations when wrong information is entered. Plan for these situations.

Eliminate Off-Site Storage. Off-site vault storage is another manual, labor-intense, error-prone, costly computer center function that can be replaced by electronic vaulting. Electronic vaulting is the ability to electronically store and retrieve DASD back-ups and historical information off-site. Electronic vaulting improves reliability and makes the information more accessible in event of a disaster or equipment failure.

Most computer center staff are competent and conscientious. Yet, most computer centers rarely have a perfect audit of their off-site vault. Rarely is everything in the vault which ought to be included. In most cases, somebody has forgotten to take something off-site, and it is sitting in the computer room. Furthermore, conventional vaulting procedures result in delay. Backups are processed, and those backups sit in the computer room for hours waiting for someone to pick them up. When they are picked up, a van driver hauls them in an unsecured van to some secured location. There is a real need to move toward electronic vaulting, and this can be achieved with high density storage devices such as mass storage systems and automatic tape libraries.

SUMMARY

The objective of unattended computer center operation is to improve quality by automating the computer center. Of all the names, *computer center automation, dark room processing, lights-out operation,* the name that seems to best describe this process is *unattended operation.*

The objective of unattended computer center operation is to improve quality by removing the fault points, and the most conspicuous fault points are the repetitive, manual activities performed by the computer center staff and the computer users who send or receive information from the computer center. These fault points include centralized batch job scheduling, operator intervention, print, data entry, input/output control, change coordinators, quality control coordinators, the help desk, JCL specialists and off-site storage.

Unattended computer center operation removes all the manual intervention between the computer user and the computer. Unattended computer operation improves quality by removing the source of error.

Chapter 6

Prerequisites for Unattended Computer Center Operation

INTRODUCTION

Implementing the three strategies for achieving unattended computer center operation (value added data handling, self-service computing and computer center automation) requires an increased emphasis on computer center security. As the functions of the computer center are distributed to a wider and wider base of users, it is increasingly important that the integrity of information is secured from accidental or intentional corruption. In addition, increased dependence on the computer center for vital business functions demands that management rethink the way in which they view the computer center. Security is a vital resource which requires a contingency recovery plan in event of an extended interruption.

Finally, the absence of human intervention in the computer center requires continuous computer center availability. The services must be available twenty-four hours a day. Unattended computer center operation returns the responsibility for work management to the originator of the information. With no one in the computer center, the users need the flexibility of tailoring their computer work schedule to their departmental work plan. There is no one in the unattended computer center to schedule exceptions; hence, continuous on-line processing is essential.

Therefore, three computer center management functions are required before unattended computer center operation can be implemented: data security, computer center disaster contingency planning and continuous on-line availability. The driving force for these functions is usually *good business practice*, and, as a result, they are not part of the unattended computer center planning process, they are prerequisites to unattended computer center operation.

DATA SECURITY

Did you ever stop to think about why computer centers develop elaborate sign-off documents? Authorization documents are required for schedule changes, library moves, report distribution changes, parameter changes and terminal access. Have you ever examined how much time it takes to prepare and distribute these documents, how many people handle the documents and how many opportunities for error and delay are created?

Computer centers are trying to ensure that only authorized users and staff have access to computer based information. What computer centers accomplish is a false sense of security. Signatures are reviewed, source documents are filed, documents are audited and security appears to be under control. However, the chances of a computer center detecting unauthorized information access through all this paperwork handling are slim.

Computer centers need to use data security software as a method for ensuring that only authorized users are changing schedules, moving programs into production, querying or updating information and reviewing reports. Security software is a positive control over the computer center. It eliminates the need to maintain files, to look for approved signatures and to audit paperwork. Security software provides a complete audit trail. Furthermore, security auditors already have confidence in this audit trail. Most importantly, this approach ensures that the computer center is automatically protected seven days a week, twenty-four hours per day.

In light of the issues raise by unattended computer center operation, the challenge for the computer center is to develop effective tactics for managing both administrative and operational information security.

Administrative Tactics

Security administration starts with a management commitment that security is important. In most organizations this commitment is obtained by funding a security administration function. Where there is no funding for security, it is fair to assume that there is little or no management commitment.

The second administrative tactic is to establish a security function with a formal mission and charter. The security function selects, maintains and administers security software. It also performs internal security consulting, investigates potential security violations and audits the security procedures for conformance and improvement opportunities. Furthermore, the security administration function participates in the computer center disaster contingency plan.

The third administrative tactic is to form a committee comprised of representatives from security administration, application development, technical services, the computer center and EDP auditors to develop a security policy for approval by the organization.

Finally, security standards and guidelines are communicated to the organization through a security manual. This security manual provides guidance for physical security, security services external to the computer center, data and software security, personnel security, computer center disaster contingency planning and insurance. These standards and guidelines can be prepared by the security administration group or with the assistance of external consultants. After publication, the security manual is maintained by the security administration function and should be reviewed in its entirety once a year and updated as frequently as necessary.

Operational Tactics

Management approval for security administration sets the framework for putting computer center security into operation. The operation of security administration involves using audit trails, developing incident reports, maintaining site files, providing centralized consulting, interjecting security into the application development process, selecting and administering security software, developing an encryption policy, maintaining a security library and maintaining a high security profile.

Audit trails are a useful security tool. The data collected by security software, the operating system or application systems can be examined. It is useful to examine these audit trails periodically and systematically for patterns such as the frequent execution of sensitive utilities and unsuccessful attempts to log onto the computer. Audit trails can be used in conjunction with extract utilities for exception reporting. However, it is generally not practical to enforce security compliance through the review of large volumes of audit trails.

Security administration uses a formal security incident report to define an incident for further investigation by the security administration function. A security incident is not necessarily a violation; it is an action or situation that could indicate a violation. Incident reports, therefore, require further investigation. A file of these incident reports, including the final disposition, is kept on the computer center site. If multiple sites are involved, set up multiple site files.

The security administration function is the focal point for all security consulting (physical, network, and data security). It provides security consulting services whenever required. Furthermore, security administration should maintain a file of outside consultants in areas where internal expertise is not sufficient. Security administration needs to be part of the application development process. One or more security checkpoints should be part of every application project. This practice will ensure that new application software conforms with security policies and procedures. It avoids potential security breaches and costly software rework.

Security software should be purchased and installed in the computer center early in the process. Security software operates like a protective umbrella over application software, data and other computer center automation tools. Security software is a prerequisite for a self-service computing environment. It enables users to access information and software without interfering with the integrity of other users and without relying on central computer center administration.

If justifiable, based on the sensitivity of the data and the risk associated, encryption software can be introduced. An encryption policy should be developed to define when and where encryption should be used. Encryption is not a panacea; it does not work in every case. It is expensive to install and operate, and it increases the complexity of the computer center and decreases data access. It is best to discuss this topic during the early stages of development. Establish a policy for when encryption is to be used, and avoid continual recurring discussion.

Finally, security administration should maintain a library of the latest changes in the security industry. As the computer users' level of skill increases, the sophistication of security practices needs to increase. This is a constant ordeal. The most successful way to stay on top of these changes is for the security administrators to maintain a high profile. Security administrators need to market security and train staff on the correct security practices. Remember, when it comes to security, out of sight is out of mind.

CONTINGENCY PLANNING

As increasing amounts of information are stored and processed on computers, the risk associated with the storage and processing of that information increases dramatically. An unattended computer center accentuates this risk, and the *prudent man rule* dictates that a computer center disaster recovery contingency plan needs to be in place as a prerequisite to unattended computer center operation.

Implementation of a disaster recovery contingency plan is a three step process: evaluation, procedurization and validation. This three-step implementation approach is characterized as a closed loop as illustrated in Figure 6.1. The process starts and ends with an evaluation of all computer-based systems and procedures. During the interim, a recovery method is established and

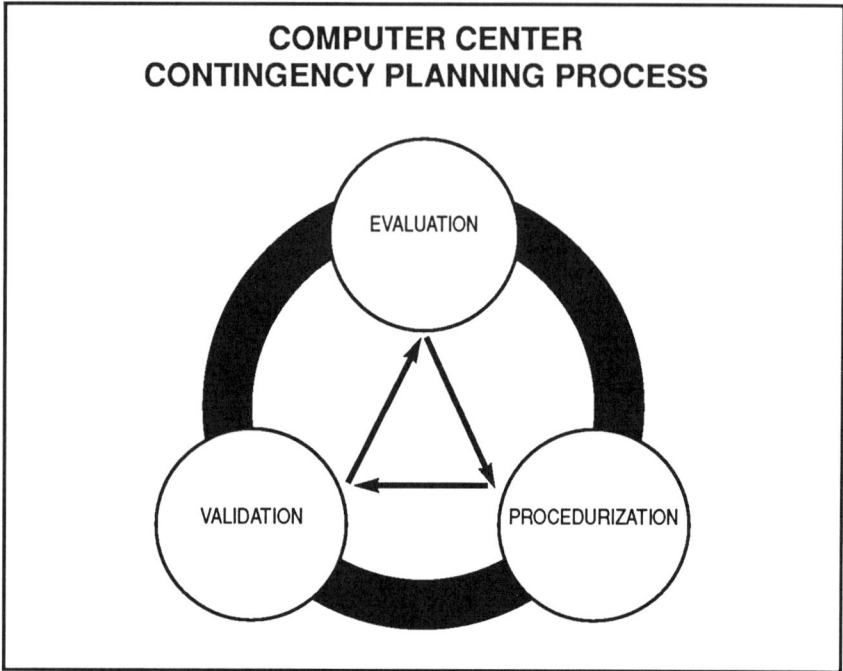

**COMPUTER CENTER
CONTINGENCY PLANNING PROCESS**

EVALUATION

VALIDATION

PROCEDURIZATION

Figure 6.1. Computer center contingency planning is a three-step, closed loop process that never ends.

validated. A data processing environment is never stagnant; new systems are added, systems are changed, systems are deleted. Periodically, everything needs to be reevaluated. Changes need to be made, and the process revalidated. For this reason, the process is a closed loop that cycles back on itself.

Evaluation

The evaluation is a six step process: (1) categorizing the systems, (2) defining an interruption, (3) setting objectives, (4) defining the resources needed to satisfy the objectives, (5) selecting/reviewing alternatives, and (6) selecting an approach.

1. *Categorizing.* The first step in the evaluation process is to evaluate all computer based systems and categorize them as critical, secondary or tertiary.
    *   Critical systems must be available within seven calendar days of the interruption. They are systems such as payroll, accounts payable, sales audit, marketing and point of sale. Critical systems are essential to the daily business operation.
    *   Secondary systems must be available within two weeks. These systems are major financial applications such as General Ledger, Finance Reporting, Accounts Receivables. They can also include test systems. No recovery system is foolproof; some testing of changes to production systems will be required to sustain the operation of a company.
    *   Tertiary systems do not need to be operational until the computer center is fully reconstructed. These systems include Human Resources, Cost Control Systems, Property Accounting, Marketing, Budgets, and Personal Computing. During the categorization process, the computer center is usually surprised at what falls into this category, and some systems may be completely discontinued.

2. *Definition of an Interruption.* Interruptions are defined as an Outage, Extended Outage or a Disaster.
    *   An Outage is the inability to process for up to twenty-four hours. It is estimated this could occur once a year. An uninterruptable power system can be installed to handle minor power fluctuations, and hardware redundancy is used whenever possible to address equipment failures. This obviously does not handle every contingency, but it does significantly reduce the risk.
    *   An Extended Outage is the inability to process for one to seven days. It is estimated that this can occur once every five years. To handle this, tools similar to those used for an outage are implemented: 1) uninterruptable power system,

2) diesel generator for more extended power outages and 3) hardware redundancy for equipment failure.

- A disaster is the inability to perform computer processing for one or more weeks with no immediate expectation of resuming this processing. Such an occurrence can happen once every twenty years. The disaster recovery contingency plan is the suggested method for satisfying this type of outage.

3. *Setting Objectives.* Having categorized the systems and having defined an interruption, the next order of business is to set objectives for recovery. This is crucial because it dictates the recovery method. If recovery must be in minutes versus hours or hours versus days, the contingency plan will vary. The objectives of the model plan are to process the critical systems within one week of the interruption, the secondary systems within two weeks of the interruption and the tertiary when the computer center is fully operational. Obviously, some organizations, such as banks, may have a requirement to recover critical systems within minutes or hours.

4. *Defining Resource Requirements.* A need has been established to process the critical and secondary systems during the period between the onset of the outage and restoration of the computer center. Isolating the processing capacity requirements for critical and secondary systems is now achieved by identifying the peak processing requirements for these systems during normal processing. Using these requirements, the computer capacity, input/output equipment, floor space (power, air conditioning, water chilling), communications (an especially significant requirement), office space, storage space, and terminals and printers requirements are established.

5. *Review Recovery Alternatives.* Having established the resource requirements, the alternatives for satisfying these requirements are evaluated. There are at least a dozen recovery alternatives ranging from service bureaus to ready conditioned at

another site within the company. Table 6.1 is a list of the twelve different recovery alternatives.

Service bureaus require that application systems conform to the standards of the service bureau. Even in an IBM VM operating system environment, this process can be very labor-intense. Parallel communications are required since the minimum lead time to install communication lines is usually thirty days. This alternative has the least costly subscription fee, but the communications and manpower costs make it the most expensive. It does, however, have the advantage that testing is readily available and that recovery can be almost immediate. Immediate recovery can be worth the cost.

Hot Sites are a popular alternative. Hot Sites are defined as companies that provide an on-site computer and a shell site (with power, air conditioning, water chilling, etc.). They provide a dedicated computer for usually one month and the shell is available for up to six months. The company provides its own software and communications. There is usually a substantial subscription fee and a utilization fee if the facility is used. In addition, the company has the cost of communications lines. The greatest advantage to this alternative is that test time is provided as part of the subscription fee.

Another popular alternative is the *Cold Site*. Cold sites simply provide a shell site with power, air conditioning, water chilling, office space and basic communications (telephones). The subscriber provides all of its own hardware and software and must have data communications in place. There is a subscription fee and a minimum utilization fee. The most significant negative to this approach is that testing is not usually available.

Company-owned *ready conditioned* space is similar to the cold site except the company provides its own site and its own hardware and software. By rerouting communications through this site, it is possible to already have communications in place. No subscription fees are necessary, but, like the cold site, no testing is available.

The last alternative is business interruption insurance. In this alternative, the company does not set up a contingency plan — it

CONTINGENCY PLANNING ALTERNATIVE

1. **Reciprocal agreement.** An agreement between the organization and a local company whereby each company agrees to share the other's computing facility in the event of a disaster.

2. **Consortium agreement.** Also called a mutual aid agreement, this option is an expansion of the reciprocal agreement option. This is an agreement with several member firms that agree to share their computing resources with the member company that suffers a disaster.

3. **Cold Site.** A cold site or an empty shell is a computing facility that contains no computing equipment. Except for environmental support such as air conditioners, water conduits, raised floors, motor generators, power outlets and a security system, the facility is an empty warehouse that is ready for the installation of computer equipment.

4. **Company owned *ready conditioned* space.** Company owned ready conditioned space is much the same as the cold site except the company provides its own site. The company provides its own hardware and software. By rerouting communications through this site, it is possible to already have communications in place.

5. **Equipment vendor agreement.** In some cases, it is possible to contract with a computer vendor to use corporate facilities, such as a support center, to process the computer work load in event of a disaster. The optimal time to obtain such a written agreement is during the equipment contract negotiations. This option is usually limited to major non-IBM vendors (NCR, Unisys, Honeywell, DEC).

6. **Service bureau.** A service bureau is a commercial computing facility that supplies the necessary resources to process the computing work-load of an organization. Some service bureaus specialize in data entry preparation or time-sharing,

Table 6.1

while others can provide full computer services from input preparation to delivery of the necessary output products.

7. **Hot site.** This option is basically a fully equipped cold site. In this case, the computing facility is equipped with computing hardware and support equipment but is not staffed.

8. **Third party standby facility.** This is another type of hot site. It consists of a third party computing facility with short term (up to six weeks) computing capability. For longer term recovery, while the firm is reconstructing its facility, a cold site (ready conditioned space) is available to the customer. The ready space — a cold site with lights and power installed — allows the customer the continuity of processing for up to six months. To use the ready space, the customer would have to provide its own equipment — usually leased.

9. **Alternate site, co-op ownership.** This option is similar to the hot site option except that the facility is cooperatively owned by several member firms. In this option, the facility is made ready with the installation of both environmental and computing equipment.

10. **Parallel operation.** This option requires total redundancy of the computing system. This is not a common alternative because of the prohibitive cost.

11. **Assume all risks via insurance.** This option is self explana- tory — the organization assumes the risks and purchases insurance to cover the loss risks.

12. **Any combination of options.** This allows for a modular approach by selecting the best part of any option based on the organization's disaster contingency requirements. For example, hot site is used to backup batch processing; a ser- vice bureau may be used for data entry services; and the consortium agreement may be expanded to backup on-line and limited batch production requirements.

Table 6.1 Continued.

buys a large quantity of relatively low cost business interruption insurance. On the surface, this appears callous, but a disaster recovery contingency plan can be very costly and takes many resources away from other application development projects. When a company gets involved in a disaster recovery contingency plan and the costs associated with it, this alternative can become very attractive. The company is able to receive a larger return on investment by redirecting contingency planning dollars and staff into projects within the company.

Caution should be used when entering into a reciprocal agreement. This is really an obsolete concept. Most organizations rely heavily on an on-line system. Rarely does a computer center have sufficient capacity to concurrently support two different organizations without creating a disruption to the host site. Although they sound good in theory, in practice, it does not work.

6. *Select Approach.* First, evaluate your business interruption insurance. You will almost certainly find it inadequate.
   * *Business Interruption Insurance* — Buy as much as the organization can afford. As indicated earlier, money can overcome the shortfalls in a disaster contingency plan. The company will need to cover (1) the cost of replacing its equipment; (2) the cost of replacing the environment; (3) the cost of replacing media and tape and (4) it will require monies for miscellaneous expenses (travel, temporary staffs and all the other materials required to operate a temporary data center for the period of about three months.)

Next, protection should be consistent with the level of risk. The first step in selecting a recovery alternative is to measure the security risk associated with not having the primary, secondary and tertiary systems available.

The difference between the various computer center recovery alternatives is the mean time to recovery. The sooner the organization needs to have its primary systems available, the higher the cost. Immediate recovery is only achieved through parallel operation or a service bureau. Organizations that can exist with an outage of a day to a week can use almost any of the other alternatives.

A good approach is to first look for ready conditioned space within the company and to offset the lack of a testing facility by contracting your testing. One of the first places to contact for testing is with a disaster recovery company. There is a high probability that they will have time available (although it may be at an inconvenient time). If ready conditioned space is not available in your company, look to cold sites and finally to hot sites. Obviously, if the computer center must be back in service within twenty-four hours, there is no alternative to parallel operation or a service bureau.

Procedurization

Having selected a contingency processing alternative, the next step is to procedurize the steps necessary to make this process work. These procedures consist of user procedures and information service procedures.

User Procedures. User procedures are for manually processing the critical and secondary systems during the interruption period. This is probably the most difficult task to accomplish since users do not tend to place a high-level of urgency on this process. Second, an emergency supply of special forms must be maintained: payroll checks, time cards, accounts payable checks. These supplies can be easily maintained through major forms suppliers with very little preplanning. A failure to take this minor item into consideration can be a major impasse. Lastly, risk management, or whatever function is responsible for insurance, will need to evaluate all of your business interruption insurance.

The specific items necessary to support the recovery of the computer center have been addressed here. However, an interruption which impacts the data center will most likely impact the manual processing aspects of the business. A cost must be assigned to this manual processing, and interruption insurance should cover that cost.

Information Services Procedures. The disaster recovery procedures for information services consist of procedures for retaining data center documentation, developing alternative site requirements, maintaining magnetic media backup and maintaining the actual disaster recovery contingency plan.

- Document the computer center configuration; develop a very detailed hardware and software inventory. Develop a detailed list of the critical, secondary and tertiary systems. Be especially careful to define what specific jobs/programs make up the critical and secondary systems. Identify if they are daily, weekly or monthly and what are their processing requirements.
- Establish the hardware and software configuration for the contingency computer center (the CPU configuration and input/output equipment) and the support equipment necessary (air conditioning, water chilling). Most likely, an off-site vault facility is available to store backup material: ideally, this will be an electronic vault. This site is vital to the success of the overall disaster recovery contingency plan. Then, working with the administrative services group, or some similar function, identify the location for the contingency computer center, a site which will satisfy the kind of computer and input/output equipment identified.
- Develop a checklist of all activities. Identify responsible personnel and their backup. Develop the specific recovery procedures, identifying the tasks required to rebuild the operating software, to recover databases, to forward recover up to the point of the interruption and to apply changes from the change control system. To minimize written documentation, the database recovery procedures can be maintained on a computer library, accessible after the operating system is restored.
- Reevaluate backup schedules and ensure that the processing can be reconstructed from the point of the last backup to the point when an interruption occurred. An interesting side point is that new backup requirements will be identified such as backups for micro-processor software. In addition, with the

advent of personal computers, backups are needed to maintain some critical personal computer software.

- Evaluate data storage requirements. Storage is required to maintain operating system software, program libraries, on-line system log tapes, databases, historical data and special storage for such items as personal computing and other computer software.
- Evaluate documentation storage requirements. This should include systems development documentation, information center documentation, (training courses, manuals), data center procedures (including the disaster recovery contingency plan itself), and administrative documentation (such as contracts).

Validation

The last element of this whole process is verification of the disaster recovery contingency plan. This includes exercising the plan and the ongoing administration of the plan.

- Once a year set up a simulated disaster. This process should include: (1) going to the off-site tape vault and collecting backups, (2) selecting the participants (typically this is minimized, simply from a cost consideration); however, these people need to be rotated to give maximum exposure, (3) in advance, define what constitutes a disaster recovery test and what the acceptance criteria is, (4) use selected databases in the area of critical and secondary systems and run selected jobs which are representative.
- Exercise the procedures: Take the databases to an off-site location. As noted, a disaster recovery company is a good source for the computer processing time but any computer center that will sell you the computer time once or twice a year will do. Restore all databases, forward recover, and run the selected jobs. Typically, the Internal Audit Department participates in these tests. They add credibility to the test.
- After this test is complete, bring all the test results back to the computer center and review them with the users. Evaluate the

test results in a relaxed environment. Proper validation is an essential element. If the test is not correct, correct the problem(s) and repeat the test. The test may have to be repeated, but you will probably never encounter a problem which could not have been corrected during processing in the event of a real disaster.

- The second element of verification is the administration of the disaster recovery contingency plan. Annually, evaluate all of critical and secondary systems and reestablish their processing requirements. On an ongoing basis, but at least once per quarter, update the disaster recovery contingency plan manual. Update the backup system whenever hardware or software changes are made, and update the Management Information Systems (MIS) Standards and Procedures and Corporate Policies and Procedures, as required.

Conclusions

It is important to highlight that a disaster recovery contingency plan involves a tremendous amount of effort from the information technology group, not only to develop the plan but to exercise it every year. The disaster recovery contingency planning process does pay back many benefits. It causes the computer center to look closely at its operating procedures. The computer center must evaluate its methods, procedures and overall service and productivity objectives. Ultimately, the changes that are made to implement such a plan improve the computer center. Everyone hopes that they will never have to exercise such a plan, but the computer center must feel secure that if it does, this plan will work.

CONTINUOUS ON-LINE AVAILABILITY

One of the strategies for achieving an unattended computer center is to provide a self-service environment. In a self-service environment, computer center users enter their own data, schedule their processing and control the distribution of their output. It is an environment where the computer user has complete control of their information from creation through processing and consumption. In order to achieve such an environment, it is necessary for the computer center to have on-line systems available twenty-four hours a day.

On-line Scheduling

In a self-service environment, the computer center provides the computer user with the ability to change the routine computer processing schedule or to process ad hoc work without computer center intervention. This is achieved through an automated computer job scheduler. The automated scheduler eliminates the need to submit paperwork to schedule or reschedule routine or ad hoc work. The system provides the facility and security to submit job control parameters directly into jobs without any knowledge of JCL or without assistance from computer center personnel. Furthermore, computer users should be able to query the status of their own processing. Computer users need to know whether something has processed correctly. In a self-service environment, the last thing the computer center wants is hundreds of calls asking the status of a job.

A distributed automated scheduler provides the ability to view other scheduled work. This aids the computer user to schedule work that has cross-system dependencies and ensures that jobs will not be submitted when capacity is available. It establishes a basis for modeling the computer schedule and gives both the computer center and computer user a high level of confidence that their desired schedule can be met.

Once scheduling is distributed to the computer user, the computer center needs to keep the on-line systems available most of the day. In a multi-user environment, it becomes very labor-intense to survey users to find out when they want to work or if their jobs are complete. The system must be available at least sixteen hours a day, therefore, why not make it accessible twenty-four hours and completely avoid scheduling problems.

On-line Query

Over the last decade virtually all new computer hardware has been designed for on-line processing. Computer users are becoming accustomed to viewing information on-line. They are now capable of creating some of their own queries and reports. This situation is further complicated by flexible work schedules and working at home. It is no longer possible to assume that staff will work a normal 9:00 A.M. to 5:00 P.M. schedule.

Once again, the computer center has a very good case for keeping the on-line systems available most of the day. It is almost impossible to survey computer users needs when they work at home or when they work a flexible schedule. Therefore, the computer system has to be available almost twenty-four hours a day.

On-line Reports

When reports are required, centralized printing should be discouraged. Output should be stored on a direct access device and viewed on-line at a terminal as an electronic report. Electronic report distribution software directs reports to a disk device rather than to a printer. Once on disk, it can be retained for a predefined period, viewed and, if necessary, printed under the control of an end user. This is not a substitute for on-line query, but it is an outstanding intermediate step. It gets the computer user to begin to think in terms of the information they require rather than in terms of reports. However, the computer has to be available at the computer users' convenience, and in a world where users have the option of working flexible hours or from terminals at home, this can be twenty-four hours a day.

On-line Data Entry

Data entry is an accepted computer center function, although functionally, it is best performed at the source of the information. Each person who handles information reduces its accuracy and increases its cost. The ideal situation is to collect data at its point of creation via point of collection machines (electronic cash registers, automated tellers and the like), data collection devices and on-line data entry. To effectively accomplish on-line data entry, application systems need to be updated concurrently with batch processing, and the computer needs to be available twenty-four hours a day.

On-line data entry is achieved first by designing new computer applications for source data entry, by converting existing applications and by using easy-to-use on-line data entry systems that interface directly to computer based systems. Dismantle the data entry function and integrate data entry into the skill set of the computer user. A word of caution is in order; if the on-line systems are not available without restriction on work hours, much of the benefit of source data capture is lost.

On-line Quality Control

Self-service eliminates the need for control functions. The computer center is substituting automation for inspection. The computing center is using tools such as automated report balancing and control, automatic job scheduling and electronic JCL review to build quality. These are on-line tools, and automated quality is not an eight, twelve or sixteen hour a day job. It is a twenty-four hour a day job.

On-line Change Control

On-line change control is part of unattended computer center operation and a move toward self-service. Changes can be made on-line through the automated computer job scheduler. Program and support library management can be performed by programming and technical support staff using library support software under the protection of a security package. Programming and technical support staff can move modules into production libraries as part of the application development process.

Using the security system as the substitute for authorization, the computer center can allow programming and technical staff to maintain their own libraries. This eliminates labor in the computer center and expedites the task of the applications or technical person. Remember that application programmers correct computer problems at almost any hour of the day, frequently from their homes.

On The Horizon

What is on the horizon for computer centers? One device that is becoming common is Touch Tone Interface (TTI) or the ability to use a touch tone key pad on the phone to access information on the computer center. Too advanced? Well, it is being used by banks to query accounts and to pay bills. TTI is being used by insurance companies to query status and financial service companies to purchase stock. Universities are using it to register for courses. Retailers use it to make phone orders. TTI requires that systems be available twenty-four hours a day. Furthermore, there is support for robotics, on-line manufacturing systems and data collection. Twenty-four hours a day on-line processing is on the horizon for most everyone.

Conclusions

Computer centers need to provide twenty-four hours on-line system availability. They need to design or redesign applications to support concurrent batch and on-line processing, and they need to bring pressure to bear on vendors to support concurrent system and database backup, terminal implementation and operating software changes without interrupting computer processing and fault-tolerant computer architecture. This technology is available or technically feasible and can become universally available with sufficient pressure from commercial computer users. Don't wait until you need twenty-four hours a day on-line processing. The lead time for twenty-four hours a day, non-stop on-line processing can be years, and when you need it, it will be too late.

SUMMARY

Unattended computer center operation is achieved by eliminating unnecessary data handling, by providing a self-service computing environment and by automating the computer center. The computer center is eliminating the procedural steps which add no value to the data entered into the computer or produced by the computer. It is allowing computer users to enter their own data, schedule their processing and control the distribution of their output, and it is automating itself. The computer center is eliminating the fault points which are created by human intervention between the computer center and its users.

Implementing these strategies requires an ever increasing emphasis on physical and data security. It is increasingly important to insure the integrity of information from accidental or internal corruption. Furthermore, the wider use of the computer results in a greater dependence on the computer. This dependence demands that computer professionals implement a contingency recovery plan for extended service interruptions. Finally, the absence of human intervention in the computer center makes twenty-four hours a day on-line services a must.

Therefore, three computer center management functions are required before unattended computer center operation can be implemented: data security, computer center disaster contingency planning and twenty-four hours on-line availability. The value of the data security program exceeds the protection value of an individual program or device. The sense of security that is derived from a fully tested computer center disaster recovery contingency plan is worth the investment of time and monies. Finally, twenty-four hours a day on-line processing furthers the computer center's objective of self-service which improves the quality and service of the computer center.

Each of these are worthwhile business objectives in and of themselves. They are easily justified as stand-alone projects, and they are critical prerequisites to achieving unattended computer center operation.

Assessing Your Security Risk Index

INTRODUCTION

As discussed in Chapter Six, unattended computer center operation creates a renewed need to emphasis computer center security. Furthermore, the rapid advances in information technology and the increased need to process large quantities of information, as well as the greater availability of computing, is also increasing the need to secure computer based information. In support of this requirement, a series of security procedures are usually developed to circumvent the potential risks associated with increased access to computer based information and information processing. These procedures seek to maximize protection from areas of vulnerability. The procedures minimize the aspects of security that inhibit the use of information processing and the distribution of information while maximizing security, integrity and privacy.

Management plays a key role in security by ensuring that an organization is adequately secured through a series of prudent checks and balances. For corporate officers and other management, such as data processing management, there are legal implications in exercising prudent security management including the safeguarding of computer facilities, computer based information systems and information vital to the organization. Numerous court cases in which disgruntled share holders sued corporate officers have solidified this prudence management concept into a standard called the *Prudent Man Rule*. It requires that officers and other agents discharge their duties with the diligence and care that an ordinary prudent man would exercise under similar circumstances.

The specific conduct required to manage and protect information assets varies depending on the circumstances of any given organization. However, when little or nothing productive is done in connection with information technology security, the objectives of the organization are placed in increasing jeopardy. With the (1) extensive reliance on computerized accounting and record keeping, (2) the operating dependence on computer generated information, (3) the complexity of computer-based systems and control procedures, (4) the difficulty and cost of recovering from a serious error or catastrophic incident and (5) the fact that this far reaching risk is typically concentrated in a small area and in the hands of relatively few people, management can hardly ignore the need to evaluate security risk.

While 100% security remains elusive, a great many prudent policies, procedures and practices are possible to narrow security risks. The audit of policies and procedures is a common practice in most organizations. However, assessment of policies and procedures for risk is far less common. The following three-step risk assessment procedure isolates the areas in jeopardy and, therefore, reduces security risks:

1. Diagnostic procedures to assess and evaluate the level of risk associated with a potential security exposure.
2. Rating the effectiveness of existing checks, balances and protection measures.
3. Prioritizing corrective measures to address high risk areas and to avoid the adverse impact should a potential hazard materialize.

Having accomplished this three-step risk assessment procedure, management implements the corrective measures and audits for compliance. Routinely, management repeats the assessment and evaluation of the on-going level of risk associated with security measures.

SECURITY ASSESSMENT

The security assessment is a systematic method for assessing potential jeopardy to computer centers and computer based information systems. It enables management to take immediate steps to deal with information technology security by (1) evaluating risk, (2) establishing programs to minimize risk and (3) correcting or minimizing security risk.

Assess scope. The security assessment is a practical, low cost way to meet the prudent responsibilities of management. A security assessment can be carried out quickly, effectively and economically by in-house personnel. Designed to assist management, the scope of the security assessment typically includes a review of security, integrity and privacy.

1. Security is defined as the protection of computer centers, computer processing systems and data from accidental or unintentional destruction or disclosure.
2. Integrity is the verification of information, information processing or information storage for accuracy.
3. Privacy is the assurance of the right of an individual or organization to determine to what extent information is made available to others.

Reasonable use. The goal of information technology is to provide access to information and information processing services in support of organizational objectives. Information systems are not developed to inhibit the access and distribution of information. Management must guard against practices that convolute the goal of information technology such as:

- Guarding computer centers like a fortress and distributing media via public courier services.
- Storing the backup copy of critical information in the same building or in the immediate proximity of the computing site.
- Developing password procedures to restrict access to on-line facilities and then publicly posting the password.

- Implementing security procedures which are more complex or restrictive than comparable manual procedures.
- Limiting the electronic access to data when similar data is available to the same audience in paper form.

Attitude. People are not concerned with weight until they are overweight; they are not concerned with household security until they are burglarized, and they are not concerned with information security until there is a security breach. Security is a form of protection and like all forms of protection, be it insurance, police, armies and so forth, it is hard to get enthusiastic about it until it is needed. However, like all forms of insurance, the sicker you get, the harder it is to find insurance. Prudence dictates that it be there before it is needed.

The effectiveness of security, therefore, depends heavily on awareness and attitude. Employees need to become and stay security conscious. In the absence of security consciousness, a security program rapidly falls into disuse. Recognizing the need to be security conscious and then implementing a program of security consciousness is as important as the methods for becoming and staying secure.

THE SECURITY TASK FORCE

A security assessment can be informal, with information technology management and a systems analyst or analysts performing the assessment. For some organizations, this may be more than adequate. More commonly, however, the circumstances call for discussion and planning among a number of people.

This larger group of people can comprise a security task force or advisory board whose role is to plan the security assessment, open the right doors, secure the necessary cooperation, review oral and written assessment reports and recommend corrective action.

Task force representatives may encompass both line and staff organizations, among them information technology, internal audit, computer security, insurance, law and personnel. The chairperson for the task force varies by organization and, to a large degree, is determined by who initiated the assessment and whose leadership provides the greatest benefit to the mission of the task force.

At a minimum, however, the task force is charged with implementing the following eight steps:

1. Orient the task force to the mission and scope of the assessment and to the assessment procedures.
2. Select the individual(s) to perform the assessment.
3. Establish the ground rules for conducting the security assessment.
4. Develop, refine and expand the assessment items.
5. Assign weights to assessment items.
6. Review and critique the oral and written assessment reports.
7. Direct immediate corrective measures, review proposed alternatives and recommend priorities to management.
8. Schedule and initiate follow-up assessments.

Selecting an investigator. Of all the activities of the task force, selecting the individual to conduct the assessment is the most important. The committee should strive to appoint someone whose judgement, ability, objectivity and probing nature can be depended upon. This individual conducts interviews, reviews written materials and observes operations in and around the computing center. The assessment includes computer software development, and requires a knowledge of programming. The task force should select a technically proficient person, who is able to extract himself or herself from the technical details in order to organize his or her thinking and prepare a coherent report for review by the task force. If the organization has an Electronic Data Processing (EDP) auditor, the selection of the auditor or auditors is obvious.

Investigation methods. If the security task force feels it would benefit from the observations of more than one person during the security assessment, several approaches can be considered.

1. *Two person team with one evaluation.* Two investigators conduct every step of the security assessment, each hearing answers to questions posed by the other and probing areas of mutual or individual interest. They arrive at a single evaluation on each security item and record pertinent comments as required.
2. *Two person team with two evaluations.* This is the same approach as above except that each investigator makes his own evaluations and comments. The results are not disclosed to the other investigator. The reports may be separate or joint, but the differences in evaluation and comments are shown. Differences are most typically resolved by the security task force in the final report.
3. *Redundant assessments.* Two completely independent assessments are conducted. They are rated, commented and reported separately. The redundant assessment ensures complete objectivity and independent appraisals but may excessively tax the subjects of the assessment. With the *two-person team with one evaluation* approach, the investigators may compromise their findings to the degree that a single evaluation might prove more effective. *Finally, the two-person team with two evaluations* approach provides independent evaluations and does not add much burden to the subjects of the assessment. This method facilitates more reliable ratings, but it is crucial that team members do not share their evaluations.

Finally, the assessment can be conducted in any order that is convenient. Investigators should carefully review each security item in advance to be certain that they understand what is required and plan the assessment sequence to minimize the need to interview the same people multiple times. It is acceptable to plan the sequence of the assessment around the availability of staff.

DEVELOPING SECURITY ITEMS

Security items are the security topics that will be investigated. Table 7.1 is a sample of some of the items that should be included

SECURITY ITEM LIST

ADMINISTRATION	RATE	WEIGHT	ACTUAL SCORE	MAX SCORE	INDEX VALUE
• Is there an organization-wide policy for computer security?	4	4	16	20	.8
• Is a single individual responsible for computer security?	1	3	3	15	.2
• Is a single individual held accountable for each key element of computer data?	5	4	20	20	1.0
• Are procedures established to identify security violators?	5	4	20	20	1.0
• Have punishments been predetermined for security violations?	3	2	6	10	.6
• Are security violators punished?	3	3	9	15	.6
• Are software security procedures implemented?	3	3	9	15	.6
• Are software security procedures faithfully administered?	3	3	9	15	.6
• Are physical security safeguards adequate to protect computer facility?	4	4	16	20	.8
• Are employees instructed on how to enforce security procedures?	5	4	20	20	1.0
• Have adequate safeguards been taken to protect resources and data from vendor personnel?	5	2	10	10	1.0
• Does a disaster contingency plan exist, and is it tested annually?	1	4	4	20	.2
• Is attention to security a criterion used in evaluating personnel performance?	3	1	3	5	.6

Table 7.1.

in the security assessment. Developing this initial list of security items is the most significant obstacle to performing a security assessment. Perpetuating the assessment thereafter is much easier. After the first assessment, it is relatively easy to add, delete or modify security items.

For purposes of organization, it is convenient to categorize the security items into the following groups; however, they can be arranged any way that makes sense to the organization.

1. *Personnel.* Includes pre-employment investigations, employee and contractor bonding, personnel policies, employee orientation, exit interviews and similar personnel issues.
2. *Physical Security.* Includes computer center and ancillary area access controls, security activities, fire prevention, short and long-term power interruptions and intrusion alarm systems.
3. *Computer Center Operation.* Includes procedures for equipment use, preventive maintenance, environmental conditions, change controls for hardware and software, financial checks and balances, assessment trails, data entry, use of outside services, computing equipment backup and help desk procedures.
4. *Communications Security.* Includes time sharing network, the open or public communication network and the local area network (LAN) or wide area network (WAN).
5. *Data Security.* Includes data library access controls, data loss and error detection, modification and change controls for databases, data storage facilities and data retention, archival and destruction.
6. *Software Development.* Includes management and review of systems design, software development, software and system testing and software maintenance.
7. *Security Program.* Includes disaster contingency planning, security policies, the test of backup provisions, insurance coverage and security program responsibility.

Developing a list of security items is the most labor-intense aspect of the security assessment. The labor associated with developing the list can be minimized by collecting copies of recent literature on security. By analyzing the articles, the investigator can gain insight into the areas which other experts have identified as areas of vulnerability. These areas are translated into concise statements to be assessed by the investigator.

After the initial list is developed and classified, present them to a working session of the security task force. Use this working session as an opportunity for brainstorming. Expand the list to include as many new items as make good business sense, and remember, there is no limit to the number of which that can be investigated; therefore, be concise and avoid duplication and overlap.

The security assessment is an ongoing process. It is replicated as frequently as necessary, usually annually. Thus, the list of security items is dynamic. In each cycle, new items are added, and other items are dropped. Therefore, it is suggested that the list be maintained on a spreadsheet (LOTUS or Excel for example). In this way, items can be added or dropped. Furthermore, as ratings are developed, they can be calculated, and follow-up lists can be sorted with little or no manual effort.

Making the Evaluations

Each security assessment item is evaluated by the investigator or investigators. An item can receive an evaluation of yes or no or an evaluation of excellent, good, adequate, poor or very poor. Based on the evaluation, a numerical value is assigned as follows:

VALUE	CRITERION
5	*Yes.* The yes condition exists more than 90% of the time.
4-2	*Partial.* A partial rating is applied where a yes or no is not appropriate. A single value is determined from a range of 2 to 4. The high end means that the rating tends toward being yes, while the low end means that the rating tends toward no.
1	*No.* The no condition exists more than 90% of the time.

OR

---

5   *Excellent.* Carried out with superior effectiveness, or complete in all respects; evaluation applies more than 90% of the time.

4   *Good.* Effective or better than average performance; evaluation applies more than 80% of the time.

3   *Adequate.* Effective in most respects or satisfactory performance; evaluation applies more than 70% of the time.

2   *Poor.* Mediocre effectiveness or unacceptable in some important respects; evaluation applies more than 60% of the time.

1   *Very Poor.* Serious flaws and deficiencies, unacceptable in many important respects; rating applies more than 50% of the time.

All the evaluations are the best assessment of the investigator of security conditions at the time of the assessment. The evaluations are based on a judgement as to the degree to which something exists rather than being based on measurable fact. This means that complete agreement on the evaluations is usually not possible.

Unless the investigator has a tendency to make erratic evaluations, judgements will tend to be consistently high, low or on target. The security task force needs to be cognizant of such *halo* effects and discount subjective judgements when they become evident. Consistently severe judgements need to be avoided, but when they are detected, they need to be adjusted. Redundant evaluation methods are ideal for detecting and adjusting biased judgements.

Assigning Item Weights

As each item is developed, the security task force determines the weight it deserves.

Weight is a measure of importance; it is a multiplying factor. Its value depends upon the importance of the security item to an organization. Weight is not related to the evaluation, the evaluation is a measure of condition.

Weights. Weights may be assigned either before or after the security assessment is performed. Assigning weights before the assessment lets the investigator know what is important and could cause him to probe more deeply on highly weighted items. Assigning the weight before could also be undesirable in at least two ways:

1. A higher weight could influence a rating based on the predisposition of the investigator.
2. A lower weight could result in superficial treatment instead of the evaluation it deserves.

Assigning weights after the security assessment avoids these potential drawbacks, but it may create another problem: the assigned ratings may influence the assignment of the weights. The choice of approach, therefore, depends upon the judgement of the security task force. As a practical consideration, weights are not generally reassigned to security items after the first assessment. Therefore, it makes a lot of sense to assign weights before the assessment since that is the condition that will prevail after the first assessment.

Security items with a weight of zero should be excluded in advance so that the investigator will not waste time on assessments that are considered to be irrelevant or unimportant. Again, if a spreadsheet is used, this can be done with a minimum of manual effort.

Assigning Weights. Suggested weights should be based on the importance of the security item to the organization. The following criteria are suggested for assigning weights:

WEIGHT	CRITERION
0	Not relevant (exclude)
1	Normal
2	Important
3	Very important
4	Critical

All weights are set at normal (1), and a judgement is required to increase it or decrease it. Realistically, few items are categorized under 2, 3 or 4. However, because the assignment of weight is a judgement, individual variations may be expected. Such variations result from oversights, differences in knowledge and experience and other factors. One job of the security task force is to resolve such conflicts. To the extent possible, the task force ensures that the criteria for assigning weights is applied consistently. If the task force feels that the criteria need to be expanded or changed to support local conditions, the security task force can accept modifications.

Quantitative Scoring

Five columns are positioned on the right side of the security assessment document or spreadsheet for the following entries: (See Table 7.1).

- *Rating.* The investigator's numeric evaluation (1 to 5) of security conditions based on the assessment and entered during the assessment.
- *Weight.* A numeric measure (1 to 4) of the importance of the security item, typically entered before the assessment.
- *Actual score.* A calculated value (rating times weight).
- *Maximum score.* A calculated value (the highest rating possible times weight).
- *Security Index Value.* A calculated value (actual score divided by maximum score).

The relationship between the actual and the maximum score is important. This relationship is the security index and it is easy to calculate for each individual security item when a spreadsheet is used. The security index is determined by a simple calculation: divide actual score by the maximum score (actual/maximum). If the assessment is being manually compiled, this calculation will be labor-intense. It is not uncommon to have a couple hundred security items. The significance of the relationship between the actual and maximum score is essential for prioritizing the items for correction. Again, manually prioritizing the security items into priority sequence will be very labor-intense and a spreadsheet is highly recommended.

Index values may range from 0.00 to 1.00. In general, the following meanings may be given to any security index:

SECURITY INDEX VALUE	LEVEL OF SECURITY
1.00 – 0.90	Excellent
0.89 – 0.80	Very Good
0.79 – 0.70	Good
0.69 – 0.60	Adequate
0.59 – 0.50	Poor
0.49 – and below	Very Poor

It is important to recognize that the security index is a calculation based on a numeric value assigned to a judgement and has all the limitations of judgement. As such, its usefulness is restricted to providing a simple indication of overall condition for an item, classification or organization.

The goal of the assessment is to improve security and security awareness. When the rating and scoring are done, sort the items by the security index value from lowest value to highest within classification (personnel, physical security, data security and so on). The items that are most in need of correction are listed first in each security classification. They are the items with the lowest security index value. At a minimum, correct each item with a score of less than good. Give priority to correcting the security items that have a low security index value and a high weight since these items are designated as important but have been assessed as having low compliance.

Cautions and Recommendations

Assessment Recommendations. During the security assessments there will be a tendency to offer suggestions for remedial action. Resist this temptation unless there is clear and imminent danger. The mission of the security assessment is to present an accurate picture of existing conditions. Straying from this mission by offering on-the-spot recommendations typically creates more problems than it solves since all the facts have not been gathered and thoughtfully analyzed. Furthermore, on-the-spot recommendations can create a defensive condition and there may be no follow-up on such recommendations. Specific recommendations for improvements should be recorded as a comment for later review.

Comments. Comments should be used extensively if the security assessment is to provide a practical basis for corrective action. Unless a security item is so explicit that further comment is unnecessary, observations should be recorded as they occur. Not only do comments indicate the specific reasons for a rating, but they also serve to stimulate report narrative. Listed below are some situations that could require comment:

1. To disclose reasons for high or low evaluations.
2. To explain the evaluation for critical items.
3. To make explicit a judgement, especially where an assessment item can be interpreted in different ways.
4. To describe recommendations, why they were made and to whom they were made.

Journal. Lastly, it is convenient to keep a couple of journals. The first is a list of assignments to show which assessment items were covered by which investigator. The second is an interview journal to record names, places, and dates of meetings and appointments. These, like the comments, will serve to assist in developing the narrative that accompanies quantitative ratings.

SUMMARY

The success of unattended computer center operation depends heavily on implementing the three strategies of value added data handling, self-service computing and computer center automation. These strategies in turn operate under a security umbrella. Steps need to be taken to ensure the integrity of this security umbrella. The security assessment achieves this goal.

The effectiveness of a security assessment in turn depends upon the steps taken by management to ensure a free exchange of information throughout the assessment. The assessment requires the cooperation of the specialists within the organization, and it further requires that management communicate their determination to conscientiously execute and follow up on the security assessment.

The benefits that can be reasonably expected from a security assessment and the subsequent corrective actions include the following:

- Increased security consciousness.
- Compliance with prudent security measures.
- Increased management comfort about security adequacy.
- Improved protection from accidental or intentional security penetration.
- Structured analysis of continuing security requirement.

In order to derive these benefits, it is essential that security be continually tested. Therefore, prudent management requires that the assessment be repeated regularly, at least annually. Further, security items receiving a high weight should be reviewed independently and at more frequent intervals.

Finally, it is common for the primary emphasis of such an assessment to be on physical security. However, the increased demands for personal computing, decentralized programming, end user query computer center automation and source data entry shift the emphasis to security. Further, the nature of computing is changing; on-line processing, computer networks, interactive processing, distributed databases and so on are creating new opportunities for security breaches. In the future, it will be necessary to shift the emphasis of the assessment again to eliminate these and other new opportunities for security breaches. The security assessment is an evolutionary approach to security, and it can accommodate such requirement changes.

The
Tape
Escape

INTRODUCTION

The most significant technical obstacle to unattended computer center operation is tape usage. Although there are no simple, inexpensive replacement alternatives to tape, there are ways to significantly reduce the use of tape, to automate the manual handling of tape cartridges, and replacement alternatives are available with more on the horizon.

One company that operated a 15 MIPS class IBM mainframe computer, twenty-four hours a day, seven days a week reduced its staff to eight. The center operated with one operator per twelve hour shift or five operators. It had two people on the day shift, a scheduler and a utility person, and one management person. A total of eight people to operate a 15 MIPS class computer center. Had the computer center been able to eliminate tape, it could have operated with no operators. Unattended computer center operation is possible and tape continues to be one of the technical obstacles.

Software to manage and reduce the size of tape libraries has been available for a long time. Automatic tape cartridge loading and picking systems are available to assist or eliminate the manual handling of tape cartridges. The per unit cost of DASD is decreasing, making it a more reasonable alternative to tape for many applications. Finally, mass storage devices are available which store up to a terabyte of data in a very small foot print and optical disk is becoming commercially available. For most computer centers, a significant amount of, if not all, tape usage can be eliminated through the use of such technologies.

Solutions for other technical obstacles such as computer scheduling, operator interaction with the computer and hard-copy report distribution are available. In some cases, they do not provide a complete solution, but the inadequacies can be solved or easily skirted.

THE IMPACT OF UNATTENDED OPERATION ON DATA STORAGE

There are many steps to implementing unattended computer center operation but for purposes of discussion they can be summarized into three strategies which have a direct impact on data storage. In one respect, they are eliminating the need for tape storage while simultaneously increasing the demand for direct access storage.

One of the first impacts of unattended computer center operation is an increased reliance on on-line processing. Over the last decade, all new computers have been designed for on-line processing. It is a recognized fact that providing computer users with the ability to directly update and retrieve information contributes to improved productivity and creativity.

If computer professionals are designing batch-orientated systems, they are spending their most valuable resource, the ability to generate software, on something that is obsolete before it is even off the drawing board. Unattended operation is giving the computer user the ability to interact directly with the computer, and this is increasing the demand for on-line systems.

Second, unattended computer center operation is increasing the reliance of the computer center on automation software. Automation software is being used to remove the fault points between the computer center and the computer center user. The computer center is suffering from shoemaker's children syndrome. While the information technology professionals are automating other business functions, the needs of the computer center have been ignored. The operation of the computer center ends up being a strange combination of manual and automated techniques, thereby, decreasing its effectiveness and the confidence level of the computer center user.

Lastly, unattended computer center operation is increasing the self-reliance of the computer center user. It is nice to provide a support service but experience demonstrates that individuals and organizations are most productive and most creative when they are self-reliant. Unattended computer center operation is based on the concept of self-reliance. It does not remove the life-net, but it does remove the crutches.

Unattended computer center operation is, therefore, increasing the demand for direct access storage. To better understand this growth, direct access storage is classified into three categories: on-line data storage, working storage and support software storage.

- *On-line data storage* is information storage: databases, VSAM files or flat files used to store operational or historical information.
- *Working storage* is the reusable storage that is used by the computer to support on-line or batch-production on the computer. Working storage is the DASD used for page-swap datasets, spool datasets, for temporary datasets, test datasets, for even some productions data and for temporary-production datasets, data sets that go away after a production cycle.
- *Operating software storage* is the operating system, the teleprocessing monitor or monitors, all of the computer center operation support software and the application software.

When the direct access storage is analyzed in terms of these three categories, the typical database environment uses approximately one third of its DASD for on-line database storage, one third for working storage and one third for operating software, as illustrated in Figure 8.1. The surprising aspect of these statistics is that only one third of the direct access storage is being used for on-line information storage in support of application systems. The majority of the direct access storage is being used for working

DASD STORAGE

ON-LINE STORAGE
(DATABASE, ETC)

WORKING
STORAGE

OPERATING
SOFTWARE

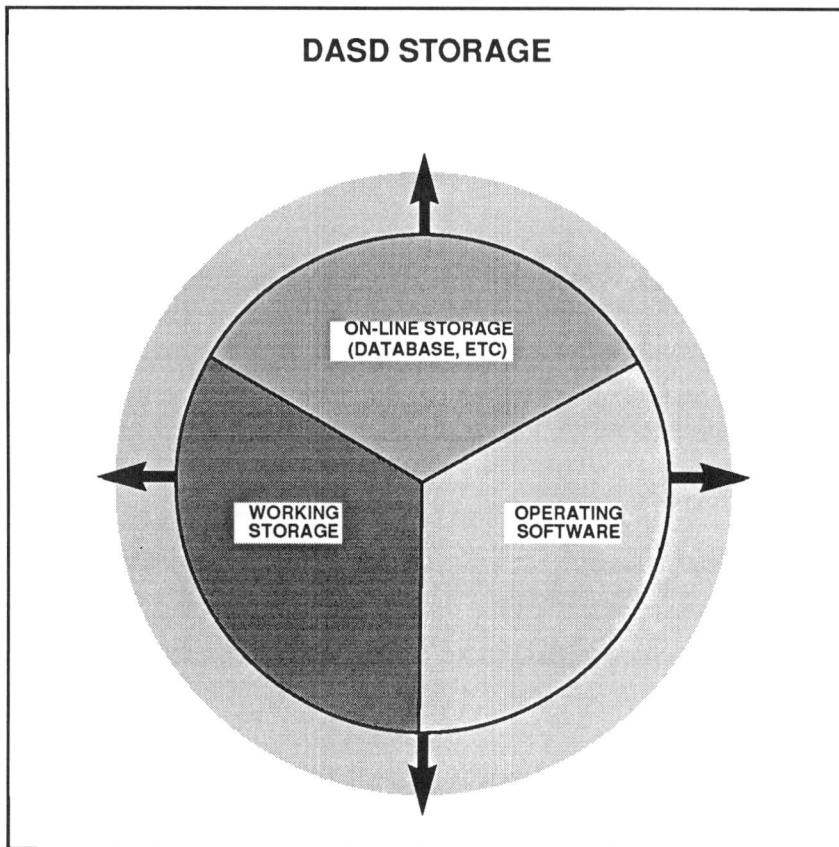

Figure 8.1. DASD is used for storing on-line information, for working storage and for operating software storage. The total pool is increasing at 20-30% per year.

storage to improve the performance of the systems and to store operating software and software libraries. Finally, irrespective of the direct access storage category, the DASD storage is increasing at a rate of twenty to thirty percent per year and, in some cases, it is actually reaching forty percent per year.

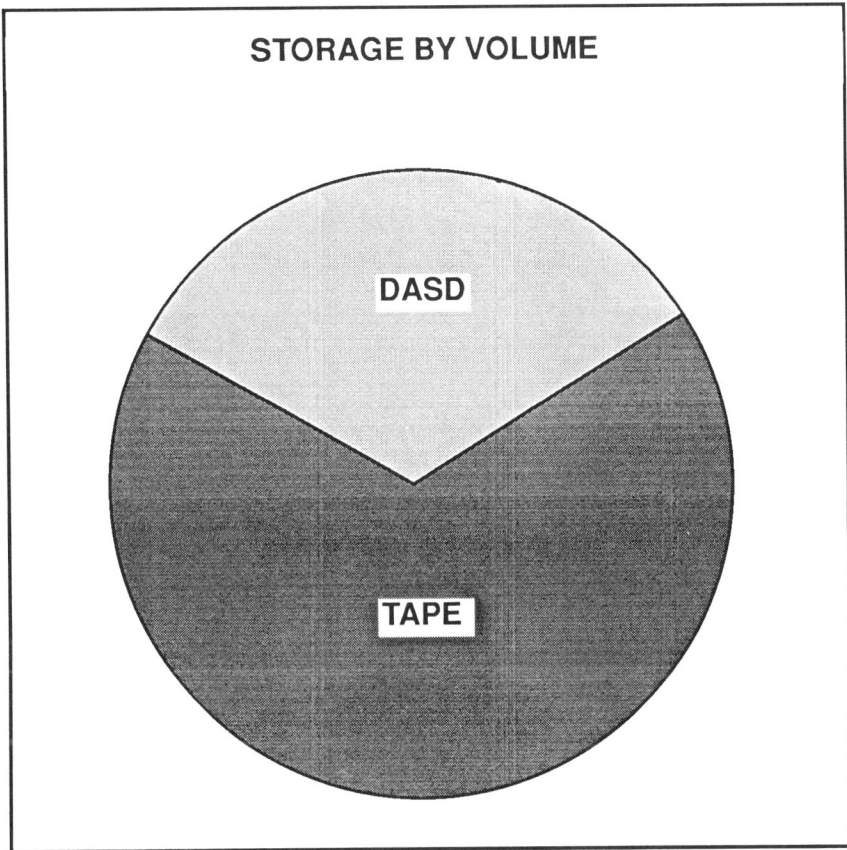

STORAGE BY VOLUME

DASD

TAPE

Figure 8.2. Storage by volume.

So far, this analysis has addressed the impact of unattended computer operation on direct access storage. However, when the total storage requirements of a computer center are analyzed, a different picture results. In the typical computer center, as shown in Figure 8.2, about one third of the storage is DASD and about

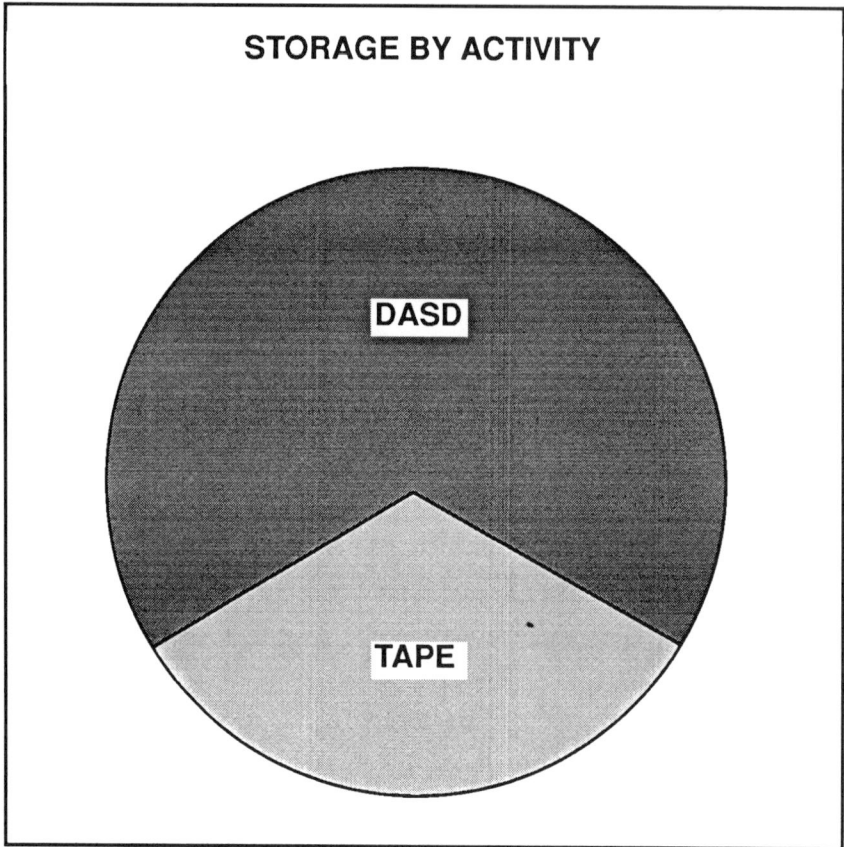

STORAGE BY ACTIVITY

DASD

TAPE

Figure 8.3. Storage by activity.

two thirds is tape. This ratio can change dramatically depending upon the status of application software. Typically, a database environment tends toward a two to one ratio while a batch environment may have a tape to disk ratio as high as ten to one. Computer centers having a preponderance batch oriented systems or older tape based systems have more tape storage.

However, when storage is analyzed by activity, as shown in Figure 8.3, the picture is exactly the opposite. The vast majority of

---

STORAGE CLASSIFICATIONS

- **TIME DEPENDENT STORAGE (DASD)**
  Requires short response time on-line access, and is high utilization

- **TRANSITORY STORAGE (TAPE)**
  High volume information that has low utilization and is used for batch-processing.

- **TIME INDEPENDENT STORAGE (MASS STORAGE, OPTICAL DISK)**
  Information that can be accessed on-line when sub-minute response time is acceptable.

Figure 8.4. Storage Classifications.

the activity is against direct access storage devices. About two thirds or more is against the direct access storage and only one third is against tape. As with storage volume, the DASD activity may reach 90% and tape activity may be as little as 10%.

The two common ways of viewing storage are, therefore, storage by volume and storage by activity. Unattended computer center operation, however, is creating the new way of looking at storage time independent storage. Time independent storage is information storage that needs to be on-line but where response time requirement does not need to be instantaneous. The response time can be sub-minute rather than sub-second.

Using this new category of storage as a base, as shown in Figure 8.4, we can view how tape and disk fit into this new scheme. First there is *time dependent* storage, direct access storage, DASD. The attribute of time dependent storage is high-utilization, on-line access and short response time. Computer center users expect time dependent storage to have response times in the range of seconds or even sub-seconds.

The next category is *transitory storage*. Transitory storage is tape. It is a one time medium. It is used for transportation, and it is typically used to store large volumes of data. The vast majority of the tapes in most computer centers are used to backup direct access storage. In computer centers which rely heavily on database technology, tapes are not commonly part of the production process. Tape is used for storing historical data. The computer center writes out a tape and puts it into storage, never using it again. At best, the tape is used infrequently. Tape is also used as a medium to get data into the computer center from a service bureau or another computer center. It is used as an output medium to send data to another computer center. In some cases, it is being used as part of a production process, but again, the norm is to write it out once and read it in once. In this sense it is a one time, transitory medium.

Lastly, there is the new category of storage: *time independent storage*. Its attributes are low utilization, on-line access but rapid response time is not critical. Time independent storage can have sub-minute response time. Time independent storage is high-density storage mediums such as mass storage devices.

Using Time Independent Storage

Another obstacle to unattended computer center operations is the distribution of reports. Typically, the computer center produces reports using a machine that operates in nanoseconds, and then it takes hours and even days to get reports produced and distributed to the people who need the information.

An example of this is a company in the Midwest where the computer center is located in one building and the rest of the staff is located in four other sites, one in a city hundreds of miles away. This company installed an electronic report distribution system and attached low cost line printers onto its communication network. By storing high-volume reports on the electronic report distribution system and giving the staff the facility to print out exception reports and sections of very large reports on their local printers, it was able to expedite distribution, reduce print and improve the quality of the service.

Electronic report distribution changes the way in which the staff thinks about information. Over the last twenty-five years computer users have become acclimated to think in terms of reports when they require information. They ask for a report, not for specific information. In most cases, the same information could be available much more quickly on-line. Staff have become conditioned to having a piece of paper; it gives them a warm, fuzzy feeling. Electronic report distribution causes people to start to think in terms of information on a screen. It is a good transition medium for getting the staff to operate interactively with that computer. Electronic report distribution increases the requirement for on-line storage.

Time independent storage provides on-line access to historical information. Most organizations have on-line systems to update and view current information. However, the minute historical information is required, the systems are batch-oriented. If an accountant wants to look at ledger information that is a couple months old or a registrar wants to look at student information five or six years old or the marketing department wants to analyze marketing information for the past few years, or if any kind of historical data is required, the systems are batch-oriented.

In this scenario, the organization doubles the time and the cost to design a system. A batch oriented system is designed to get the older data, and an on-line system is designed to handle the current information. Computer users must have two sets of procedures, one for retrieving historical data, and one for interacting with current data. The real cost of that historical information is in duplication. Computer users are forced to accept this duplication because tape is low cost. This is false economy. In most cases, the strategic value of historical information is in the ability to analyze historical information, and it is this information that we have made difficult to retrieve. In a self-service computer center there is a greater demand to keep more historical information available on-line but immediate response time is not mandatory.

In an unattended computer center, there are no people to respond to problems, and no matter how efficient the computer center, something will go wrong. Under those circumstances, technical staff need access to the voluminous log information on the system. Furthermore, production applications tend to have the same kind of historical audit trail, and this also needs to be accessible in the event of a system failure. Log information is voluminous and needs to be on-line, but immediate response time is not essential.

Last, there is electronic vaulting. Electronic vaulting is the ability to electronically store and retrieve DASD backups and historical information off-site. Most computer center staff is both competent and conscientious. Yet, few, if any, computer centers have ever had an off-site vault audit where everything that should be there is there. In most cases, somebody has forgotten to take something off-site, and the tapes are sitting in the computer room.

Furthermore, conventional vaulting procedures result in delays. Backups are processed, and those backups remain in that computer for hours waiting for someone to pick them up. When they are picked up, a van driver hauls them in an unsecured van to some secured location.

In summary, there is time dependent storage (DASD), transitory storage (tape) and a new category of storage, time independent storage. Time independent storage is high-density on-line storage such as the Masstor System M960 or M1000 mass storage devices or optical disk storage devices (See Appendix A). Today, time independent storage is a very small fraction of the total storage market, but as time passes, it is going to become an increasingly larger percentage of the storage market. Both time independent and time dependent storage will continue to grow, taking the market share from tape. In fact, tape is an obsolete media that computer centers hang onto because of false economics.

The Tape Escape

In order to achieve unattended computer center operation, it is necessary to eliminate the dependency on tape. This requires a going, going, gone tactic. The computer center needs to take every opportunity to reduce the use of tape, to automate tape handling and to implement tape replacement solutions.

Reduce The Use Of Tapes. The first step is to reduce dependency on tape. If the computer center has a large number of tapes, (5,000 or more) it is almost mandatory that the computer center have a tape management system. Tape management systems, such as the Computer Associates CA-1, TMS, control the inventory and disposition of tapes. Tape management systems are valuable tools isolating the use and reducing the inventory of tape volumes.

Start the process of reducing the inventory of tapes by discontinuing the design of software systems that require tape as a processing medium. Eliminate the use of tape as a storage medium from existing systems whenever possible. Look for ways to reduce the numbers of tape volumes. Statistics indicate that 80% of all tapes use only a few inches or feet of the tape reel. Install software to stack multiple datasets on a single reel using software such as the Tape Dataset Stacking Utility offered by U. S. Denver, Colorado. Stacking datasets increases the access time to retrieve a dataset, but there is also a very good chance that the tape will never be used again or at worst, that it will be used infrequently.

The first step toward eliminating tape is to limit the scope of the problem. Stop developing new applications that require tape, and decrease the number of tapes in the inventory.

Automate Tape Handling. The second step is to reduce the manual handling of tapes. Convert to the IBM 3480 cartridge tape system. Further, by installing a tape stacker, it is possible to significantly reduce the manual operator intervention required for tape cartridge handling.

Another alternative for reducing manual tape handling is the automated tape library (ATL). Automatic tape libraries are essentially tape cartridge picking systems that reduce or eliminate the operator labor required to pick and load tapes. Two such systems have been announced: the StorageTek 4480, Cartridge Subsystem, and the Memorex-Telex 5400, Automated Tape Library. The StorageTek unit has a minimum capacity of 6000 cartridges while the Memorex Telex has a minimum capacity of 658 and expands to a maximum of 5152 in increments of 600.

Since most computer centers do not exclusively use cartridge tapes, it is difficult to eliminate all computer operators through such systems. However, computer centers which have large volumes of tape mounts and multiple operators per shift can significantly reduce the need for operators with such systems.

Eliminate Tape. The final step is the elimination of tape through the use of high-density, time independent storage. One such device is the Masstor System M960 that stores data on bullet-shaped cartridges and is capable of storing 110 Gbytes of data per unit (220 Gbytes compressed) and the M1000 that stores 1.6 terabytes of data on a tape cartridge. Both devices have a footprint smaller than a refrigerator. These devices provide sufficient storage to totally eliminate the use of tape as a storage medium. Further, the devices are capable of staging data on a direct access storage device. Access time is quick enough that they can become a substitute for disk for time independent storage.

Another emerging technology is optical disk. The sale of twelve-inch Write Once Read Many (WORM) drives is increasing at a rate of about 30% per year. International Data Corporation forecasts that 6,500 twelve-inch WORM drives will be sold worldwide in 1988 and that annual sales will reach 13,500 by 1992. Optical technology has recently received a boost from IBM's announcement of Imageplus that will eventually allow corporations to store and retrieve text and graphics from the AS/400 midrange mainframes.

DATA/WARE Development Corporation in San Diego, California offers an optical storage subsystem that plugs directly into IBM s/370 and PCM computer systems as a direct replacement for DASD. The DW 34800 Optical Storage Subsystem has a capacity of from 190 to 760 gigabytes. Since this device is write once read many, it is still not a replacement for all DASD. It is most valuable for the storage of static information.

Another optical device from Filenet Corporation in Costa Mesa, California marries magnetic devices with an optical library. The Filenet on-line storage subsystem holds up to 64 twelve-inch optical disks each holding 1 Gbyte of storage per side or 128 Gbyte per library. Since such optical devices are write once and read many, they are limited to the storage of static information.

For this reason, optical disk has serious limitations as vehicle for time independent storage.

SUMMARY

Unattended computer operation is achieved through value added data handling, automating manual computer center functions and self-service computing. These strategies are changing the way that computer center looks at storage. It is increasing the demand for on-line storage while simultaneously decreasing the demand for tape storage.

Historically, tape has been a very labor-intense and error-prone storage medium but it is viewed as inexpensive. However, when batch systems are created to specifically take advantage of tape, it becomes a very expensive medium. On-line systems are created to access current information and batch systems are created to retrieve and analyze historical information.

The most expensive aspect of information technology is developing application software and duplicating the effort because tape is inexpensive. Furthermore, if organizations are developing batch, tape-oriented systems, these systems are obsolete before they are implemented and again we are wasting our most expensive resource.

Therefore, the major technical obstacle to achieving unattended computer center operation is tape storage. In order to eliminate tape, the computer center needs to first reduce the dependence on tape. Next, it needs to automate the handling of tape, but most importantly, an alternative for tape storage needs to be installed. Computer centers need to install storage that can be accessed on-line but do not necessarily need immediate response time. Such storage is available in the form of mass storage devices and is on the horizon in the form of optical disk.

The objective of unattended computer center operation is to improve the quality of computer center products and services through automation. This translates into decreased labor cost in the computer center and in the computer user's department. Unattended computer operation is improving the quality of products and services by removing the fault points and one of the major fault points is tape.

Electronic Vaulting

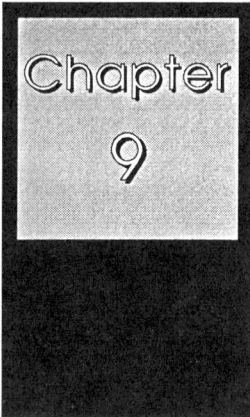
Chapter 9

INTRODUCTION

The requirement for adequate, controlled, off-site storage of critical information is apparent to all information technology professionals. Any organization, regardless of size, which depends upon computing for its operation cannot risk the chance that active or historical information may not be available when required. Acts of God and the volatile nature of computer-based information make it very likely that even the best managed computer center will require the reconstruction of computer based information. A failure to properly protect this information is simply a case of dereliction of duty on the part of computer center management.

The protection of critical information is further exacerbated by the increasing numbers of departmental computers, personal computers and word processors. While computer center management may not be responsible for these types of information, computer center management is usually well versed in backup and storage techniques and should take appropriate steps to communicate that information.

The time and effort required to plan, implement and maintain effective off-site vault storage protection procedures need not be great. Once in place, the effort to maintain the plan becomes routine. The total amount of time and money expended on off-site storage is usually minuscule in comparison to the total computer center budget.

Despite the expanded requirements for off-site storage and the availability of competent, conscientious staff, rarely are off-site vaulting procedures perfect. The off-site vault rarely contains everything that should be there. In most cases, somebody has forgotten to take something off-site, and it is sitting in the computer room. This situation is further compounded by delay. Backups are processed, and remain in the computer room for hours waiting for someone to pick them up. When they are picked up, a van driver hauls them in an unsecured van to a secured location. There is a real need to automate the off-site storage of magnetic media.

ELECTRONIC VAULTING ALTERNATIVES

Off-site vault storage is a manual, labor-intense, error-prone, costly computer center function that can be automated through electronic vaulting. Electronic vault storage is the ability to electronically store and retrieve back-ups and other historical computer based information in a site remote from the computing center. The electronic vault is connected to the computing center via a direct channel connection, a phone line or a Local or Wide Area Network (LAN or WAN). On the other end of this communication connection is one or more of the following devices: Direct Access Storage, Mass Storage, Optical Disk or Automatic Tape Library.

Direct Access Storage Devices (DASD). The cost of DASD is decreasing and, as a result, it is possible to keep more information available on-line than ever before. Most organizations have on-line, DASD based systems to update and view current information. However, when historical information is required, the system is batch-oriented and tape-based. If an accountant wants to look at ledger information that is a couple months old, or a registrar wants to look at student information five or six years old, or the marketing department wants to analyze marketing information for the past few years, or if any kind of historical data is required, the systems are batch-oriented.

In this scenario, the organization doubles the time and the cost to design a system. A batch-oriented system is designed to retrieve the older information, and an on-line system is designed to handle the current information. Computer users must have two sets of procedures, one for retrieving historical data and one for interacting with current data. The real cost of that historical information is in this duplication. Computer users are forced to accept this duplication because tape is low cost. This is false economy. In most cases, the strategic value of historical information is the ability to manipulate and analyze historical information, and it is this information that computer centers have made difficult to retrieve.

The introduction of double and triple density IBM 3380 disk drives and channel extenders make it possible to increase the availability of strategic information by keeping more of it on-line. Furthermore, it is now technically possible to backup all disk storage onto a mirror image located in another location apart from the main computer.

Using DASD to backup DASD is still an expensive alternative. As a result, information storage must be well managed: the number of backups needs to be minimized, information duplication and unnecessary information need to be eliminated. The availability of electronic backups increases the speed that information can be retrieved, allowing some of the information stored on tape to be eliminated. For example, backup information is usually stored locally and in an off-site vault because of the long retrieval time should it be required. Electronic vaulting eliminates the need to keep a copy of this information in the computer center.

Few computer centers are able to use DASD for their electronic vault. However, DASD as a backup medium for DASD is an opportunity to streamline information storage, to provide greater access to historical but more strategic information and to reduced application development cost. The reduced cost of DASD hardware is making this alternative feasible for some computer centers.

Mass Storage Devices. Another alternative for electronic vaulting is the mass storage device. This type of storage device uses helical scan recording common to video recorders and the flight recorders in modern military and commercial jet aircraft. Masstor Systems of Santa Clara, California markets a unit that is capable of packing up to 700 megabytes of storage in a bullet shaped cartridge about 3.5 inches long and up to 220 gigabytes of storage into a box the size of an IBM 3380 type disk drive. A single system comprised of two control units and eight storage units is capable of storing up to 1.76 terabytes (trillions of bytes) of data in the footprint of approximately ten 3380 type disk drives. One east coast user of this technology determined that a configuration of three storage units and two control units had sufficient capacity to replace a tape library of more than 10,000 tapes. For the really storage hungry computer center, Masstor Systems has announced a second device scheduled for delivery in the middle of 1990 that provides 1.2 terabytes of storage in the footprint of a single 3380 disk drive.

The Masstor device is a fully automated storage and retrieval system. The device can be located in the computer center or in a remote site up to 1.8 miles from the host site. For remote connection it uses channel extenders and 4.5 megabytes per second data-streaming channels. Furthermore, the device has dual write capabilities permitting two copies of data to be created from a single write command. This permits a second backup copy of information to be created without consuming computer cycles.

These features make the device ideal for both unattended computer center operation and electronic vaulting. A storage unit can be located in the computing center and another at a remote site up to 1.8 miles away. When backups are created one copy can be created for the central site and one can be created for the electronic vault with a single pass through the data. The small footprint and the high capacity of the device provide a unique opportunity to automate another aspect of the computer center, the off-site vault.

Automatic Tape Libraries. Computer center automation is a high priority for many large computer centers. Computer centers are experiencing budget crunches as organizations try to get more for their computing dollars. Two of the most labor-intense aspects of the computer center are print and tape processing. As much as

25% or more of the labor required to operate a computer center can be committed to tape processing: retrieving, hanging, filing, cleaning and transporting tapes.

Other than speed and compression, tape technology has changed little over the last three decades. The most significant change is the introduction of the IBM 3480 cartridge tape drive. The IBM 3480 improved the situation in two ways: it has reduced tape handling, and it has led to the introduction of the automatic tape library. Tape drives have always required a two for one intervention ratio for every tape. For each tape, a person intervenes once to hang the tape and and once to remove the tape. The 3480, when used with a tape stacker, reduces this intervention ratio to one for one or less. This is the first major advance in labor reduction for tape processing since the self-loading tape.

Second and even more significant, the tape cartridge has led to the introduction of the automatic tape library. Automatic tape libraries (ATL) are automatic tape cartridge picking systems. The system uses robotics to select tape cartridges and inserts them into a read/write station, returning the cartridge to the appropriate inventory slot when the processing is complete. The ATL virtually eliminates all human intervention and creates an opportunity for a near on-line storage condition.

In near on-line storage, information is stored in batch files on tape and as required the ATL provides the opportunity to quickly load the information onto DASD for on-line processing. The ATL can be used as an electronic vault. The down-side to the ATL is that they require a relatively large amount of computer room floor space and the burden of improving the storage utilization of a tape cartridge is still a computer center burden.

Two automatic tape library (ATL) systems have been announced: the StorageTek 4480 Cartridge Subsystem and the Memorex Telex 5400 Automated Tape Library. A similar announcement seems to be imminent from IBM, thereby giving creditability to the ATL technology. The StorageTek unit has a capacity of 6000 cartridges while the Memorex Telex has a minimum capacity of 658 and expands to a maximum of 5152 in increments of 600. Since an ATL looks like a 3480 type tape drive to the computer, one can be located in the computing center and another can be located in a remote site. When backups are created, a copy can be created for the central site and a second copy can be passed to the remote site, thereby creating an electronic vault. The storage capacity (circa 6000 tapes) and the large footprint diminishes some of the value of the ATL as an electronic vault, but, nevertheless, it is a workable solution.

Since most computer centers do not exclusively use cartridge tapes, it is difficult to eliminate all computer operator intervention through such systems. However, computer centers which have large volumes of tape mounts and multiple operators per shift can significantly reduce the need for operators in the computer center and can totally automate their off-site vault.

Optical Disk Storage. One of the continuing challenges of the computer center is to find more efficient ways of storing and retrieving information. At the heart of this challenge is the need to combine the rapid access of image type data and the data files associated with the data. Optical disk technology, which permits storage and fast retrieval of this data, appears to be part of the long term solution to retrieving documents and related data.

Optical disk systems are a good solution for storing and retrieving documents since many of the problems associated with commercialization have been solved. These include such solutions as the availability of scanning, digitizing, display and manipulation equipment, the refinement of mass production techniques for high-quality, low cost optical disks, and the development of disk library systems. Disk libraries are jukebox type devices which store and retrieve disks with storage up to a terabyte (a trillion bytes or a million megabytes) of data in a single cabinet, significantly increasing the storage density. The sale of twelve-inch write once read many (WORM) optical storage drives is increasing. Plug compatible optical replacements are available for magnetic disk and optical disk has recently received a boost from IBM's announcement of Imageplus that will eventually allow corporations to store and retrieve text and graphics from the AS/400 midrange mainframes.

Another optical device from Filenet Corporation in Costa Mesa, California, combines magnetic devices with an optical library. The Filenet on-line storage subsystem holds up to 64 twelve-inch optical disks each holding 1 Gbyte of storage per side or 128 Gbyte per library. Since such optical devices are write once and read many, they are limited to the storage of static information.

However, the optical disk unit tends to be a stand-alone device and is usually connected to the mainframe by some type of communication. This feature, as well as the high density of the storage, are desirable features for an electronic vault. However, the static information restriction of optical disk is a serious limitation to the electronic vault concept.

Benefits of Electronic Vaulting

Electronic vaulting improves reliability and makes the information more accessible in event of an interruption and automates the recovery process in the event of a disaster. Electronic vaulting is consistent with the goals of unattended computer center operation. It eliminates human intervention and improves the reliability of the backup and recovery process.

Improved Reliability. The process of off-site vaulting is a manual, labor-intense operation. During the development and support of computer based applications, data files are identified for off-site storage. Computer software is developed, and tape copies of these data files are produced for off-site storage. The copies are physically transported to a remote location. In most cases, this is a commercial site that is shared by many different computing centers. Routinely, these tape copies are returned to the computer center after being replaced by the current cycle. This manual, labor-intense operation is subject to error every step of the way.

Electronic vaulting irrevocably alters this process. After the backup process is defined to an automatic computer job scheduler, it is executed without human intervention, and copies are moved to the vault electronically. The electronic vaulting is immediate. It ensures that backups are not forgotten, that everything which should be in the vault is in the vault, that the wrong tapes are not returned to the computer center prematurely and that the commercial site does not jeopardize the information. Electronic vaulting significantly improves reliability.

Faster Retrieval. Electronic vaulting makes information in the off-site vault available for immediate retrieval. It reduces retrieval time from hours to minutes when time is most valuable during an interruption. Computer centers pay a premium for a delay in retrieving information. Technical staff and computer users lose the use of the computer until information is retrieved and restored. In most cases, the computer center abrogates this problem by making multiple copies: one for the computer center and one for the off-site vault. They double the processing, the human handling and the media cost in order to have immediate recovery and security from disaster. The electronic vault permits immediate retrieval of off-site information.

Reduced Backup Storage. Immediate storage and faster retrieval can significantly reduce the amount of backup data that is required to ensure the integrity of computing center processing. If data can be retrieved immediately from the off-site storage, less is required in the computer center. Furthermore, the ability to quickly retrieve historical information makes it feasible to reduce the amount of current information that is maintained on-line in the computer center. Less storage is less cost, and less storage is less opportunity for human error.

Disaster Recovery Contingency Planning. In the event of a computer center interruption, electronic vaulting can cut days off the recovery process. A list of eleven different alternatives for computer center disaster recovery contingency planning were presented in Chapter Six. In each instance, an electronic vault located at the recovery site or in a third party location would expedite the recovery process. Furthermore, increased reliability improves the likelihood that all the information required is available at the electronic vault. During a crisis situation, time becomes money and an electronic vault could make the difference between an organization's survival or failure.

Opportunity to Vault all Computer Based Information. The electronic vault is an opportunity to secure information from departmental computers and personal computers. The direction of computer technology is to install personal computers, departmental computers and special purpose computers and to network these computers together. Via a network, the data on such computers can be protected through copies that are initiated centrally and are archived in the electronic vault. This secures the information stored on these remote computers and automates one of the labor-intense aspects of computer network.

Expense Reduction. The electronic vault can be cost-justified. The vault eliminates the cost of an outside vaulting service, the cost of tape media and the courier and transportation cost. The electronic vault is part of the process for limiting the rapid growth of DASD storage in the computing center. It is an essential element of the computer center automation process. Without electronic vaulting, the staffing cannot be removed from the computer center. As an independent project, an electronic vault might be difficult to cost-justify, but as part of unattended computer center operation and in support of a disaster recovery program, it is easier to justify.

Unattended Computer Center Operation. Electronic vaulting is essential to unattended computer center operation. As much as 25% of the labor in a computer center is associated with the handling of tapes. If this labor is to be eliminated, it is necessary to find an alternative for automating the protection of vital computer based information.

Implementation Strategy

It is likely that most large computer centers will require more than one of the electronic vaulting devices to satisfy its needs. There are computing centers where the DASD alternative will work. Such computer centers will include computers dedicated to a single application, heavily on-line computer centers or centers that need to be back in operation almost instantaneously.

Some computing centers have a limited requirement for tape storage. These computing centers include those that rely heavily on database technology. Such computing centers can totally eliminate the use of tape with a mass storage device. However, in large, complex, multi-computer computing centers, it is likely that the electronic vault could consist of a combination of mass storage, automatic tape library (ATL) and optical disk: mass storage to copy DASD, the ATL for tape and optical disk for document storage.

Furthermore, the location of the electronic vault will vary based on the disaster recovery contingency planning alternative chosen. The device could be located in a site designed specifically to house the electronic vault; it could be located in a hot/cold site, or it could be located in an alternate computing site. The electronic vault could be part of a commercial off-site storage facility. To a large degree, the computer center disaster recovery plan determines the site for the electronic vault.

The planning and implementation of an electronic vault are usually spearheaded by the computer center management. However, the implementation team needs to include members of the technical service, database management, application services and security departments. The electronic vault creates new security requirements. It is necessary to insure that the communication link between the computing center and the electronic vault is physically secure. The electronic vault impacts the amount of data and the frequency of backups. It alters the way application systems are designed. The best alternative is to set up a task force of representatives from each of these areas.

SUMMARY

As a practical matter, computer centers must remain cognizant of the real risks in a poorly administered off-site vault storage program. The requirement to support the on-going needs of the business are real and increasing. Organizations which have suffered the loss of data files they were unable to reconstruct have been forced to stop doing business and some have gone out of business.

A study by the University of Minnesota (*Computerworld*, 1988) claimed that 93% of the organizations which lost the use of their computer center for 10 days or more filed for bankruptcy within a year of the event, and half filed immediately. Even those organizations which have been able to survive a disaster without a solid off-site vault storage plan, have faced severe hardships in maintaining their business.

On a somewhat less intense scale, the loss of records casts the organization in a poor light. Loss of business and customer goodwill cannot be treated lightly. There are instances where the loss of information has had a rather minor effect on the overall organization, yet the negative ramifications to the organization's image have been quite severe.

The need for an effective off-site vault storage plan is critical. It is, therefore, incumbent upon computer center management to move away from the manual techniques and to automate off-site vault storage. The computer center manager has the clear responsibility for seeing that an effective off-site vault storage plan is in operation and the most effective plan is achieved through electronic vaulting.

Rethinking Computer Center Design

Chapter 10

INTRODUCTION

Building or expanding a computer center is not an every day project for most computer center management. A well-managed computer center may only build a new or expand an existing computer center once every five to ten years. Furthermore, the typical computer center manager may only implement one such project during his or her entire career. Such projects are both complex and expensive. Construction includes site selection, architectural design, electrical, plumbing, security, and air conditioning work, as well as consideration for such directional issues as unattended computer center operation. It is not uncommon for a computer room to cost from $125 to $350 a square foot. A typical 100 foot by 100 foot (10,000 sq./ft.) room can cost between $1,250,000 and $3,500,000 without any computing or ancillary support equipment (air conditioning and electrical power conditioning).

The complexity of a computer center construction project is easily abrogated through a checklist approach to computer center design. Such checklists are readily available in data processing handbooks and are occasionally summarized in technical journals or periodicals. Philip C. Cross, a vice president at Group Health Insurance in New York City, is the author of an excellent series of computer center construction checklists. The checklists appear in Auerbach's loose-leaf *Data Processing Management* handbook.

Computer centers typically consist of four areas: the computer room, operation support area, electrical-mechanical support area and ancillary areas. Construction or remodeling of these areas usually include security considerations and frequently require site selection. Checklists minimize the risk associated with computer center construction because very little of the conceptual design for computer centers has changed over the last 25 years. Some aspects of computer center design have changed: the increased emphasis on physical security and the impact of the unattended computer center. These are the aspects of computer center design which need to be rethought.

COMPUTER CENTER ATTRIBUTES

Computer Room. The computer room is the heart of the computer center. All of the environmentalized computing equipment such as the central processing unit (CPU), direct access storage (DASD), tape, communication controllers, printers and and control units are located in the computer room. Typically, the computer room includes the master console or command center for operating the computer as well as the tape and media libraries and vendor service engineering area. The computer room is the most expensive area of the computer center to construct or expand.

Computer center automation and unattended computer center operation are having the most significant impact on the computer room. Reduced reliance on tape and the introduction of automated tape libraries and high-density storage such as the Masstor M960 and M1000 are reducing the number of tape drives and the size of tape libraries. The automated console response software and automated job schedulers are eliminating the computer console and the operation command center while electronic report distribution software is reducing the need for printing.

Unattended computer center operation is removing the people from the computer room. The work flow is changing, and more consideration is being given to optimizing space, to equipment change and to expansion rather than to human efficiency.

Operation Support Area. Another area impacted by computer center automation is the operation support area. The operation support area includes job setup, job balancing, troubleshooting, media pickup and the help desk. One of the strategies for achieving unattended computer center operation is to provide a self-service computer center. Self-service means that the computer center user is able to do their own for job set-up and scheduling. Computer job balancing is accomplished by the computer user assisted by an automated balancing tool, and media pickup is eliminated by an electronic report distribution system.

The objective of unattended computer center operation is to improve the quality of the computer center service and products. The introduction of computer center automation tools is building quality into computer center processing and quality reduces the need for quality control coordinators, trouble shooting and the help desk. The most efficient way to operate a computer center is to service the computer user correctly the first time. As the computer center achieves its quality objective, fewer support personnel are required, therefore, freeing valuable space for computer center expansion.

Electrical/Mechanical Support Area. The operation support area is being phased out while the electrical/mechanical support area is receiving *more* emphasis. The electrical/mechanical area is the area in the computer center which houses the support equipment for the computer center: electrical power, air conditioning, motor generators, water chillers, Uninterruptible Power Supply (UPS) and diesel generators.

Consistent and near perfect availability is an essential aspect of modern computer center management. The dependence on computer centers is increasing, and the cost of an outage is increasing. As a result, computer centers are installing redundant air conditioning, emphasizing clean power supplies and installing UPS systems to assure this reliability and availability. More than ever, the electrical/mechanical area is being emphasized.

Ancillary Areas. The ancillary areas are the reception area, guard station, staff lounge, janitorial room, locker room, elevator and restrooms. Despite the emphasis on computer center automation, the computer center is managed by people, supports people and will continue to be used by people. The computer center will receive visitors, it will continue to get dirty and it will continue to have equipment moved in and out.

The quality of the ancillary support areas can make a big difference in the overall efficiency of the operation of the computer center. A sloppy or ill maintained computer center reflects the attitude of management, and employees tend to reflect this in the way they perform their duties. The objective of the modern computer center is improved quality. To achieve this goal, well engineered ancillary areas are required.

Overall Considerations. Site selection and security join with the design and construction of each of the four major computer center areas. Developing a new computer center is a rare opportunity to select a site with adequate utility service, secure from natural disaster and complete with adequate parking and access. It is an opportunity to construct a building that minimizes the risk of fire, vandalism, water damage and security breaches while providing an opportunity for controlled growth.

Security considerations are becoming increasingly important during the construction and remodeling of computer centers. Security decisions are becoming career decisions. This is emphasized by the University of Minnesota study (*Computerworld*, 1988) that claimed that 93% of the organizations that lost the use of their computer center for ten days or more filed for bankruptcy within a year of the event and half filed immediately.

EMPHASIS ON PHYSICAL SECURITY

Early computer centers were show places. Computers were placed in glass cages and were shown off to customers, visitors and employees. However, as organizations became more dependent on computing centers for their very existence, they became cognizant of the risk associated with exhibiting the computer center. The computer center changed from showplace to fortress. There is less to see in the computer center and more reasons for not exhibiting it.

Computer centers are more heavily on-line oriented, and computer center management has tended to become so data-oriented that physical security is either overlooked or the protection is delegated to an existing security organization: a plant security or private police force.

Unlike other corporate assets, computer centers deal with information, and information has unique characteristics. It is intangible, transmittable and often irreplaceable. Too often, computer center security is considered solved by the acquisition of a physical access control system, completely overlooking the intangible nature of information. It is imperative that computer center security be planned and coordinated in conjunction with the unique characteristics of information security, and a period of construction or remodeling is an outstanding opportunity to achieve this.

The most important aspect of computer center security is that protection should be consistent with the level of risk, and the first step in developing computer security measures is to measure the security risk index of the computer center. A security risk index is achieved by conducting a vulnerability survey to identify the weaknesses in physical security. The mechanics for conducting such a survey are readily available in security literature (see "Assessing Your Security Risk Index," Miller, January 1989). Generally the survey involves a checklist of vulnerable areas and a systematic review of each area. Such a survey would normally include a survey of computer center location, construction, access control, fire and water protection and electrical power and environmental systems.

Once the security risk analysis is complete and the areas of vulnerability are identified, the next step is to evaluate effective safeguards and countermeasures. It is important to remember from the outset that approximately 20% of the security budget results in 80% of the protection and that any additional protection is very expensive. The cost of protection between the 80% and 99% level increases exponentially, and absolute (100%) security is impossible.

There are four tactics available for developing effective computer security safeguards and countermeasures during the construction or remodeling of a computer center: containment, deterrence, obscuring and recovery.

- *Containment* is safeguarding the computer center by isolating it from the view of the general public. Computer centers can be located in remote locations or in buildings that are easy to secure. The computer center can be located in a remote or inconspicuous site or in an existing site that has been made inconspicuous or more defensible.
- *Deterrence* is an active approach to safeguarding the computer center while containment is a passive approach to computer center security. Deterrence involves actions such as advertising stiff penalties for perpetrators, activities which increase the chances of being caught, installing early warning devices, active detection mechanisms or reviewing audit trails for patterns.
- *Obscuring* is a totally different tactic for securing the computer center. It calls for actions such as encrypting information, hiding physical assets, restricting the flow of information. It also can include activities which cut losses in the event of a breach of physical security. This could include backup and recovery, alternate processing sites and multiple locations.
- *Recovery* is the ability to cut losses to a minimum and restore the computer center in the event of a total disaster. Recovery is the process of developing and exercising a computer center disaster recovery contingency plan (Miller, 1986).

Location and Construction. Creating a secure physical environment starts with the physical site. Obviously, the computer site should be in an area that is not prone to physical disaster. When a computer center is located in such an area (earthquakes in California, hurricanes in Florida, or tornados in the Midwest) the nature of the disaster needs to be taken into consideration, and appropriate countermeasures can be taken to avoid or minimize the negatives. This is especially important for assessing the risk associated with disaster contingency planning.

The computer facility is best located in a stand-alone building, at ground level for easy access. When the location is shared with other occupants (even other data processing staff), it should be physically segregated from other occupants. Most computer center administrators do not have the luxury of choosing the computer center site. They inherit the site or economics force it on them. However, a clear understanding of the strengths and weaknesses of a site can go a long way to improve security and abrogate the negative of a site.

Access Control. Access control is based on (1) excluding unauthorized access to the computer center, (2) prohibiting unauthorized use of the computer center and (3) recording unauthorized access or use of computer center resources. Computer centers consist of many physical and logical areas. Physical areas are the computer room, the entrance, the lobby, the support area and the ancillary area. Logical areas are individual areas or clusters of areas that are available for restricted periods or unrestricted periods (9:00 A.M. to 5:00 P.M. weekdays or twenty-four hours a day seven days a week). Access control techniques are designed to limit access to sensitive areas while permitting access to legitimate computer center users and staff.

The most widespread access control devices are lock and key, keypad and card access systems. The strength of these approaches is that they are inexpensive and cover 80% or more of the requirements. The weakness is that keys and cards can be lost or given away. Other approaches are available such as retina scan and finger print or palm print scanning, but the cost of these devices increases exponentially and the risk must be there to justify them.

Fire Protection. Fire is the single most feared physical hazard to the computer center. A computer center can be threatened by fire originating in the computer center or in any other part of the building. There are three aspects of fire protection. The first is prevention: remove combustibles, use fire retardant furniture and eliminate smoking. The second is early detection to save lives and help reduce the damaging effects of the fire: smoke detectors and alarm systems. Third is extinguishing the fire: halon system, carbon dioxide (CO_2) and water sprinklers.

Water Protection. Water protection is similar to fire protection: the best defense is avoidance. The best defense against water damage is to locate the computer center away from potential hazards such as flood plains and underground springs. Locating the computer centers in basements, under restrooms or near kitchens should be avoided. Ceilings should be watertight and floors should have adequate drainage. Water detectors should be located under raised floors.

Electrical Power. Computer centers require consistent, reliable power supplies. Electrical problems can include brown outs, power spikes, power fluctuations and power interruptions. Power conditioning equipment can range from inexpensive voltage regulators to motor generators that maintain power for brief interruptions. Power conditioning equipment includes diesel generators and Uninterruptible Power Systems (UPS). A UPS is the most expensive and the most secure alternative. A UPS provides consistent power through a set of batteries charged by the utilities. If power is interrupted, the batteries provide from fifteen minutes to one hour of protection so the computer system can be shut down. If used in conjunction with a diesel generator, the computer center can be maintained indefinitely.

Environmental Systems. Computer centers require clean, filtered air at a constant temperature and humidity. The potential damage from problematic environmental equipment is very great. This is especially true for devices with close tolerances such as direct access storage devices. However, the risk of such occurrences is not high since there is usually warning of impending danger.

Some preventive actions can be taken. Air conditioning units should be modular to preclude complete outage. Air intake should be equipped with dampers to shut off outside pollutants. Units located outside the building (heat exchangers and air conditioners) should be secured and protected. Air intakes should be out of reach to avoid having harmful elements sprayed into the ducts (tear gas or mace).

A physical security program for the computer center is more than the protection of a fire alarm system or physical access control. The main element is the security risk analysis that determines the physical security requirements. The care which computer center management applies to the security risk analysis is rewarded in the form of a secure computer center and a minimum of security problems.

IMPACT OF THE UNATTENDED COMPUTER CENTER

Unattended computer center operation is a relatively new strategy based on the concept of self-service. Both the computer center and the computer center user achieves the highest level of quality and productivity when the computer user interfaces directly with the computer. The direct dialog between the computer user and the computer decreases the need for computer center staffing and changes the physical design requirements for the computer center.

Dark Room Processing. One of the concepts of unattended computer center operation is the *dark room*. Computer equipment which does not require operator intervention such as the CPU, DASD, control units and so forth are segregated into a separate room that is darkened. A second variation of this concept is to segregate non-critical processing into the second or third shift or weekends and to darken the room during these periods.

Computer center construction or redesign is an opportunity to adapt the construction of the computer room. The computer room can be designed to isolate the computer equipment and to accommodate the electronic monitoring equipment required to notify service or support staff of the impending or imminent failure of unattended equipment.

Dark rooms can be adjacent to the command center, or they can be located either above or below the command center. With channel extenders, it is now conceivable for the dark room to be located in a building apart from the command center. Regardless of the location, dark room operation is a departure from the traditional computer room layout, and more than ever, it is critical that the areas selected are secure, impervious to water damage and structurally sound. It is especially important to be sensitive to floor loading. More and more equipment is being concentrated into a smaller and smaller area with little or no human intervention.

Automated Problem Solving. The ideal computer room is one that is populated by equipment which never fails. Despite significantly improved reliability, such perfect operating conditions are not likely to be available for the dark room computer center. In the absence of perfection, computer center, technical service, application staff and hardware service staffs need to be available, and the computer room needs to be equipped with a mechanism to automatically recognize the symptoms of hardware failure and notify the appropriate personnel.

Computer room construction is an excellent opportunity to introduce an automatic problem notification system into the design of the computer center. As a stand-alone project, a notification system could be difficult to justify and might appear to be an unnecessary luxury. As part of the unattended scheme and imbedded in a construction project, its value is obvious.

Tape Elimination. The only significant technical obstacle to unattended computer center operation is the continued use of tape. Tape processing is a manual, labor-intense, error-prone and costly aspect of operating the computer center. It is not uncommon for 25% of the computer center staff to to be dedicated to tape handling. In addition, 10% or more of the computer center problems, such as missed deadlines, job rerun and lost information can be linked to tape handling.

The elimination of tape has a significant impact on the physical design of the computer center. Tape libraries and tape hardware consume large blocks of computer room floor space. They are usually strategically placed close to the computer console or command center to minimize the amount of operator travel. The alternative to tape is one or more different technologies: the Automatic Tape Library, an automatic tape cartridge picking system, the mass storage device, a high density tape storage device or the optical disk, a high density storage for image or document storage. These devices are a whole new class of unattended computer input/output devices which need to be planned into the computer center.

Some of these new devices reduce the requirement for floor space while others, such as the Automatic Tape Library (ATL) require large amounts of floor space (500 sq./ft.or more). Taking into account that the tape storage library goes away, the net increase in floor space is negligible. However, during the transition period, both the tape library and the ATL are required. In most cases a short-term increase in computer room floor space is as difficult to satisfy as a permanent increase in floor space.

Electronic Vaulting. Despite the expanded requirements for storage of magnetic media and the availability of competent, conscientious staff, rarely are off-site vaulting procedures perfect. The off-site vault rarely contains everything that should be there. In most cases, somebody has forgotten to take something off-site, and it remains in the computer room. This situation is further compounded by delay. Backups are processed and stay in the computer room for hours waiting for someone to pick them up. When they are picked up, a van driver hauls them in an unsecured van to some secured location. There is a real need for electronic vault storage to automate the off-site storage of magnetic media.

Off-site vault storage is a manual, labor-intense, error-prone, costly computer center function that can be automated through electronic vaulting. Electronic vault storage is the ability to electronically store and retrieve back-ups and other historical computer-based information in a site remote from the computing center. The electronic vault is connected to the computing center via a direct channel connect, a phone line or a Local or Wide Area Network (LAN or WAN). On the other end of this communication connection is one or more of the following devices: Direct Access Storage, Mass Storage, Optical Disk or an Automatic Tape Library.

The location of the electronic vault varies based on the disaster recovery contingency planning alternative chosen. The device could be located in a site designed specifically to house the electronic vault, it could be located in a hot/cold site or it could be located in an alternate computing site. The electronic vault could be part of a commercial off-site storage facility. To a large degree, the computer center disaster recovery plan determines the site for the electronic vault.

Regardless of the location, electronic vaulting impacts the design of the computer center. It creates the need for an alternate environmentalized site for the electronic vault. It also reduces the staffing in the computer center and streamlines manual tape handling procedures while eliminating the need for a tape staging area.

Increased Growth. One of the common design errors when constructing or expanding a computer center is to ignore expansion. A site is selected with rigid computer room boundaries that do not permit easy vertical or horizontal expansion. The computer center is constructed without adequate electrical power and air conditioning to support expansion. Common error such as these can turn expansion into a nightmare.

Unattended computer center operation eliminates such functions as data entry, schedulers, quality control, media distribution and so forth. By recognizing that these functions are targeted for elimination and by locating them adjacent to areas of the computer room that will expand, it is possible to accommodate future expansion with a minimum of construction. Furthermore, as computer center quality increases, and as computer center availability and reliability increase, the likelihood of a computer room expansion increases.

SUMMARY

Constructing a new computer center or remodeling an existing computer center is an opportunity to make the design of the computer center conform to the direction of information technology. Organizations have become increasingly dependent on computers for processing information, while the size and complexity of computer centers have increased. Dependency has increased the requirement for computer center security. Computer center construction is an opportunity to evaluate security risk and to ensure that physical security precautions conform to the risk.

Furthermore, the increasing size and complexity of the computer center has increased the difficulty of maintaining high-service levels using traditional manual techniques while simultaneously computer center automation is receiving a lot of attention. Computer center automation changes the work flow in the computer center while making space available for future expansion. It is an opportunity to introduce automatic hardware and support equipment monitoring, to isolate equipment that does not require human intervention and to recapture space to handle expansion without increasing the capacity of the computer center.

When constructing or remodeling a computer center, computer center managers need to weigh the increased demand for computer center security while gauging the impact of computer center automation on the current and future space demands.

Automating The Computer Center

Selecting Purchased Software

INTRODUCTION

The inability to develop low cost, high-quality software is inhibiting the rapid expansion of information technology. As development methodologies, high-level languages and similar techniques have failed, organizations have increasingly turned to purchased software as an alternative. The automation aspect of unattended computer center operation is following the same pattern.

Purchased software is very important to computer center automation, and its importance continues to increase. Virtually all of the operating and support software for computer center are purchased. A thorough understanding of the methods for selecting purchased software is critical to the success of an unattended computer center project.

THE PURCHASED SOFTWARE DILEMMA

Purchased software is not without problems. It is no less difficult for a vendor to develop software than it is for anyone else. The advantage of purchased software comes from an economy of scale; the vendor develops the software only once and then distributes the cost of development and ongoing maintenance over a large, installed base. The down-side to this is reverse economy of scale, the *Tower of Babel Effect* and obsolescence.

- Commercial software is typically developed using the most widely accepted and installed technology. For IBM mainframe users, this technology is typically CICS and VSAM. The selection of this technology is a marketing stratagem; use technology that reaches the largest base of potential users. The same holds true for departmental computer or personal computer users; develop software for the largest installed base of computers. In most cases, purchased software does not support such state-of-the-art concepts such as unattended data center operation. Further, since it is developed for the largest installed base of computers, it may not run efficiently on any one computer or operating system. The result is that most commercial software is not using the best technology and in many cases it is using obsolete technology.
- There is a resistance to making major functional changes to commercial software. As the cost of development and maintenance is reduced by spreading it across a large installed base, the cost of implementing major improvements is also magnified by spreading it across that same large installed base. This is reverse economy of scale. If a large installed base reduces cost, then major changes to this large base is, conversely, very costly.

    Further, the solutions to this dilemma are no less desirable. The supplier can maintain multiple versions of the software and lose maintenance economies of scale, or the supplier can drop support for users that do not maintain a specified level of currency and, therefore, lose ongoing revenues. Neither is attractive and the logical outcome is that purchased software becomes slow to evolve and obsolescence is accelerated.
- Recently, there has been a large amount of confusion and instability in the software market. Software suppliers have gotten into financial trouble and have curtailed support and development activities. Other software vendors have merged with larger vendors: UCCEL and Cullinet have been purchased by Computer Associates, and Duquesne and Morino have combined to become LEGENT. Software vendors with similar products are attempting to reduce the number of software products they support by consolidating their client base

into fewer products. Others are merging products into larger, more comprehensive, systems.

The result is that purchased software users are being forced to think in terms of reinstalling software, are experiencing large increases in on-going support cost and are finding it increasingly difficult to get assistance from software vendors.

• Another down-side aspect of purchased software is the *Tower of Babel Effect* or the use of multiple programming languages. The direction of data processing for the last two decades has been to standardize on a single programming language (COBOL, FORTRAN, PL/1). However, in an effort to reduce maintenance and improve flexibility, vendors are writing all or part of their software using in-house report writers or fourth generation languages (4GL's). This works well when the first software package is purchased and installed but becomes a problem with the second and a nightmare with the third, fourth and so on.

What happens is that each vendor provides a language, and usually the data processing group also purchases one or even more general purpose 4GL's. These languages add overhead to the operation of the system support staff; each language has a learning curve, requires cross training and results in dependence on trained individuals. The languages do not talk to one another, therefore, the name *Tower of Babel Effect*.

There is virtually no solution to this dilemma. Software suppliers use the languages for the custom part of their installation, therefore, it is difficult, if not impossible, to avoid using them. Suppliers use these languages as a further enticement for purchasing more than one of their offerings, forcing organizations to sacrifice functionally to avoid the problem of incompatibility. In some cases, the languages differ from package to package even from the same vendor. And in most cases, the vendor 4GL's do not substitute for general purpose languages, and even these cannot be eliminated.

• Finally, the use of database software has become common. Rarely is purchased mainframe software designed specifically for a database management system (IMS, IDMS, ADABAS, TOTAL). The installed base for each database management system is only a portion of the entire database market. Therefore, if used, the database limits the potential market for the software package.

The result is a choice between selection based on functionality or database compatibility. The ability to satisfy both is limited. The widespread use of purchased software is severely limiting the likelihood of having a single image corporate database of information. Further, it is severely limiting the flexibility of the organization to adjust software to the changing needs of its business.

The risk associated with purchased software is substantial. And in addition to the above directional, business and management problems, there are many other vendor related issues. These include such issues as vendor stability, mergers, acquisitions and simple nonperformance. There are also organizational issues such as software modifications, training requirements, budgeting considerations and installation standards.

The Benefits of Purchased Software

Yet with all the associated problems, the popularity of purchased software is increasing. Why is purchased software becoming more popular, and why would computer professionals complicate their life by installing something as risky as purchased software? The answer is productivity.

Purchased software provides an opportunity to deliver a complex system in a comparatively short time. Many of the more common applications are available in many different colors and flavors. In most cases, the software has a large installed base of users and a proven track record of success. It is common for them to be extensively documented. Further, the users are able to visualize the screens, reports and forms required to operate the system; they are given the opportunity to touch and feel them. Potential clients are given the opportunity to meet other clients; they share experiences and avoid installation problems.

Further, the benefits continue after the software is installed. The ongoing maintenance overhead for purchased software is far less than for in-house developed software. Staff is released to address issues that can only be satisfied with custom-developed software. New releases of the software satisfy new or legal requirements with little or no requirements definition. The users have an opportunity to continue to meet and share experience and to exert influence over the future direction of the software.

ESTABLISHING REQUIREMENTS

It is obvious that regardless of improvements in the ability to develop software, purchased software is here to stay. In order to effectively select purchased software, an organization needs to understand the functions and technical specifications that the ideal software would possess. These functions and technical specifications are the software requirements. By systematically analyzing available software and comparing the functional characteristics to the requirements, it is possible to select purchased software which maximizes the above benefits while minimizing the problems.

Selecting a software package is the end result of a long series of compromises. Some functions of the software are a perfect fit, other functions require compromise and some functions are missing. Therefore, it is important to understand what is required and which of these requirements are critical and which are not. When the time comes for compromise, it is, therefore, possible to select the software that best satisfies the critical requirements and will not be influenced by the satisfaction of superficial requirements.

It is best to group like-requirements into general classifications. The most common classifications are as follows:

Product Capabilities. Includes functional requirements for the type of software required (computer operating system, utility, sort, banking, inventory, and so on).

Technical Support Information. Includes such information as product documentation, communication monitor, operating system support and technical support information.

Implementation Information. Includes information about report set-up, hardware requirements, software prerequisites, implementation effort and complexity to change.

Miscellaneous Information. Include pricing, discounts and maintenance schedules, installed base of users, vendor information and user group information.

After the initial list of requirements is developed and classified, present them to a group composed of user representatives, information technology professionals and management. Make this a brainstorming session, and expand the list to include as many functional requirements as possible. Remember, there is no end to the number of items that can be added to a wish list, therefore, be concise and avoid duplication and overlap as much as possible.

The functions of the vendor software are compared to the list of requirements and are numerically evaluated for compliance. Calculations are required. Furthermore, as the process proceeds, requirements are added while others are dropped. It is, therefore, suggested that the requirements list be maintained on a spreadsheet (LOTUS or Excel for example). In this way, items can be added or dropped, ratings can be calculated and the list can be sorted with little or no manual effort.

Making the Ratings

Each requirement is rated by the analyst. A requirement can receive a rating of yes or no or a rating of excellent, good, adequate, poor or very poor. These are assigned a numerical value as follows:

VALUE	CRITERION
5	*Yes.* The requirement is satisfied more than 90% of the time.
4-2	*Partial.* A "partial" rating is applied where a "yes" or "no" is not appropriate. A single value is determined from a range of 2 to 4. The high end means that the rating tends toward being yes, while the low end means that the rating tends toward no.

1   *No.* The requirement is not satisfied more than 90% of the time.

OR

---

5   *Excellent.* Carried out with superior effectiveness, complete in all respects; consistently very effective enforcement, superior performance throughout, exemplary, outstanding accomplishment. Rating applies more than 90% of the time.

4   *Good.* Effective, commendable, better than average performance, carefully executed in all respects, well done, more than adequate quality throughout. Rating applies more than 80% of the time.

3   *Adequate.* Effective in most respects, deals in an acceptable way with situations, satisfactory performance, carried out properly with no serious deficiencies, sufficient, at least passable quality in all important aspects. Rating applies more than 70% of the time.

2   *Poor.* Intermittent effectiveness, mediocre, unacceptable in some important respects, not carefully executed, insufficient quality in key areas, needs improvement. Rating applies more than 60% of the time.

1   *Very Poor.* Serious flaws and deficiencies, carelessness, unacceptable in many important respects, consistently inadequate, generally unacceptable, poor quality, sloppy, generally ineffective, unsatisfactory. Rating applies more than 50% of the time.

All the ratings are the analyst's best assessment of how well the software meets the requirements. The ratings are based on a judgement of the degree to which something exists, rather than being based on measurable fact. This means that complete agreement on the rating is not possible. The selecting organization needs to be cognizant of halo effects and discount subjective judgements when they become evident. This halo effect includes decisions influenced by vendor promises of *future enhancements.*

Enhancements are rarely as extensive as promised and rarely occur when promised. Consistently skewed judgements need to be avoided and when detected they need to be corrected.

Assigning Weights

As each requirement is developed, the analyst determines the weight it deserves.

> Weight is a multiplying factor. Its value depends upon the importance of a requirement to a particular environment. Weight is a measure of importance; it is not related to the rating, which is a measure of condition.

Weights. Weights may be assigned either before or after the analysis is performed. Assigning weights before the evaluation lets the analyst know what is important and could cause him to probe more deeply on highly weighted items. This could also be undesirable. If the analyst is inclined to look for justification to improve a rating, the higher weight could influence his thinking. Furthermore, some risk exists that the lower weighted items could get superficial treatment and not the probing analysis they deserve.

Assigning weights after the evaluation avoids these potential drawbacks, but may create another problem; the assigned ratings may influence the assignment of the weights. The choice of approach, therefore, depends upon the judgement of management. Requirements with a weight of zero should be excluded in advance so that the analyst will not waste time on evaluations that are considered to be irrelevant or unimportant. Again, if a spreadsheet is used, this can be done with a minimum of manual effort.

Weighting criteria. Suggested weights should be based on the importance of the requirement to the organization. The following criteria are suggested for assigning weights.

WEIGHT	CRITERION
0	Unimportant or not relevant (exclude)
1	Normal
2	Important
3	Very important
4	Extremely important or critical

All weights are set at normal (1) and a judgement is required to increase it or decrease it. Realistically, few items are categorized as 2, 3 or 4. However, because the assignment of weight is a judgement, individual variations may result from oversights, differences in knowledge and experience and other factors. One task of management is to resolve such conflicts.

Quantitative Scoring

Five columns are positioned on the right side of the spreadsheet or evaluation document for the following entries (See Table 11.1).

- *Rating*. The analyst's evaluation of requirements based on how well the software meets the requirements.
- *Weight*. A measure of the importance of the requirement, typically entered before the evaluation.
- *Actual score*. A calculated value (weight × rating).
- *Maximum score*. A calculated value (weight × 5).
- *Index Value*. A calculated value (actual score/maximum score).

The relationship between actual and maximum score is the compliance index. The compliance index is determined by a single calculation: divide maximum score into actual score (actual/maximum). If a spreadsheet is used, this calculation is easily done for each requirement, for the sum of the requirements within a classification and finally for the complete analysis.

Index values may range from 0.00 to 1.00. In general, the following meanings may be given to any compliance index.

REQUIREMENTS INVENTORY

	RATE	WEIGHT	ACTUAL SCORE	MAX SCORE	INDEX VALUE
PRODUCT CAPABILITIES					
• Is there a tutorial function?	4	4	16	20	.8
• Does it provide print driver support for remote printers?	1	3	3	15	.2
• Is the software capable of being used by non-technical staff?	4	4	16	20	.8
COMPLIANCE INDEX					.64
TECHNICAL SUPPORT CAPABILITIES					
• Has the product been on the market long enough to mature (two or more years)?	5	4	20	20	1.0
• Does the software package provide on-line documentation?	5	4	20	20	1.0
• Does the software run with your TP monitor?	5	4	20	20	1.0
COMPLIANCE INDEX					1.00
IMPLEMENTATION INFORMATION					
• Are JCL or PROC changes required to install the software?	3	2	6	10	.6
• Are modifications required to comply with data center standards?	3	3	9	15	.6
• Is the software easy to maintain?	3	1	3	5	.6
COMPLIANCE INDEX					.60
MISCELLANEOUS INFORMATION					
• Have you included an acceptance test as a condition of acceptance?	3	3	9	15	.6
• Do you have the product cost?	3	3	9	15	.6
• Do you have the maintenance cost?	5	2	10	10	1.0
• Is a deferred payment plan available?	4	1	4	5	.8
COMPLIANCE INDEX					.71
SOFTWARE PACKAGE COMPLIANCE INDEX					.76

Table 11.1.

INDEX VALUE	LEVEL OF COMPLIANCE
1.00 – 0.90	Excellent
0.89 – 0.80	Very Good
0.79 – 0.70	Good
0.69 – 0.60	Adequate
0.59 – 0.50	Poor
0.49 – and below	Very Poor

It is important to recognize that the compliance index is a calculation based on a numeric value assigned to a judgement and has all the limitations of judgement. As such, its usefulness is restricted to providing a simple indication of overall compliance for an item, classification or software package.

The goal of the analysis is to select the software that best meets the requirements identified by the analyst. When the rating and scoring is complete, compare the compliance index for each software package selected, and select the two packages with the highest ratings. Schedule a site visit for each, and select one of the two for a 30 day trial period, if applicable. If the results of the site visits or trial period are not satisfactory, choose the next highest alternative.

Before you schedule a site visit, secure a copy of the purchase contract and submit the contract for legal evaluation. Ensure that warranties are adequate to protect your interests during and after installation. Complete books have been written on negotiating purchase contracts for data processing hardware, software and services. Do not ignore this aspect of the selection process.

SUMMARY

Virtually all of the computer operating software, utility software, computer management and application development software (languages, methodologies) for a mainframe computer are purchased. Further, an ever increasing percentage of the application software is also purchased. As a result, good selection procedures for purchased software are becoming increasingly more important.

The key to successful software selection is establishing requirements. A requirements list is a wish list of all the business functions desired, assuming the opportunity was available to include these functions. Once developed, it is fairly easy to assign relative importance to the requirements. This is called weighting. By comparing the functions of the available software to the requirements list, it is possible to differentiate how well one software package conforms to your ideal. Further, it is possible to quantify this evaluation and to select the software that has the best score or compliance index.

Some words of caution are in order. In many cases, the potential purchaser does not truly understand his or her requirements. This results in one of two potential types of errors:

* The purchaser selects a software package based on the specifications presented by a single vendor.
* The purchaser looks at many different software packages without first fully developing a list of the organization's requirements.

In the first case the organization selects the software without having a set of requirements, without a clear idea of what is available and without a clear point of reference. Software vendors will always try to get you to focus in on their product to the exclusion of all others. In the second case, the organization looks at so many software packages that its requirements tend to be developed by availability rather than need. Further, it becomes very difficult to differentiate the importance of one requirement from another.

When selecting software, look at the ratings and evaluations in trade journals like *DATAPRO*. Do not hesitate to ask others in your industry what experiences they have had with purchased software. However, avoid making site visits until you have limited the selection to one or two vendors. The purpose of a site visit is not to identify the functionality of the software but to gain insight into variables which are difficult to assess from a requirements evaluation. For example, it is possible for a requirement to be satisfied in more than one way. One way may be more labor-intense than another, and although it meets the requirements, it is less valuable. It is possible to ascertain this kind of information from a site visit.

Never bring in a software package for a thirty day free trial unless it is your finalist. Installation of software is rarely as easy as the software supplier intimates. Installation takes longer than expected, evaluation staff is seldom available on the desired schedule and there are often technical problems. Resolution of all these issues makes it very unlikely that the software will ever be removed from your computer. Increase the likelihood of success by only installing your finalist.

The benefits of purchased software are clearly seen in its increasing popularity for mainframe applications and in its virtual dominance of personal and departmental computer applications. The selection process for purchased software is a long series of compromises, and there are many risks associated with these compromises. However, with a little planning and a little structure, the chances of a successful selection are greatly increased.

Automating the Computer Center

INTRODUCTION

Automated computer center management tools are central to achieving unattended computer center operation. In most cases, automation tools are already installed in the computer center. Some, like tape management and batch job scheduling have been around, in some form, for a long time. In most cases these tools have been installed to automate the computer center and not to automate service to the computer center user. The objective of computer center automation is not to make the computer center staff more efficient but to install tools that will make the computer center user more efficient.

Where the software is already installed, it may be necessary to modify the installation or replace the software in order to achieve the functions necessary for self-service computing and to implement value added data handling. For example, a scheduling system may not provide the ability for computer center users to schedule their own work or to determine the status of their processing. In this case, the function needs to be added or the software needs to be replaced in favor of one that can provide the function.

Computer center automation software is almost always installed as an automation tool for the computer center staff rather than for the computer center user. In such cases, it is necessary to dissolve central staff in favor of distributing the functions of the software to the computer user. This is the human side of automation, and in many cases, rebuilding organizations is a far more difficult task than selecting and installing software.

Where software is not already installed, the computer center needs to identify the requirements and select the specific software necessary to achieve unattended computer center operation. Three software packages are central to the computer center automation process: the automated computer job scheduler, the automated console response system, and the electronic report distribution system. These software packages address the three most labor-intense and error-prone activities of the computer center: scheduling batch jobs on the computer, managing the operation of the computer and distributing hard-copy output media. Once these software tools are in place, there is a wealth of other special purpose automation tools available.

SOFTWARE CLASSIFICATION

There are three classes of computer center automation software: primary, secondary and support. Figure 12.1 is a diagram of how these computer automation software packages form a comprehensive computer center automation model while Appendix A is a comprehensive list of the software packages that fit into each category.

Primary automation software products are those software products that interface directly with the computer (see Figure 12.2). They are targeted at automating a great deal of the functions of the computer operator, the production control group and the distribution group. Primary products include the automated computer job scheduler, the automated operator, and electronic report distribution. The primary products are briefly outlined in this chapter and other chapters are dedicated to each later on in the book.

Secondary automation products are products that interface and enhance the functionality of the primary products. As the concept of unattended computer center is embraced by more and

```
┌──────────────────────────────────────────────────────────┐
│                                                            │
│   COMPUTER CENTER AUTOMATION PRODUCTS                      │
│   ╭──────────────────────────────────────────────╮        │
│   (                  SECURITY                      )       │
│   ╰──────────────────────────────────────────────╯        │
│                                                            │
│  ┌──────────┐   ┌──────────┐                               │
│  │AUTOMATED │   │AUTOMATED │◀──────────┐                   │
│  │ RERUN    │◀─▶│          │           │                   │
│  │RECOVERY  │   │SCHEDULER │           │                   │
│  └──────────┘   └────┬─────┘           │                   │
│                      │                 │                   │
│                      ▼                 │   ┌──────────┐    │
│  ┌──────────┐   ┌──────────┐   ┌───────┴──┐│ SYSTEM   │    │
│  │ELECTRONIC│   │          │   │AUTOMATED │◀▶│MONITOR  │    │
│  │ REPORT   │◀──│MAINFRAME │◀─▶│          │ └──────────┘    │
│  │DISTRIBUTION  │          │   │OPERATOR  │ ┌──────────┐    │
│  └──────────┘   └────┬─────┘   └───────┬──┘◀▶│AUTOMATIC│    │
│                      │                 │    │ PROBLEM  │    │
│                      ▼                 │    │ NOTIFIER │    │
│  ╭───────────┬───────────┬───────────┬──────────╮          │
│  │  TAPE     │DISK SPACE │ ON-LINE   │          │          │
│  │MANAGEMENT │MANAGEMENT │DATA ENTRY │ JCL SCAN │          │
│  ├───────────┼───────────┼───────────┼──────────┤          │
│  │ LIBRARY   │  REPORT   │DISK SPACE │TAPE DATA │          │
│  │ MANAGER   │ BALANCING │  ABEND    │SET STACKING         │
│  ╰───────────┴───────────┴───────────┴──────────╯          │
│                                                            │
└──────────────────────────────────────────────────────────┘
```

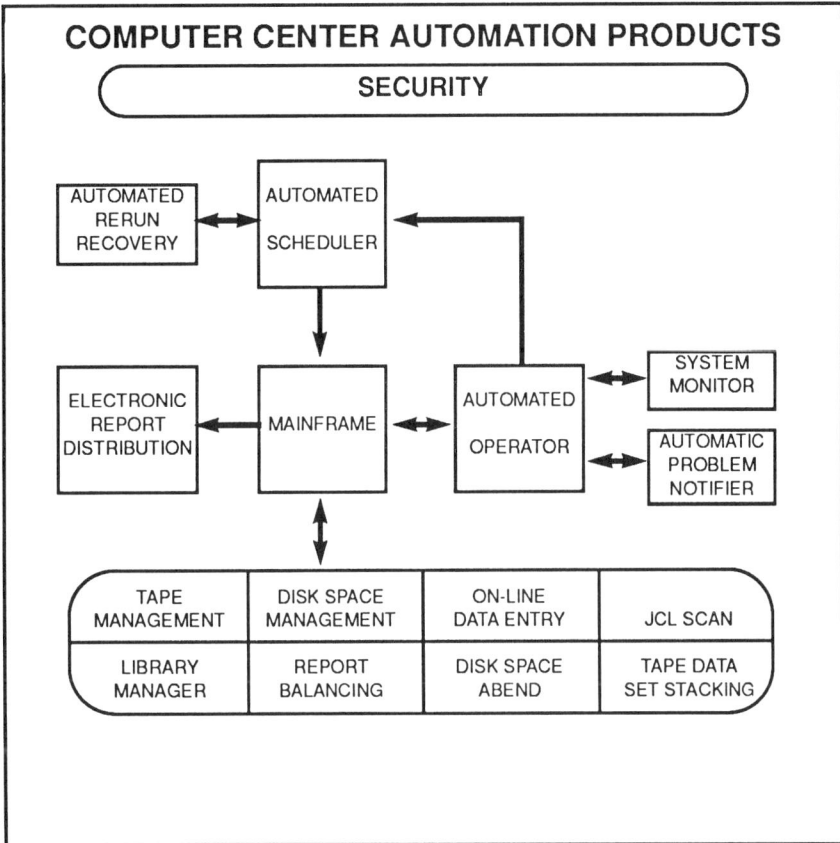

Figure 12.1. Computer center automation is achieved through an array of products which interface with the computer and support the conversion to unattended operation.

more software vendors, some of the features of these products will be integrated into the primary products.

The strategies for achieving unattended computer center operation include providing a self-service computing environment and value added data handling. To implement these strategies, a security system needs to be installed which allows computer cen-

PRIMARY PRODUCTS

AUTOMATED SCHEDULER

ELECTRONIC REPORT DISTRIBUTION

MAINFRAME

AUTOMATED OPERATOR

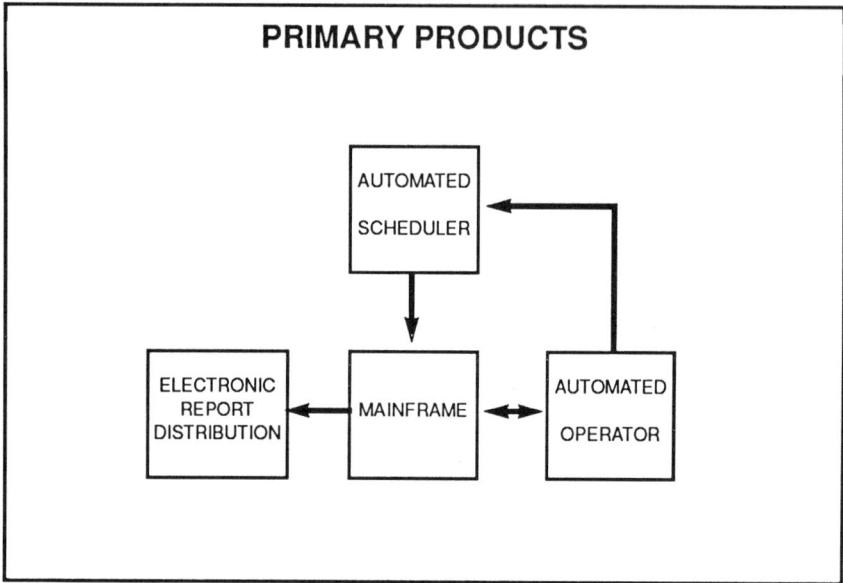

Figure 12.2. The primary computer center automation products are the products which interface directly with the computer.

ter users to access computer center automation tools the way they access application software. Therefore, the secondary software tools include security software as well as software to manage performance, to automate rerun/recovery and to automate problem notification when automatic rerun/recovery is not possible.

Finally, the support products are those products which enhance the conversion to unattended computer center operation. These tools depend on the hardware and software configuration of the computer center. This chapter discusses eight of the secondary software products: tape management, tape dataset stacking utility, disk space abend software, disk space management software, automated report balancing and control, on-line data entry software, JCL scan utilities, and application software library management software. Some computer centers will use more of these products than others.

The Central Software Systems

Three software packages are essential for implementing unattended computer center operation: automated computer job scheduler, automated console response system and electronic report distribution system. These systems are discussed in more detail in this section.

Automated Computer Job Scheduler. The automated scheduler manages the routine, daily batch computer processing schedule. In an unattended computer center, it is essential that the features of this software be available to the computer center user. The objective is to provide computer center users with the ability to change the routine schedule or process ad hoc work without computer center intervention.

Automated computer job schedulers should provide the following functionality:

- Allow computer center users to schedule their own workload. The objective of the scheduler is to provide self-service scheduling support to the computer center user.
- Permit the scheduling and rescheduling of computer processing on-line.
- Provide the facility to submit job control parameters directly into jobs without any knowledge of JCL or without assistance from computer center personnel.
- Provide users with the ability to know the run status of their own work. The user needs to know whether or not something ran without having to call someone in the computer center.
- Provide the ability to see all scheduled work. This aids in scheduling work that has cross-system dependencies and ensures that jobs will not be submitted when capacity or availability is not there.
- Provide the ability to model the production schedule, allowing computer center users a high level of confidence that their desired schedule can be met.

Automated Console Response System. The objective of a console response system is to eliminate all routine interaction between the computer operator and the computer. It is important to impress upon hardware and software vendors that console traffic is viewed as both error-prone and labor-intense and is, therefore, unacceptable. Yet, these activities have become so ingrained in software and hardware that suppliers do not even realize they are designing or perpetuating this kind of activity. Let them know their objective is to eliminate the console.

An automated console response system should support the objectives of unattended computer center operation. It binds together the numerous software packages that are used to achieve unattended computer operation. It improves the quality of the service of the computer center by eliminating the human intervention between the application software systems and the computer and between the computer operation software and the computer.

In most cases, many software packages are required for unattended computer center operation, and the console response system acts to integrate these software packages into a fault-tolerant environment. Automated console response systems provide the following features:

- Handle all routine console messages.
- Trap console messages and provide an automatic response.
- Perform all computer or master console operator functions.
- Automatically cancel and reset hardware components of the computer (terminals and similar devices).
- Automatically balance the system workload when system thresholds are exceeded or system standards are violated.

Electronic Report Distribution System. Software to electronically manage and distribute hard-copy reports is available. This software directs reports in an output queue to a disk device rather than to a printer. Once on disk, it can be retained for a predefined period, viewed and, if necessary, printed under the control of an end user. This is not a substitute for on-line query, but it is an outstanding intermediate step. It gets the computer user to begin to think in terms of the information they require rather than in terms of reports.

Electronic report management and distribution systems should provide the following functionality:

- Enable the user to view reports on-line, to administer their own report distribution and to print exception reports locally or at the central computer site.
- Provide LOTUS-like capabilities for formatting and reformatting reports. Most reports are not designed for an 80 column screen; therefore some formatting capabilities are necessary to effectively view these reports.
- Offer the possibility to define *logical reports* and the capability of using *implicit* instead of *explicit* report description definitions.
- Offer retention and archival facilities for reports and thereby not only eliminate the need to print reports but also eliminate the need to rerun them when they are lost.

The Second Level of Software Systems

The automated computer job scheduler, the automated console response system and the electronic report distribution system are central to computer center automation. However, at the next level, there are four additional software systems that enhance the features of the primary products: security software, automated rerun/recovery systems, automated computer monitoring systems .

Security Systems. Security software operates like an umbrella over the top of all the other computer center automation tools. Security software is a prerequisite for a self-service computing environment. In order to provide a self-service environment and source data entry, the computer center needs to allow users to access their information and software that they need for their job without accessing or interfering with the integrity of the information of others. Furthermore, the computer user should not have to rely on central computer center administration. The most common security software is RACF from IBM and CA-Top Secret and CA-ACF2 from Computer Associates.

Automated Rerun/Recovery Systems. Rerun/recovery software enables the automatic restart of batch jobs without technical support, database or computer center personnel assistance. Automated batch job restart is crucial to unattended operation. It enables automatic housekeeping (uncataloging datasets, restarting TMS for GDG's, determines restart step and so on) so that the only intervention required is to correct the problem and restart the job.

In an unattended computer center, batch jobs are scheduled and controlled by end users; reliance on computer center staff for clean-up and restart is unacceptable. Software is available to handle these conditions and new applications should be designed with this as a prerequisite requirement. In many cases, the forethought required to set up a rerun/restart job reduces the need for restart.

Automated System Monitors. Interactive computer system monitors such as OMEGAMON have been available for a long time. This software provides the technical services staff and computer operator with the ability to interactively monitor the performance of the computer system. Within the software, thresholds are set for computer performance and when exceeded, corrective actions can be taken. This software permits the computer operator to manage the operation of the computer.

When the automated system monitor interacts with an automated console response system, conditions that exceed threshold can be automatically corrected through an automated response. The combination of the automated console response system and the automated system monitor offer the opportunity to automatically correct performance imbalances before they impact the computer user.

The features of the automated system monitor typically include:

- The ability to define the parameters for normal computer operation (response time, CPU utilization, resource utilization, elapsed time and so on).
- Identification of abnormal processing, and provides diagnostic features to isolate problems.

- Statistics for historical analysis of abnormal conditions.
- Status identification for all processing on the computer with the flexibility to provide additional resources to highly sensitive processing.
- The ability to pass messages to and receive messages from the console response system to balance computer workload. The console response system can take steps to correct abnormal work-load balance conditions based on predetermined rules, frequently before an operator would recognize their existence.

Automated Problem Notification. Security and environmental monitoring devices are available to monitor the vital aspects of the computer center in the absence of computer room staff. Such equipment can recognize failing equipment or intrusions and phone designated staff or maintenance personnel using voice synthesizers. Furthermore, the devices can be queried by cautious or inquisitive management.

A very low cost way of achieving this objective is to use a home alarm system. For example, when the alarm for an air conditioner goes off, the home alarm system detects the noise and places a call to a station that is staffed. The person can then investigate the source of the alarm. Since most support equipment has some sort of audible alarm, this can become a very low cost way of providing surveillance.

A similar device is available for the computer, the TIC-2000 from Votek. TIC-2000 operates as an automated operator. Messages are passed to a microcomputer where they are logged and filtered. Messages which require no action are ignored, those requiring a response are answered, and those that cannot be satisfied initiate a phone call to on-call support personnel. Regardless of the action, all messages are logged. When the computer center is unattended such a device becomes indispensable to follow-up on the software failures that are sure to occur in the best run computer centers.

Currently, some computer centers which operate one or more unattended shifts do not respond to computer job failures; they let those jobs go uncorrected until the next staffed shift. The objective of unattended computer center operation is to improve the quality of the computer center's products and services and this is not acceptable.

Other Automated Computer Operation Software

Achieving unattended operation requires that the power of the computer be used to manage itself. For at least a couple of decades or more, information technology experts have been applying their skills to managing all aspects of the business. It is time for computer center professionals to do the same for the computer center. There are many other areas where automation can be applied to the computer center that will facilitate the conversion to unattended computer center operation.

On-line Data Entry Software. Centralized data entry is an obsolete function. A 1989 AFCOM survey indicates that only 48% of the computer centers surveyed had a centralized data entry function. In 1984 over 90% of the computer centers had a data entry function, a decrease of almost half (42%). Furthermore, alternate methods of data collection such as Automatic Teller Machines, bar code scanning and the like have replaced data entry as the predominant method of data collection. Finally, for more than a decade, all new computers have been designed for the on-line update and retrieval of information. The day of off-line batch data collection is over.

The typical data entry function operates something like this: information is written up on an input document, the documents are batched, the batches are logged and sent to data entry for key entry and processing by a batch system. The information is processed by the computer and an exception error report is returned to the originator for correction. The whole process is then repeated for the corrections. In an on-line system, the originator of information does not rewrite the content of source documents but enters data into the system directly, correcting errors as they occur. This is a far less labor-intense process. However, all systems are not on-line and a reasonable low cost alternative is on-line data entry software.

On-line data entry software provides the information originator the same opportunity to directly enter data. The edit and
update facilities are not equal to those of custom on-line update
systems, but the software usually offers some logical editing
(numerics, date ranges and so on). These products also offer personal computer functionality with uploading and downloading
capabilities and even stand-alone updating to diskettes. Further, if
the software is used in conjunction with a report management
system, it eliminates the need to return exception error reports.
Keymaster from TSI International, with more than 50% of the on-
line mainframe computing data entry market, is the most common on-line data entry software package. Other on-line data
entry software packages are listed in Appendix A.

Automated Report Balancing and Control. Report balancing is the
source of a significant amount of effort in many computer center
production control operations. Frequently, ten or more years of
effort are expended on the efficient design of application systems,
and little or no effort is spent on automating the balancing process. An entire processing stream will be halted for hours or even
days waiting for computer users to review and balance their
system.

Computer centers need to automate the report balancing process. Banks, insurance companies and other companies which
process much report balancing and have large staffs to accomplish it have been moving in this direction. For the most part, this
has been accomplished through in-house developed software, but
there is at least one purchased software package on the market to
accomplish automated report balancing: U/ACR from UNITEC
Systems, Inc. in Oak Brook, Illinois.

Report balancing software, like all other computer center software, should support a self-service philosophy. The recipient of
the information should have the ability for computer users to
define balancing rules and to change them as necessary. It should
automatically check and balance reports where required.

Library Management. Software library management should be
performed by the computer center user under the protection of a
security package. Installing new software or making changes to
existing software is a labor intense, error-prone process. The fail-

ure rate for new systems and for changes to existing systems is very high. Correcting these problems requires much from computer center and support programming staff.

Programming and technical support staff should move modules into production libraries. This presupposes an electronic signature and an audit trail. Remember that computer center librarians do not know what a new software module can do, only that the proper forms were provided and that they had proper authorization.

Using the security system as the substitute for paper-based documentation, the computer center can allow programming and technical staff to maintain their own libraries. This reduces the staffing requirements in production control, improves the reliability of the turnover process and reduces the maintenance support requirements. It is time for computer centers to emulate the computer center users in effectively taking advantage of the security system.

JCL Scan Utility. JCL is another labor intense and error-prone activity. JCL is the source of a significant portion of the computer center's interruptions and problems. Scanning JCL for syntax errors and/or conformance with computer center standards should be part of building the computer center batch-operation schedule, library maintenance and production and test job submission. Syntax checking is part of the operating system, some automated job schedulers include it as an integral part of their software and stand-alone software is available for scanning JCL. There is no excuse for not reducing the error due to JCL through one or another of these products.

Disk Space Management. One of the alternatives that is becoming more and more cost effective as a trade-off for tape processing is to substitute disk or Direct Access Storage Devices (DASD) for tape. It is not uncommon for departmental machines to not have any tape. Furthermore, as on-line systems become more indispensable, it is becoming more common for on-line databases to be backed up with disk.

As a result of these and other uses, the data stored on disk media are growing at a rate of 30% or more a year. This growth pattern has resulted in the increased use of disk management software to ensure that sufficient disk space is available, that it is used efficiently and that its use is not dependent on human intervention.

Disk Space ABEND Software. Disk space abend software stops space-not-available DASD abends during step initialization. These conditions are associated with disk space availability and management, and arise when the IBM MVS operating system is not able to satisfy space allocations for a new dataset. These abends are found in the best run computer centers. Since they are not part of the programming staff's area of responsibility, recovery from these types of abend conditions can place a significant burden on computer center operation, technical service or database staff.

Tape Management Systems. In order to achieve total computer center automation, it is necessary to completely eliminate the dependency on tape. Tape elimination is a three step process: reduce dependency on tape, automate tape handling and provide an alternative storage media.

To achieve the first step, a couple of software packages are required. If the computer center has a large tape inventory, it is almost mandatory that the computer center have a tape management system. Realistically, tape will be with us for a long time, and tape management software helps to improve reliability and reduce the direct labor associated with the use of this media. Remember, tape management systems make tape labeling a thing of the past — unnecessary labor. Tape management systems, such as the Computer Associates' CA-1, TMS (tape management system), control the inventory and disposition of tapes.

Tape management systems are valuable tools for isolating the use and reducing the inventory of tape volumes. They should reduce the labor associated with tape handling, improve the quality of the retention process and assist in identifying ways to reduce tape usage. Tape is a data storage medium that is likely to be with us for a long time. Start reducing the inventory of tapes by no longer designing software systems which require tape as a processing medium.

Tape Dataset Stacking Utility. Computer centers need to eliminate the use of tape as a storage medium from existing systems whenever possible. Look for ways to reduce the numbers of tape volumes. Statistics indicate that 80% of all tapes use only a few inches or feet of the tape reel. Install software to stack multiple datasets on a single reel using software such as the Tape Dataset Stacking Utility offered by U.S. West of Denver, Colorado. Stacking datasets reduces the access time to retrieve them, but there is a very good chance that the tape will never be used again, or at worst, that it will be used very infrequently.

Tape dataset stacking software should be used in concert with tape management software. Many tapes are backups used only in exception processing. Furthermore, many of these backups use only a fraction of a tape volume. By stacking these kinds of tape datasets, the computer center can reduce the physical handling of tapes, reduce the volume of tape inventories, decrease off-site storage cost and improve cost containment.

The first step toward eliminating tape is to minimize the problem. Stop developing new applications which require tape and decrease the numbers of tapes in the inventory.

SUMMARY

To achieve unattended computer center operation, many different software tools are required: a batch job scheduler, automatic rerun/recovery software, electronic report distribution, security software, an automated computer system performance monitor, an automatic call-back system and so forth. However, the computer center automation tool that ties all the computer center automation tools together is the automated console response system.

The automated console response system intercepts messages from the operating system. By forcing out messages from the application software, the console response system can activate the scheduler and restart jobs which have failed or initiate action to correct the performance of the computer. The system can send messages to a call-back system to initiate human intervention when no other recourse exists. If restart was not possible, it has invoked analysis tools for human evaluation and manual restart.

It can assist in isolating permanent solutions.

The console response system can recognize messages from performance monitors and respond to abnormal work-load balance conditions. It can take steps to correct abnormal work-load balance conditions based on predetermined rules, frequently before an operator could even recognize that it exists. Usually, the console response system is viewed as a way of reducing console traffic, but it is much more. It is quality assurance. It ties together the automated functions of all the other computer center automation tools, and in doing so, automates the automation.

Although the console response system only displaces a small amount of labor in the computer center, it pulls together the three primary and four secondary automation products. The knitting effect of the console system makes it possible to automate the computer center with products from different vendors. With the assistance of the conversion products, computer center automation is achievable today.

The objective of unattended computer center operation is quality, and quality is achieved by identifying and eliminating the points of human intervention. Without computer center automation this improved quality is not possible. Remember, computer centers are in the service business and their customers expect a consistent high level of quality.

Automated Computer Job Scheduling Systems

Chapter 13

INTRODUCTION

The emphasis on computer center automation has caused a resurgence in the popularity of the automatic computer job scheduling system. The automated computer job scheduling system has been around for at least a couple of decades and, although it has benefited many computer centers, it has never achieved its full potential. As an advocate of unattended computer center operation, it would be nice to think that the reason for the reemergence is the increasing support for the concepts of unattended computer center operation.

However, the vast majority of the media hype for the scheduler comes from representatives of software development companies that market computer job scheduling systems. They attempt to leverage the concepts of unattended computer center operation to sell their product, and yet simultaneously they contend that removing the staff from the computer center is not achievable. The reason is that most schedulers are very labor-intense: they are difficult to install, difficult to maintain and they require dedicated computer center staff. Most computer job schedulers add staff to the computer center.

According to studies by Computer Intelligence Corporation, only about 20% of the IBM mainframe computer centers in the United States are using an automated computer job scheduler. In addition, the average computer job scheduler can range in cost from $12,000 to $120,000. The purchase cost is not the end; the cost of on-going maintenance support for such systems is from 12% to 15% of the current purchase price or another $1,500 to $20,000 a year, and future price increases will increase the cost even more. With such a lucrative market at stake, it is difficult to attribute the increased popularity of computer job scheduling systems to the concept of computer center automation.

One of the major missions of computer center management is to promote and expand the use of information technology in support of enterprise goals and objectives. Not once over the last twenty-odd years has management asked me to curtail the use of information technology. Management essentially believes in the goodness of information technology and wants more of it.

However, one of the major obstacles to achieving this objective is a lack of confidence on the part of users, management and even the computer center staff that the computer center can provide expected service, availability, response time and high-quality service. When installed correctly an automated computer job scheduler improves service and quality while reducing staff and cost.

The problem is that computer centers are automating the duties of the computer center staff instead of automating the source of the schedule at the source, the computer center user. When the computer center adds staff to the computer center, they are inspecting quality into the computer center. However, computer centers have become so complex that even with automated assistance of the scheduler, they are not capable of inspecting quality into the computer center.

The solution is to build *quality* into the computer center by automating the source of the computer schedule and thereby eliminating the points of human interface. An automated computer job scheduling system is a major asset to achieving unattended computer center operation when used to automate the computer user.

THE SCHEDULING SYSTEM

Job scheduling is a delinquency that has existed since IBM first introduced the OS operating system in 1967. The OS operating system has the capability of running batch jobs, but it cannot control the processing sequence or insure that it runs correctly. It has a short memory, therefore, it cannot remember what was processed last night, this time last week or this time last month. IBM has developed operating system components such as JES3 to provide some very basic job scheduling capabilities. However, for the most part, the lack of scheduling capabilities still exists in MVS, VM and DOS/VSE. The solution to the scheduling delinquency was delegated to independent software vendors. Appendix A provides a comprehensive list of these software packages.

In an attempt to fill a vacuum software vendors developed batch job scheduling systems. Some were more sophisticated than others, but, for the most part, they were not designed to run in an on-line environment or to support end user control of the schedule. It is from this base of batch oriented, centrally controlled systems that today's schedulers developed.

Attributes

If the automated computer job scheduling system is to meet the expectations of unattended operation software it needs to:

- Provide the majority of users with the ability to schedule their own workload. The scheduler should have appropriate security to ensure that one computer user does not violate the plan of another. The objective is not to support the computer center but to support the computer center user.
- Eliminate the need to submit paper documents to schedule or reschedule routine or ad hoc work.

- Provide the facility to submit job control parameters directly into jobs without any knowledge of JCL or without assistance from computer center personnel.
- Provide users with the ability to know the run status of their own work. The user needs to know whether something ran or did not. The last thing the computer center wants is hundreds of calls asking the status of a job.
- Provide the ability to see other scheduled work and provide the facility for one computer user to communicate with another. This aids in scheduling work that has cross-system dependencies and ensures that jobs will not be submitted when capacity or availability is not there.
- Provide the ability to review the processing history. This assists planning and results in fewer last minute scheduling changes.
- Provide the ability to model the production schedule, allowing computer center users a high level of confidence that their desired schedule can be met.

Benefits

The automated job scheduler provides three benefits: it improves quality, saves time and reduces cost.

1. *The computer job scheduler improves quality.*
   - It ensures that jobs are not forgotten, that jobs do not run out of sequence, that the wrong input data is not used with job streams or that special processing is not omitted.
   - It reduces job setup error and missed deadlines.
   - The job scheduler can be set-up to guarantee priorities and prevents jobs from being run late or totally omitted.

2. *The computer job scheduler saves time.*
   - The scheduler eliminates the time required for daily job set up, schedule preparation, schedule monitoring and the dia-

log with the computer center users. It also saves the same kind of time for the computer center user.
- The scheduler helps avoid unnecessary lag time between batch jobs. The computer does not sit idle waiting for the computer operator to release the computer job.
- The scheduler allows the computer to run at machine speed, not at human speed. The system can improve the ability to make automatic replies by setting up responses in advance, again saving machine time.
- It can save computer user time as well as scheduler time by allowing the computer user to interact directly with the computer. This saves the time to complete and process paper on the front end and the logging and status checking on the back end of the scheduling process.

3. *The computer job scheduler saves money.*
- The computer job scheduler saves lag time between jobs. If this is only one minute per job, and 200 jobs per day are processed, the scheduler will save in excess of 1,200 hours per year. 1,200 hours per year translates into a $24,000 a year savings for a computer center with a hardware budget of 2 million dollars per year.
- Attach a dollar value of $250 per rerun. If the automated computer job scheduler were to save, for example, 2 reruns per week, a very modest savings, this translates into $25,000 per year.
- If you estimate that a computer scheduler spends six hours a day on manual job setup, schedule preparation and schedule monitoring in one year, a scheduling system can save 750 hours. If the scheduling system allows computer center users to set up their own work, it can save 1000 hours in the computer center and another 1000 in the user departments. This is another $10,000 to $26,000 per year.
- The total is an annual savings of 60 to 85 thousand dollars for each year. Even at a cost of $120,000, the software pays for itself in one and a half to two years. Assuming a life expectancy of five years, the savings are $180,000 to a quarter million dollars. Further, quality means no more meet-

ings to discuss problems, no calls in the middle of the night, improved quality of life and less staff turnover. These benefits also have a dollar value.

Expectations

The requirements for a computer scheduling system are essentially the same from organization to organization. However, the importance of different computer center technical and operating procedures makes one feature more important than another. An organization which supports a strategy of computer center users scheduling their own work will attach more significance to on-line features, parameter edits and on-line job submission than will one that advocates central computer center scheduling. Some of the universal and computer center specific requirements are as follows:

Universal Requirements. The following requirements are the types of features a computer center can reasonably expect from an automated computer scheduling system.

• The ability to initiate started tasks as well as batch jobs using existing JCL, based on time of day, day of week, specific date, the completion of the predecessor jobs, resource availability, and the completion of prerequisite off-line events.
• The ability to schedule manual events as well as computer events and the ability to update or change the current schedule: add, delete or change jobs, without recreating the entire schedule. Most schedulers now allow this capability, but it is worth checking for the feature.
• The ability to interact with the on-line system, to bring it up and down, open and close on-line files as required by the production control schedule, and the use of these events as prerequisites to the release of jobs.
• The ability to provide the majority of the computer center users with the ability to schedule their own workload. The ability to notify users of the successful or unsuccessful com-

pletion of a job. The objective is not to support the computer center but to support the computer center user.

- The ability to forecast and simulate the automated schedule and to forecast and simulate the effect that changes in hardware and software would have on the automated schedule.
- The ability to balance the processing workload to optimize the hardware resources. Use resource availability as a scheduling criteria.
- Provide a central repository for operation documentation, accessible to all areas of the computer center including computer center users. This assures that operation documentation can be easily updated, audited and followed.
- The best products are easy to install. They should require no system hooks, user modifications to the operating system and should not require a rewrite of JCL.
- Consider the history and quality of vendor enhancements. New releases should be neither too close nor too far apart. New releases should include enhancements not corrections to problems. New releases tend to increase the size and complexity of the product; verify the track record of the vendor for the reliability and performance of past releases.
- The product should have a service organization and specifically a contact person to answer questions and resolve problems. Remember the objective is not to have problems, so verify the frequency of demand on this area. If one or two people handle a large installed base you probably have a stable product. All products have some problems.
- Is the product owned and supported by the original developers? There has been a lot of fallout and consolidation in the software industry, and support is one of the victims. Support for problems could be lackluster and future upgrades may be nonexistent. Products that do not grow are dead.

Computer Center Specific. These requirements are computer center specific. Based on the operating environment and the direction of the organization, these requirements may either be very important or have little or no importance. Some features such as automatic restart and automatic console responses may be better satisfied with stand alone software, making the installation of the scheduler easier.

- The ability to control and schedule events in a multiple CPU and virtual system environment and across operating systems. With the advent of the IBM 9370, this becomes particularly important. The departmental processors will most likely operate under VSE and will be linked to a host mainframe running MVS. If your shop is a single CPU, consider your future growth.
- The ability to work with multiple on-line systems such as CICS, TSO, IMS, IDMS, Roscoe, Com-Plete or VTAM. One should be able to access, control, and maintain the schedule through any or all of these systems.
- The ability to provide automatic replies to console messages and the ability to issue a response to system commands as they affect scheduled jobs.
- The capability to not only restart abended jobs, but also to perform necessary restore/recovery procedures. Some schedulers claim to provide this capability within the product, and others consider it a separate product, at an additional cost.

Establishing Expectations

There are many automated job scheduling systems on the market and Appendix A is a list of some of the more common IBM mainframe-based systems. These and other automated computer job scheduling systems can be differentiated by the following groups of features:

Product Capabilities. Include such capabilities as the ability to schedule by day of week and hour of day, control processing dependencies and the operating characteristics of the software.

Technical Support. Includes such information as product documentation, telecommunication monitors, operating systems supported and technical support information.

Implementation Information. Includes information about schedule set-up, JCL changes, hardware requirements, software prerequisites, implementation effort and the complexity to change set-up. This is one of the most important aspects of selecting a computer job scheduler. A difficult installation can negate all the positive product capabilities. If it cannot be installed, it cannot be used.

Miscellaneous Information. Includes pricing and maintenance schedules, discounts, installed base of users, vendor financial information and user group information.

In order to differentiate between automated computer job scheduling systems, develop a detailed list of expectations or requirements. Developing such a list is the most labor-intense aspect of selecting a computer scheduling system. However, the effort can be minimized by analyzing vendor literature and by surveying articles such as this one. The analyst can identify different features offered by different vendors, and these features can be translated into concise statements of requirements. The requirements are then grouped into the four classifications listed above (Table 13.1 is a sample list of requirements).

After the initial list of requirements is developed and classified, present them to a group composed of computer center users, information technology staff and management representatives. Make this a brainstorming session, and expand the list to include as many functional requirements as possible. Remember, there is no end to the number of requirements that can be added to a wish list; therefore be concise, and weed out duplication and overlap as much as possible.

The features of the vendor software are compared to the list of requirements and are numerically evaluated for compliance. Some calculations are required. Further, as the evaluation process proceeds, some requirements are added while others are dropped. It is suggested, therefore, that the list of requirements be maintained on a spreadsheet (LOTUS or Excel for example). In this way, requirements can be added or deleted, ratings can be calculated and the list can be sorted with little or no effort.

The objective of the evaluation is to select the computer scheduling software that best meets the requirements identified by the analyst. When the rating and scoring are complete, compare the score for each automated computer job scheduling

---

AUTOMATED COMPUTER JOB SCHEDULING SYSTEM
REQUIREMENTS INVENTORY

	RATE	WEIGHT SCORE	ACTUAL SCORE
PRODUCT CAPABILITIES			
• Is there an on-line tutorial or help facility?	*	1	**
• Can the scheduler monitor activities outside the scheduling system?	*	1	**
• Is the software capable of being used by the computer user?	*	1	**
• Is the system flexible?	*	1	**
• Is the system easy for the computer user to control?	*	1	**
• (see the additional features in the body of this article)			
TECHNICAL SUPPORT CAPABILITIES			
• Is there vendor product support?	*	1	**
• Is the support staff size adequate and competent to support the installed base?	*	1	**
• Has the product been on the market long enough to mature (2 or more years)?	*	1	**
• Has there been more than one release per year?	*	1	**
• Does the software package provide on-line documentation?	*	1	**
• Does the software run with your TP monitor?	*	1	**
• Is the software easy to install?	*	1	**
• Are the number, size and type of files required acceptable?	*	1	**
• Will you require additional hardware or software?	*	1	**
• Do you receive the source code?	*	1	**

*   Score from 1 to 5, 1 = does not meet requirement and
    5 = exceeds requirements.
** Multiply rating times weight to arrive at score. The weight is set
    at 1 and can be increased to 5 based on the importance to the
    computer center.

Table 13.1.

AUTOMATED COMPUTER JOB SCHEDULING SYSTEM
REQUIREMENTS INVENTORY

	RATE	WEIGHT SCORE	ACTUAL SCORE
IMPLEMENTATION INFORMATION			
• Is there a large number of users (more than a hundred)?	*	1	**
• Are current user input and references available to assist implementation?	*	1	**
• Does it have any clients that have the computer user doing their own scheduling?	*	1	**
• Is a product users group available as a source of installation assistance?	*	1	**
• Is on-site training provided?	*	1	**
• Are JCL or PROC changes required to install the software?	*	1	**
• Are modifications required to comply with data center standards?	*	1	**
• Is the software easy to implement?	*	1	**
• Is the software easy to maintain?	*	1	**
MISCELLANEOUS INFORMATION			
• Is an acceptance test (30 day test) a condition of acceptance?	*	1	**
• Do you have the product cost?	*	1	**
• Do you have the maintenance cost?	*	1	**
• Do you have the cost of new releases?	*	1	**
• Is a deferred payment plan available?	*	1	**
• Is a discount available?	*	1	**

Table 13.1. Continued.

package, and select the two packages which receive the highest rating. Schedule a site visit for each, check vendor references and, if applicable, select one for a 30 day trial period.

If the results of the site visit or trial period are unsatisfactory, look at the package with the second highest rating and so on. Remember, despite vendor claims, no scheduling package will fit all of the requirements, and some compromise will be necessary.

SUMMARY

A computer job scheduling system should support the objectives of unattended operation. It improves the quality of the service of the computer center by eliminating the human intervention between the computer center users and the work that is processed in the computer center. The scheduling system needs to provide the ability for all users to directly schedule their own work. This includes the ability to schedule ad hoc work and to alter the schedule for routine work. Again, the objective is to remove human intervention between the end user and the computer.

In the process of installing the system, eliminate control statements from batch jobs. Whenever it is not possible to eliminate control statements, automate the process for end user creation and submission. When it is not possible to eliminate control statements, an edit facility is required to ensure that the process works correctly the first time.

Introduce a software product to scan JCL for syntax and compliance to computer center standards. The JCL scan product ensures that the computer job is correct before it is submitted into the computing environment. Again, it is important to remember that the computer center is establishing its creditability. If computer center users have the ability to submit jobs, the computer center needs to increase the likelihood of success on the first try.

It is not necessary for the computer scheduling system to satisfy all requirements. In most cases, multiple software packages are required, a JCL scan, an automated restart, an automated operator and so on. It may even be more advantageous to achieve unattended computer center operation through a series of smaller projects.

Where the scheduling software is already installed, it may be necessary to modify or replace it in order to achieve the functions necessary for unattended computer center operation. For example, a scheduling system may not provide the ability for computer center users to schedule their own work. In this case, the function will need to be added or the package replaced in favor of one that can provide the function.

Reinvest the monies that are saved by the scheduling software back into any additional hardware and software that is required to achieve unattended computer center operation. The scheduler and for that matter the whole process of unattended computer center operation is much more palatable if it is self-funding. The same applies to staffing: reinvest the staffing you save back into the process of installation and fine tuning. The staff will love it, and it becomes a training process. Remember, the real goal of the scheduling system is to automate the computer center in support of unattended computer center operation

The Tie That Binds: Automated Console Response Systems

THE CONSOLE RESPONSE SYSTEM

The required interaction between the computer operator and the computer is a delinquency that has existed in the OS operating system since IBM first introduced it in 1967. First and second generation computers were completely dependent on an operator, who in many cases, was also the application programmer. The operator managed the computer. This started a tradition of close interaction between the operator and the computer.

The introduction of OS somewhat changed the operator-computer relationship. Many of the functions which were under the control of the application programmer, such as disk space allocation, were under control of the OS operating system. Also, management functions under the control of the operator such as print and tape were now under the control of OS.

With the introduction of OS/MVS, concurrent batch and on-line processing was the most common mode of processing on large mainframe computers. MVS promised a change in the role of the operator. The operator would be a manager, balancing the resources of the computer to insure that on-line systems received adequate resources and that batched systems were balanced against one another. Furthermore, those using IMS were given a new operator, the master console operator.

This was the era of the multiple console computer system. Routine messages were spooled out to one console, messages requiring response to another console, on-line system messages to another, tape mount messages to another, system performance traffic to another and possibly a system monitor to another. The system might use a tape management system or a scheduler that operates under a TP monitor such as TSO, and another console would be dedicated to it. Seven different consoles were named, and it is not uncommon to have more than that in a large computer center. In this kind of environment, it is not possible for an operator to manage the computer system.

As the capacity of the computer increased and the workload shifted from primarily batch to on-line processing, the complexity of the computing environment increased. The solution to this complex computing environment was to split up the functions of the operator into separate categories and assign more operators to the task. This was the era of specialization. Rather than automate the operator functions, management assigned more staff to handle the increasing number of tasks. Without anyone realizing that it was even happening, this tactic resulted in a significant shift away from automating the computer center.

Rather than being able to manage the resource of the computer, the average computer operator is inundated with so much routine interaction with the computer that it is impossible to manage or balance the resources. In an attempt to fill this vacuum left by the operating system, independent software vendors developed automatic console response systems (See Exhibit A) to perform the routine message response duties of the operator. Some of the console response systems are more sophisticated than others. However, for the most part, they are designed to perform the majority of the mindless responses inherent to an IBM OS/MVS environment.

The real irony of this scenario is that IBM is one of the vendors that supplies a console response system, although they do claim that Netview is primarily a network manager. Rather than remove the useless traffic from the operating system or provide a facility to generate the responses when the system is configured and generated, IBM provides another layer of software at an additional cost. In effect, IBM markets a labor-intense and error-prone condition and charges computer users additional monies to correct it.

Further, to add insult to injury, the software consumes computer resources which cost additional monies.

Despite the irony, the correct solution to the operator intervention problem is to automate the functions of the operator. The incentive for unattended computer center operation is to improve the quality of computer operation. Every operator intervention is a fault point or a potential point of error. No matter what the skill level of the operator, there is no assurance that he or she will respond correctly to a computer operating system message. Further, there seems to be no immediate plans that IBM will correct MVS or VM; therefore, the only solution is to install one of the many automated operator response systems on the market (See Appendix A).

CONSOLE RESPONSE SYSTEM PROFILE

Attributes

If the automated console response system is to meet the expectations of unattended operation software it should:

- Handle all routine console messages. Target to eliminate all system messages either through the console response system or through application system modifications.
- Trap any system console message and provide an automatic response. Put pressure on your hardware and software suppliers (especially IBM) to eliminate these operating system activities. If the messages can be responded to automatically, they can be eliminated. IBM is the worst offender, so let them know.
- Automatically cancel and reset terminal and similar devices when a system *hang* condition is detected.
- Automatically balance the system workload when system thresholds are exceeded or system standards are violated. Computer centers have expected operators to balance work-

loads for a long time but have not provided the criteria for balancing. If the criteria can be established, it can be done automatically.

- Perform all computer or master console operator functions. The lights on the console are gone, the hard-copy console is gone, and now it is time to eliminate the console.

Benefits

The automated console response system results in four benefits: it improves quality, saves time, reduces cost and integrates the computer center tools together.

1. *The console response system improves quality.*
   - It reduces the level of experience required by the operations staff and makes the operator dispensable in an unattended computer center.
   - It ensures that routine console messages are not responded to incorrectly or that jobs do not time-out because the messages are forgotten.
   - It reduces the errors associated with messages that are generated by the application software programs.
   - The automated console response system can be set up to automatically reconfigure the system at certain times and to perform the routine functions of an operator in response to abnormal conditions such as restarting terminals.

2. *The console response system saves time.*
   - The console response system eliminates the time required to look up the answer and respond to operating and application software messages. It also eliminates the same activities for the software engineer when application systems are being developed and installed.
   - The console response system helps avoid unnecessary lag time during the execution of batch jobs. The computer does

not sit idle waiting for the computer operator to respond to the message.

- The console response system allows the computer to run at machine speed, not at human speed. The console response system can improve the ability to make automatic replies by setting up responses in advance, again saving machine time.
- It can save computer user time by responding to abnormal conditions on the on-line network such as resetting terminals. This saves the computer user the time and frustration of calling and notifying the computer center about the problem.
- It saves the computer center from analyzing the situation and resolving the problem.
- It saves countless frustrating meetings to discuss problem and problem resolution projects. There is nothing like doing things right the first time to improve productivity and the quality of work life.

3. *The console response system saves money.*
   - The console response system saves lag time during jobs. If this is only one minute per job, and 200 jobs with messages are processed per day, the console response system saves in excess of 1,200 hours per year. 1,200 hours per year translates into a $24,000 a year savings for a computer center with a hardware budget of 2 million dollars per year.
   - Attach a dollar value of $250 per rerun. If the automated console response system were to save say 2 reruns per week, a very modest savings, this translates into $25,000 per year.
   - If you estimate that you can reduce eight hours a day of an operator's time by eliminating console traffic and four hours a day of computer user time through improved reliability on the on-line network (a modest amount if you have 500 to a 1000 terminals), the console response system saves computer center users 1000 hours a year and the computer center another 3000 hours. This translates into $15,000 to $45,000 per year.

- The total annual savings is in the range of $60,000 to $100,000 per year versus a cost of $20,000 for a typical console response system. At a cost of $20,000, the software pays for itself three to five times each year. Assuming a life expectancy of five years, the savings are a quarter million to a half million dollars.
- Finally, a quality computer center means no more meetings to discuss problems, no calls in the middle of the night, improved quality of work life, less staff turnover and a happy community of computer users. These benefits also have a dollar value.

4. *The console response integrates the unattended computer center automation software tools.*
   - Unattended computer center operation uses many different software tools: a batch job scheduler, automatic rerun/ recovery software, a tape management system, a performance monitor, an automatic call-back system and so on.
   - The console response system intercepts messages from the operating system. By forcing out messages from the application software, the console response system can activate the scheduler and restart jobs that have failed.
   - The system can send messages to a call-back system to initiate human intervention when no other recourse exists. If restart was not possible, it has invoked analysis tools for human evaluation and manual restart. Hopefully, it can assist in isolating permanent solutions.
   - The console response system can recognize messages from performance monitors and respond to abnormal work-load balance conditions. It can take steps to correct abnormal work-load balance conditions based on predetermined rules, frequently before an operator could even recognize they exist.
   - Usually, the console response system is viewed as a way of reducing console traffic, but it is much more. It is quality assurance. It ties together the automated functions of all the other computer center automation tools, and in doing so, automates the automation.

Expectations

The requirements for a console response system are essentially the same from organization to organization. However, the importance of different computer centers' technical and operating procedures makes one feature more important than another. Some of the universal and computer center specific requirements are as follows:

Universal Requirements. The following requirements are the types of features a computer center can reasonably expect from an automated console response system.

- *Easy to use.* It should have a help facility, a test or simulation mode, a day/time of day limit, and a frequency limit. It should have the ability to refresh, enable and disable rules.
- *Ability to manage messages.* There should be message filtering and pattern masking as well as message suppression, message rewording and message expansion. It should have the ability to alter message characteristics and send messages to a TSO user.
- *Provides a command management.* There should be command suppression and rewording as well as command security and filtering. It should be able to intercept console commands, and it should provide a complete audit trail of its actions.
- *Provides automation features.* The product should be message, command and time driven. It should reply to a WTOR and issue WTOR/WTOH, MVS or JES2 commands. It should save and access data in variables and create MVS commands.

Computer Center Specific. The following requirements are computer center specific. Based on the operating environment and the direction of the organization, these requirements may either be very important or have little or no importance.

- The ability to respond to console messages in a multiple CPU and virtual system environment and across operating systems. With the advent of the IBM 9370, this becomes particularly important. The departmental processors will most likely

operate under VSE and will be linked to a host mainframe running MVS. If your shop is a single CPU, consider your future growth.
- The ability to work with multiple on-line systems such as CICS, TSO, IMS, IDMS, Roscoe, Com-Plete or VTAM. One should be able to access, control and respond to messages through any or all of these systems.
- The ability to provide automatic replies to console messages and the ability to issue a response to system commands as they affect scheduled jobs.

Establishing Expectations

There are many automated console response systems on the market. Appendix A contains a list of some of the more common IBM mainframe-based systems. These and other automated console response systems can be differentiated by the following groups of features:

Product Capabilities. These include such capabilities as the ability to perform message management and command management. The product should have a full array of automation features and features to make it easy to use.

Technical Support. This includes such information as product documentation, telecommunication monitors, operating systems supported and technical support information.

Implementation Information. This includes information about message response set-up, JCL changes, hardware requirements, software prerequisites, implementation effort and the complexity to change set-up. Implementation is one of the most important aspects of selecting a console response system. A difficult installation can negate all the positive product capabilities. If it cannot be installed, it cannot be used.

Miscellaneous Information. This includes pricing and maintenance schedules, discounts, installed base of users, vendor financial information and user group information.

In order to differentiate between different automated console response systems, develop a detailed list of expectations or requirements. Developing such a list is the most labor-intense aspect of selecting an automated console response system. However, the effort can be minimized by analyzing vendor litera- ture and by surveying articles such as this one. The analyst can identify different features offered by different vendors, and these features can be translated into concise statements of requirements. The requirements are then grouped into the four classifications listed above (Table 14.1 is a sample list of requirements).

After the initial list of requirements is developed and classi- fied, present them to a group composed of computer center staff, technical service staff and information technology management representatives. Make this a brainstorming session, and expand the list to include as many functional requirements as possible. Remember, there is no end to the number of requirements that can be added to a wish list; therefore, be concise, and weed out dupli- cation and overlap as much as possible.

The features of the vendor software are compared to the list of requirements and are numerically evaluated for compliance. Some calculations are required. Further, as the evaluation process proceeds, some requirements are added while others are dropped. It is suggested, therefore, that the list of requirements be main- tained on a spreadsheet (LOTUS or Excel for example). In this way, requirements can be added or deleted, ratings can be calcu- lated, and the list can be sorted with little or no effort.

The objective of the evaluation is to select the console response system that best meets the requirements identified by the analyst. When the rating and scoring are complete, compare the score for each automated computer job scheduling package, and select the two packages which receive the highest rating. Schedule a site visit for each, check vendor references and, if applicable, select one for a 30 day trial period.

If the results of the site visit or trial period are unsatisfactory, look at the package with the second highest rating and so on. Remember, despite vendor claims, no automatic console response system will fit all of the requirements, and some compromise will be necessary.

AUTOMATED COMPUTER JOB SCHEDULING SYSTEM
REQUIREMENTS INVENTORY

	RATE	WEIGHT SCORE	ACTUAL SCORE
PRODUCT CAPABILITIES			
• Is there a on-line tutorial or help facility?	*	1	**
• Can the response system respond to all messages?	*	1	**
• Is the software capable of being used by the staff with a minimum amount of technical skill?	*	1	**
• Is the system flexible to use?	*	1	**
• Is the system easy for the computer user to control?	*	1	**
• (see the additional features in the body of this article)			
TECHNICAL SUPPORT CAPABILITIES			
• Is there vendor product support?	*	1	**
• Is the support staff size adequate and competent to support the installed base?	*	1	**
• Has the product been on the market long enough to mature (2 or more years)?	*	1	**
• Has there been more than one release per year?	*	1	**
• Are user exits provided, and are SYSMODS front-ended?	*	1	**
• Does the software run with your TP monitor?	*	1	**
• Is the software easy to install?	*	1	**
• Is an IPL required to install?	*	1	**
• Will you require additional hardware or software? Is additional DASD required?	*	1	**
• Do you receive the source code?	*	1	**

* Score from 1 to 5, 1 = does not meet requirements and 5 = exceeds requirements.

** Multiply rating times weight to arrive at score. The weight is set at 1 and can be increased to 5 based on the importance to the computer center.

Table 14.1.

AUTOMATED COMPUTER JOB SCHEDULING SYSTEM
REQUIREMENTS INVENTORY

	RATE	WEIGHT SCORE	ACTUAL SCORE
IMPLEMENTATION INFORMATION			
• Is there a large number of users (more than a hundred)?	*	1	**
• Are current user input and references available to assist implementation?	*	1	**
• Is a product users group available as a source of installation assistance?	*	1	**
• Is on-site training provided?	*	1	**
• Are JCL or PROC changes required to install the software?	*	1	**
• Are modifications required to comply with data center standards?	*	1	**
• Is the software easy to implement?	*	1	**
• Is the software easy to maintain?	*	1	**
MISCELLANEOUS INFORMATION			
• Is an acceptance test (30 day test) a condition of acceptance?	*	1	**
• Do you have the product cost?	*	1	**
• Do you have the maintenance cost?	*	1	**
• Do you have the cost of new releases?	*	1	**
• Is a deferred payment plan available?	*	1	**
• Is a discount available?	*	1	**

Table 14.1. Continued.

SUMMARY

An automated console response system should support the objectives of unattended computer center operation. It is the tie that binds together the numerous software packages that are used to achieve unattended computer operation. It is the new quality assurance manager. It improves the quality of the service of the computer center by eliminating the human intervention between the application software systems and the computer and between the computer operation software and the computer. The console response system eliminates the human intervention required to operate the computer at all levels.

It is not necessary for the console response system to directly satisfy all requirements of an organization. In most cases, multiple software packages are required, and the console response system acts to integrate these software packages. It ties them together into a fault tolerant environment.

Reinvest the monies that are saved through the automated console response system back into any additional hardware and software that is required to achieve unattended computer center operation. The automated console response software and, for that matter, the whole process of unattended computer center operation is much more palatable to organizational management when it is self-funding.

The same applies to staffing: reinvest the staffing you save back into the process of installing and fine tuning the system. The staff will love it, and it becomes a training process for better positions as unattended computer operation proceeds. Remember, the real goal of the automated console response system is to automate the computer center in support of unattended computer center operation.

Exploiting Console Automation

Chapter 15

INTRODUCTION

The automated console response system is the tie that binds together the computer center automation software. Multiple software components are required for unattended computer center operation, and in most cases, these components have been developed independently. The console response system is the integrator that ties these software packages together into a fault-tolerant network. The automated console response system, therefore, improves the quality of the service of the computer center by eliminating the human intervention between the application software systems and the computer and between the network of computer operation software and the computer.

The goal of unattended computer center operation is improved quality. Every computer operator intervention is a fault point or a potential source of error. No matter what the skill level of computer operators, there is no assurance that they will respond correctly to a console message. Furthermore, there seems to be no immediate chance that IBM will reduce or eliminate the messages from operating systems such as MVS, VM, or DOS/VSE. Yet, for computer technology to continue to expand at a rapid pace, human error must be removed. The means of improving computer center performance is console automation.

THE ROLE OF THE CONSOLE RESPONSE SYSTEM

The console response system is pivotal to tieing together the computer center automation products. At Boston University, it integrates the fourteen or more software products used to achieve unattended computer center operation. Over the past two years, the University has doubled its computing capacity, increased its DASD by 60%, introduced electronic vaulting technology, improved its service levels (an index composed of availability, response time, and batch job delivery) from 97% to an excess of 99% while simultaneously reducing its computer center staffing by 60%. Boston University will attain total unattended computer center operation within the next eighteen months.

Using a console response system (AF/OPERATOR), the University is implementing what it refers to as both reactive and active console automation. The console response system reacts to messages and responds to abnormalities in the computer operating software, but more significantly, it activates other automation tools and manages the computing center. The console response system is both operator and computer system manager.

The active side of console automation provides an opportunity to exploit the software (See Figure 15.1). It permits the computer center to reach levels of quality and service that elude the human operator.

Reactive Automation

The interaction between the computer operator and the computer is a shortcoming that has existed in operating systems since the outset. First and second generation computers were completely dependent on an operator. With them began a tradition of close interaction between the operator and the computer.

In the IBM world, the introduction of OS changed the operator-computer relationship. Many of the functions that had been under the control of the application programmer, such as disk space allocation, came under the control of the OS operating system. Further, the operating system took over management func-

THE AUTOMATED COMPUTER MANAGER

REACTIVE

- ROUTINE CONSOLE TRAFFIC
- MESSAGES REQUIRING ACTION
- CORRECT ERRORS

AUTOMATIC OPERATOR

ACTIVE

- CONSOLE MONITOR
- AUTOMATED RECOVERY
- JOB SCHEDULING
- PROBLEM NOTIFICATION
- MAINTAIN SUPPORT SOFTWARE

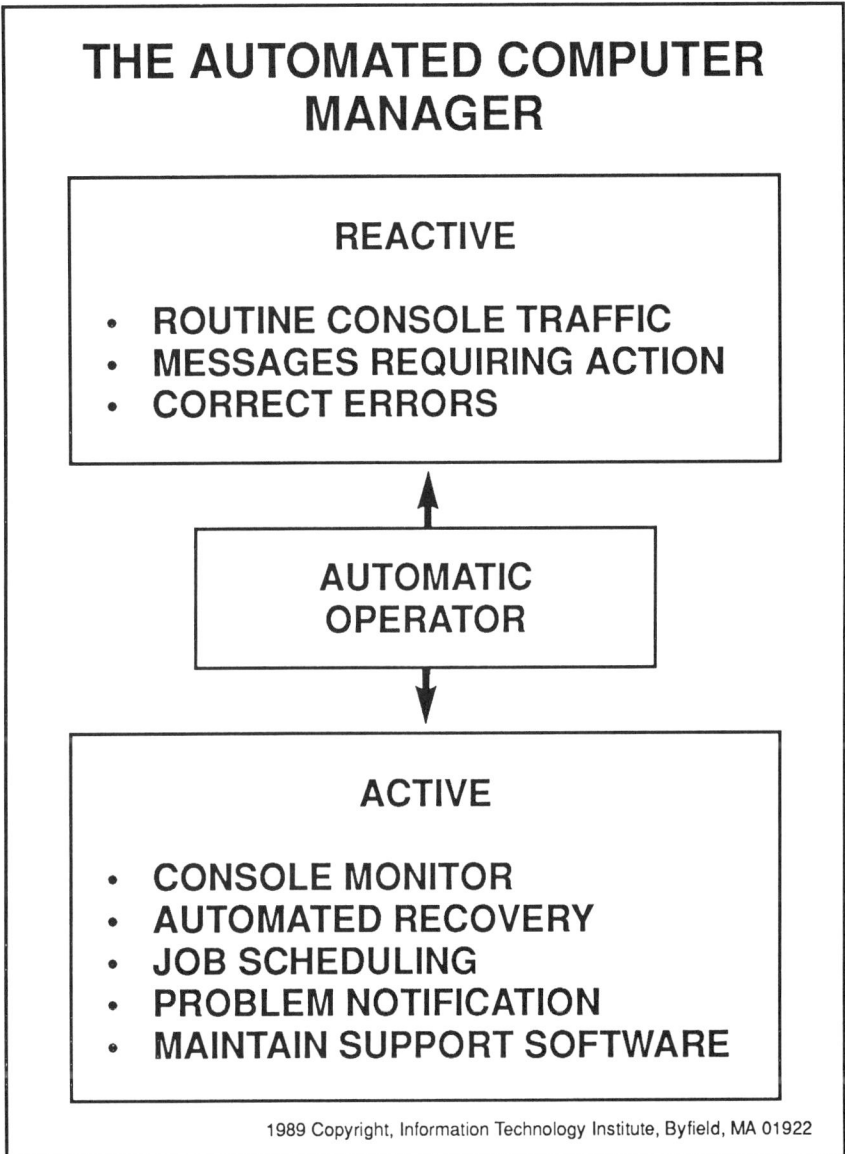

Figure 15.1. The automated computer manager.

tions formerly under the control of the operator such as print and tape.

In the OS environment, routine console messages are spooled out to one console, messages requiring response to another console, on-line system messages, tape mount messages, and system performance traffic to others and possibly a system monitor is dedicated to yet another. The automated computer center uses a tape management system and a scheduler, and another console is dedicated to each of them. This makes a total of seven different consoles, and it is not uncommon for large multi-computer centers to have more. In this kind of environment, it is not possible for an operator to manage the computer system.

Rather than managing the resources of the computer, the average computer operator is inundated with so many routine interactions with the computer that management is impossible. The automatic console response system relieves some of the management chores. It is designed to react to the majority of the mindless activity inherent in operating a mainframe computer.

- *Routine console traffic.* Boston University is eliminating all console traffic. It is spooling the 30,000 to 70,000 messages generated daily from its IBM 3090 to a repository and provides viewing capabilities through an electronic report distribution system. The messages are available in the event of a problem condition; however, they have no value for routine operation and have even less value in the unattended computer center.
- *Messages requiring a response.* The console response system responds to all messages which require a response and defaults to an automatic call-back system when a response is not available. Automatic message response is the aspect of computer center automation that receives the most press but responses to console messages represent less than 10% of the labor required to operate a computer center. Therefore, the labor reduction is not significant. What is significant, however, is that automatic responses are always timely and correct.

In addition, an automatic call-back system or problem notification system can be used as a default when an automatic response is not available. Boston University does not have operator coverage during the day shift, and, until later this year, when all tape processing is eliminated, it is using a call-back system to notify staff that a tape mount is required.

- *Correct error conditions.* Since most computer centers have become very complex, it is not uncommon to use a hundred or more different operating software packages, multiple teleprocessing monitors, database systems and even operating systems. In this environment, errors are bound to occur. There are solutions to the symptoms but no permanent solution to the root problem. At Boston University, terminals periodically *hang*, and it is necessary to reset them. Using a console response system, it is possible to recognize and correct a hang condition without operator intervention. In many cases, the correction is made before the terminal operator realizes that he or she has a problem.

The reactive side of the automated operator is the basis of console operation. It is not necessary to do more than automate these mindless activities to be successful with the automated console response system. The real opportunities for the automated console operator come, however, from the active side where the automated performs functions that humans cannot (see Figure 15.2).

Active Automation

The introduction of MVS promised a change in the role of operators. They were supposed to be managers, balancing the resources of the computer and ensuring that on-line systems received adequate resources and that batch systems were balanced against one another. The managerial role did not materialize. As the capacity of the computer increased and the workload shifted from batch to on-line processing, the complexity of the computing environment increased, and more and more intervention was required. Now, however, the automated console response system creates an

THE TIE THAT BINDS

AUTOMATIC OPERATOR

MESSAGES

REPOSITORY **ACTION**

| ELECTRONIC REPORT DISTRIBUTION | JOB SCHEDULER | PROBLEM NOTIFICATION | PERFORMANCE MONITOR |

RESTART/ RECOVERY

1989 Copyright, Information Technology Institute, Byfield, MA 01922

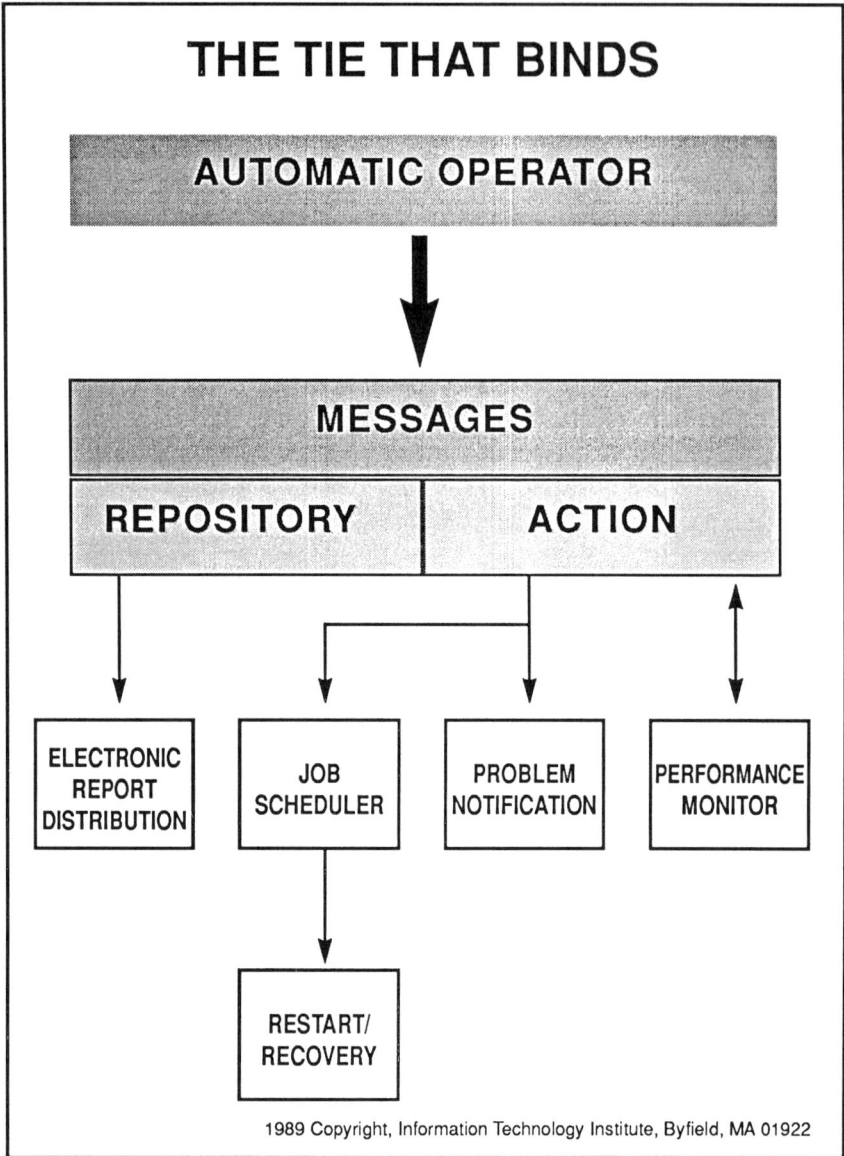

Figure 15.2 The tie that binds.

opportunity to manage the system by initiating activities at opportune times.

- *Performance Monitor.* System performance monitors such as OMEGAMON were introduced to help solve the problem of managing system resources. However, they were never used to their full potential. They were reserved for use by the technical services staff. Procedures were not established for balancing the system. Operators were not given the authority to make the changes necessary to resolve the problems. System thresholds were not reset when the system was reconfigured.

    Automated console response systems such as AF/OPERA-TOR solve this problem. AF/OPERATOR is bidirectional: it reads OMEGAMON messages and sends operator commands to OMEGAMON. Automated management of the system balancing facilities is within our grasp.

    Boston University, for example, is very excited about this development. For the first time since the introduction of on-line processing, it has the opportunity to balance the computer workload automatically. It can improve service to its users by balancing out workload spikes. Although not operational, the University is resetting its OMEGAMON thresholds and documenting its workload balancing procedures in preparation for specifying these procedures to AF/OPERATOR. For the first time since the introduction of MVS, the University is prepared to manage the computer system automatically.

- *Automated recovery.* Recovery is usually batch-oriented, even when it is automated. When a system abends and automated recovery is possible, a batch job is processed to perform the recovery. The automated console response provides an opportunity to alter this process.

    Boston University uses the automated response system to identify the need for recovery and initiates a recovery job through an automated job scheduler. Where automated recovery is not possible, a job is initiated to run the diagnostics required. It reduces the mean time to recovery. The same diagnostic facilities can be used by internal staff or by hardware and software vendors. Finally, the automatic operator can activate an automatic call-back system to notify on-call technicians when the job is critical and immediate recovery is required.

- *Job Scheduling.* The computer system standard at the University is to not issue operator messages from its application software. The University is rethinking this standard. By issuing standard WTO messages from its application software, the automated response system can initiate actions or informational messages to appropriate users through electronic or voice mail. It can also initiate any sequence of batch jobs. The scheduler can therefore initiate any sequence of batch jobs.

Boston University is using the automated job scheduler to bring-up and take-down the on-line systems. It is using the console response system to determine if there are conflicts, and it initiates or terminates on-line processing as appropriate. The University is also using the automated job scheduler to manage the scheduled or unscheduled IPL's, thereby reducing human intervention.

- *Problem Notification.* Using the automated job scheduler to pass messages to an automated call-back system, such as the TIC-2000 from Votek Systems in Richmond Hill, Ontario, Canada, as a default to the recovery process, Boston University is able to cover all exceptions. Unfortunately, all systems do not run correctly, so it is not always possible to automate the recovery process. Therefore, the messages are passed to an auto-call unit that notifies appropriate software specialists when human intervention is required.

The same problem notification facilities are used as a default for console messages. The University has reduced its operation staff to a level where 100% operator coverage is not possible. When requests, such as tape mount messages, are not filled to in a reasonable time interval, a call is placed to an area in the computer center that is known to be staffed. If that area does not respond, the notification system tries other numbers in a hierarchical fashion until on-call staff managers are notified. Involving managers is not a goal, but they form a bridge to get from a partially automated computer center to a fully automated computer center.

- *Maintaining Support Software.* Finally, the technical support and database staff use the system to schedule maintenance utilities. They perform routine maintenance to databases, reorganize databases, move data-sets, and so on. They use the automated response system to monitor the system for periods when there are no conflicts. When there are no conflicts, they can initiate housekeeping jobs from the scheduler. This eliminates the need to schedule blocks of stand-alone time and the need to schedule technical staff to come in at off hours. It also automates the routine aspects of the technical staff and improves productivity.

SUMMARY

The automated console response system improves quality, saves time, reduces cost and integrates the computer center automation tools. Whenever human intervention is required, a potential fault point is created. Automating the points of intervention between the operator and the computer improves quality and permits more efficient use of the computer. And automation translates into reduced operating cost. This is more than ample justification for an automatic console response system.

The automated operator can also tie together other aspects of computer center automation: the job scheduler, electronic report distribution, automatic restart, and problem notification. Networking these software packages permits management functions that were never possible with a computer operator.

It is possible to balance the workload of the computer, to schedule work dynamically, to tune and maintain databases, to avoid problems, to extend availability without adding capacity and generally to automate aspects of computer operation that could only be achieved through human intervention. Active console automation is an opportunity to exploit the automated console response system. Computer centers that tap this aspect of console automation will optimize their return far beyond their expectations.

Chapter 16

Electronic Report Distribution

INTRODUCTION

The popularity of on-line computers and information systems, along with the introduction of personal computing, has increased the requirement for the greater availability of computer-based information. Further, the increasing popularity of electronic mail and the advent of the concept of unattended computer operations have created a market for a new concept with a very long history — electronic report distribution.

Over the past decade, virtually all new computers developed have been designed to provide immediate input, update and retrieval of information. In addition, the majority of mainframe-based computer application software developed during this same period has been on-line application software. As a result, the business community has embraced immediate response as a mode of doing business and has increasingly demanded more timely computer-based information. This has become a self-perpetuating process. The demand has resulted in the installation of a large base of terminal-type equipment and highly reliable communication networks to tie the base of terminal equipment together.

Personal computing, either on mainframe systems or, as is more frequently the case, on stand-alone personal computers, is another factor that has perpetuated the demand for the greater availability of computer-based information. Personal computing

227

tools have provided the business person with an unprecedented ability to analyze information. However, over the short history of computing, the business community has developed a report mentality: information and reports are thought of as synonymous. Historically, reports were the only format for receiving information, and analysis was accomplished by manually transcribing information from a report to an analysis format. Computer information, therefore, became synonymous with reports.

Personal computing is changing this view of information. Business personnel now view information as something electronic that can be moved from one electronic media to another. The whole perception of information is changing.

Electronic mail has also been introduced into many organizations. Electronic mail is reducing the need for hard copy memos or letters, thus speeding the delivery of information and providing a more flexible means of communications. Electronic mail has further demonstrated a disparity between the continued dependence on printed reports for information and the ability to communicate electronically.

Finally, there is a movement toward unattended computer center operations, operating a computer processing center without any human intervention between the input or update of information and the delivery of the information. A major obstacle to achieving this goal is the continued dependence of most organizations on printed reports as the primary method for distributing information.

These trends have created an unprecedented opportunity to automate the delivery of computer output. This delivery method is commonly called electronic report distribution. Electronic report distribution is the storage of printed reports on an electronic storage media, usually a disk drive, for some predetermined period time. The electronically stored information is then retrieved on-line via an existing network of terminal equipment thereby eliminating the need to print reports. Viewing is facilitated by software that permits the manipulation of the now electronic report. Upon expiration of its useful life, electronic documents are replaced with current versions, archived or destroyed. In most cases, facilities are provided for low volume, exception printing.

Electronic report distribution is not a new concept; programmers have been using time-sharing tools to view reports, JCL and program code on-line for a long time. Furthermore, some application software systems have provided on-line report viewing for a long time. Until recently, the timing has not been right for the widespread use of this on-line report viewing by the business community. However, the number of installed on-line terminals and personal computers has created a critical mass of equipment that has put a terminal within easy reach of most key employees. This factor, along with the decreasing cost of direct access storage devices, has now made electronic report distribution practical.

It is important to understand that from a strategic point of view electronic report distribution is not a replacement for interactive data query. Electronic report distribution is a bridge to get from printed reports to electronic distribution without a huge reprogramming effort.

THE ELECTRONIC REPORT DISTRIBUTION SYSTEM

The requirements for an electronic report distribution system are essentially the same from organization to organization; however, the importance of different attributes will vary significantly based on the types of reports processed. As an example, a user with little or no data processing experience may simply wish to scan a report, selecting information in the same way they view a hard copy report. Conversely, an application programmer may desire to manipulate the format of a report to facilitate the validation process and may, therefore, be very concerned with the technical capabilities of the electronic report distribution software.

Some of the requirements common to both a technical and an end user audience will include the ability to do the following:

- View reports on-line at an existing terminal.
- Select on-line viewing or hard-copy printing as the viewing medium.
- Limit the access to confidential reports to authorized personnel.

- Share one or more reports with one or more users.
- Store reports in a compressed and sometimes encrypted database.
- Scroll report information left and right when it exceeds the capacity of the terminal.
- Produce hard-copy reports in whole or in part at local or remote printers.
- Produce report archival and restoration.
- Install the software with no modifications to operating software, application software or JCL.

Specific operating functions and capabilities vary from one software vendor to another. Further, the importance of a function will vary from one organization to another. Therefore, it is important to develop an inventory of expectations to systematically evaluate the capabilities of different software vendors.

Establishing Requirements

There are numerous electronic report distribution systems on the market. Appendix A lists some of the more common IBM mainframe-based systems. These and other report distribution systems can be differentiated by the following attributes:

Product Capabilities. Includes such capabilities as on-line viewing, remote printing, archival, report forwarding, usability, report distribution, security and product administration.

Technical Support Information. Includes such information as product documentation, communications monitor, operating system support and technical support information.

Implementation Information. Includes information about report set-up, JCL changes, hardware requirements, software prerequisites, implementation effort and complexity to change set-up.

Miscellaneous Information. Includes pricing, discounts and maintenance schedules, installed base of users, vendor information and user group information.

In order to differentiate one report distribution system from another, develop a detailed list of expectations or requirements.

Developing such a list is the most labor-intense aspect of selecting an electronic report distribution system. However, this effort can be minimized by analyzing vendor literature. The analyst can identify the different features offered by the vendors, and these features can be translated into concise statements of requirements. The statements can be grouped into the four classifications identified above. To further facilitate this process, Figure 16.1 provides a comprehensive list of the kind of organizational requirements that can be established.

After the initial list of requirements is developed and classified, present them to a group composed of user representatives, information technology professionals and management. Make this a brainstorming session, and expand the list to include as many functional requirements as possible. Remember, there is no end to the number of items that can be added to a wish list, so be concise and avoid duplication and overlap as much as possible.

The functions of the vendor software are compared to the list of requirements and are numerically evaluated for compliance. Calculations are required. As the process proceeds, requirements are added while others are dropped. It is suggested, therefore, that the requirements list be maintained on a spreadsheet (LOTUS or Excel for example). In this way, items can be added or dropped, ratings can be calculated and the list can be sorted with little or no manual effort.

The goal of the evaluation is to select the software which best meets the requirements identified by the analyst. When the rating and scoring are complete, compare the score for each electronic report distribution package, and select the two packages with the highest rating. Schedule a site visit for each, and select one of the two for a 30 day trial period. If the results of the site visit or trial period are not satisfactory, look at the next alternative.

Observations On Selection, Justification and Implementation

Early interest in electronic report distribution systems was oriented toward batch report management and tracking capabilities.

ELECTRONIC REPORT DISTRIBUTION
REQUIREMENTS INVENTORY

PRODUCT CAPABILITIES

On-Line Viewing

- Is there a maximum allowable number of pages that can be read on-line?
- Can JCL be read on-line?
- Is a separate job class required for JCL?
- In viewing mode can you search by:
  — Constants in the report body?
  — Headings?
  — Constants by row/column?
  — Use of Boolean logic?
- Is there a tutorial function?
- Is the product capable of viewing all reports (test & production)?
- Does the product have the ability to reformat & save reformatted reports?

Remote Printing

- Does it provide print driver support for remote printers?
- Does it provide mainframe to mainframe, to P/C to Mini computer distribution?
- Does it provide downloading reports to personal computers?
- Does it allow users with printers to manage their print queue?

Archival

- Is there archival to tape and/or disk?
- Is there automatic archiving?
- Is archiving done with a batch job?

Report Forwarding

- Can the user route a report to another user?
- Can the user route a report to another user, masking selected data?
- Can the user route selected pages of a report to another user?
- Can the user add comments before routing a report to another user?

Figure 16.1.

Users

- Is the product capable of being used by non-technical staff?
- Is the product menu driven?
- Is a tutorial/help function available for each screen?
- Is user education adequate for full use of products?

Report Distribution

- Are different reports going to the same area grouped together?
- Can a report be selectively distributed by searching a row or column for a variable?
- Can a report be selectively distributed by searching for changes in heading?
- Can the number of copies be altered while the job is running?
- Are there separator pages between printed reports?
- Is there an itemized list of reports by print order?
- Is there an itemized list of reports by recipient?
- Can sensitive reports be selected and printed separately?
- Are laser printers supported (IBM, Xerox)?
- Are there overrides for priority printing?
- Does software have an SMF exit to collect and store additional data?
- Does the software provide a general activity report?
- Does the software provide data on late reports?
- Does the software provide data on jobs processed or not processed?

TECHNICAL SUPPORT INFORMATION

Support Information

- Has the product been on the market long enough to mature (2 or more years)?
- Is there hot line support?
- Is there twenty-four hour support, hotline or otherwise?
- Does the product have adequate support, numbers of professional staff?
- Have there been more than one release per year of the software over the last two years?

Figure 16.1. Continued.

Product Documentation

- Does it provide on-line documentation for all or selected users?
- Does it provide technical documentation for support staff?
- Is documentation adequate to resolve routine questions without the need for vendor support?
- Are all internals documented?

Technical Issues

- Does the software run with your TP monitor?
- Is there a security interface into your security monitor?
- Are descriptions of user exits available?
- Does it provide logical versus physical viewing of data?
- Does it provide dynamic column and width adjustment of terminal image?
- Does it provide support for your current release of the spool software?
- Are operating system modifications required to install the software?
- Will the software run with your release of the operating system?
- Are storage and access methods compatible?
- Are archival and retrieval methods compatible?
- Can microfiche be created?
- Can it support simultaneous creation of reports and fiche?
- Are all documented internals operational?
- Are special JCL definitions/changes required?
- Are there interfaces with other products?
- Is the software compatible with other products?
- Will it run with other operating systems?
- Are path lengths documented for each function?
- Are there other planned upgrades or enhancements?

Implementation Information

- Are JCL or PROC changes required to install report distribution?
- Are the administrative activities required to set up a report reasonable?
- Is more than one screen required to set up a report?
- Does setup require the assistance of a programmer?
- Is the time required to set up a report reasonable?
- Is it easy to add or change a report?

Figure 16.1. Continued.

MISCELLANEOUS INFORMATION

Client Information

- Is a list of installed users available?
- Are there installations similar to yours?
- Are technical contacts available for installations similar to yours?
- Is a list of installed users available that have converted to the product?
- Is there an active users group for the product?

Contract Information

- Have you received a copy of the licensing agreement?
- Have you included a product escalation clause for timely resolution of software failures?
- Have you included an acceptance test as a condition of acceptance?
- Have you withheld monies as a condition of acceptance?
- Have you received assurance that the supplier will provide continued support?

Cost Information

- Do you have the product cost?
- Do you have the maintenance cost?
- Do you have the cost of a new release?
- Is a deferred payment plan available?
- Does the license extend to an alternate site, for example for disaster recovery?
- Have you calculated the cost of disk storage (this may vary by product based on the compression formula)?
- Are discounts available (multiple site, education)?

Other Information

- Does the product have the ability to recognize logical punch format output (from the system punch)?
- Can you phase the installation of report viewing and archiving?

Figure 16.1. Continued.

Many products were designed to support this objective rather than on-line viewing. Assuming that on-line viewing is the major requirement driving your selection, pay special attention to how flexible or user friendly your finalist is on this aspect. Remember, there are those who designed this facility into the product and those who added it as an after thought. The results are not necessarily the same.

Report preparation and distribution is a time consuming, labor-intense, high-cost process that is plagued with errors. Further, the distribution of manual reports is a major security fault point. Distribution of sensitive data by inter-departmental mail or courier is subject to error and embarrassing security violations. An electronic report distribution system is a solution to these problems.

Although cost reduction should not be the driving motivation for the installation of an electronic report distribution system, cost reduction attracts attention. It is an opportunity to raise the interest level of users and management alike. An electronic report distribution system is an opportunity to address the *real* cost associated with hard copy report distribution:

- Computer hardware processing cost.
- Print hardware and supply cost.
- Mail cost, either inter-departmental, external or courier.
- Delay in the distribution of information and the corresponding lost opportunity cost.
- Training and error cost as a result of personnel turnover.
- Management cost associated explaining why reports are lost or delayed.
- The cost associated with a loss of confidence in computer center directions as a result of lost or delayed reports.
- The cost of reruns or report recovery.

Electronic report distribution systems are an opportunity to improve administrative procedure; they reduce dependence on computer centers. Some distribution systems advertise complete end user administration capabilities without data center personnel intervention. Most products provide on-line viewing, exception printing and volume printing at remote locations that eliminate dependence on data center personnel for printing and distribution.

Some user guidelines are appropriate for implementation of an electronic report distribution system.

*   The implementation process is an opportunity to assess the need for a report, its frequency and distribution. It may be possible to eliminate or reduce the frequency or distribution of a report.
*   Set up guidelines that define exceptions:

    — Retention default.
    — Archival default.
    — Data center hard copy printing volumes.
    — Remote hard copy printing volumes.
    — Service level standards.

*   Periodically report exceptions to guidelines to the user community and management.
*   Use departmental coordinators. Provide the initial training to the departmental coordinators, and the coordinators provide direct training and consulting to their department.
*   Initiate the implementation of the electronic report distribution system in the computer center or even better in the whole MIS Group. Eliminate the printing of *all* reports in the computer center. Establish a do as I do attitude, not a do as I say attitude. This will go a long way to developing a positive user attitude.
*   Communicate the tangible and intangible benefits of an electronic report distribution system to management. Make management understand that it is integral to the objectives of unattended operation, and that it is a bridge to on-line information access. Don't let management get caught up on outdated notions about the cost of Direct Access Storage. Identify that the cost of storage is going down, and the cost of manpower is going up.
*   When implementing, start with the high volume weekly and monthly reports and with the most receptive users of the tech-

nology. You are looking for the areas that have the highest return and will generate the most positive impact.

SUMMARY

Electronic report distribution is an excellent opportunity for any organization with a large installed base of on-line terminals and a large volume of printed reports to improve the productivity of its users. The ability to eliminate the manual effort and error associated with the manual production and distribution of reports, to reduce expenses through the elimination of paper and printer related costs and to expedite the distribution of computer generated information is very enticing.

Installing electronic report distribution is not particularly difficult. Unlike other software selection projects, organizational requirements for electronic report distribution do not vary much from organization to organization. Further, software variations tend to be variations in approach rather than in real capabilities. The major inhibitor to installing electronic report distribution software tends to be the lack of awareness on the part of data center management of the potential contained in electronically distributing printed media.

Finally, there is a movement toward unattended data center operations. A major obstacle to achieving this goal is the continued dependence of most organizations on printed reports as the primary method for distributing information. Electronic report distribution eliminates this obstacle. It eliminates lost and misplaced reports, reduces job rerun and accelerates the availability of computer-generated information. In addition, it eliminates manual intervention by data center personnel while improving security.

Obstacles to Achieving Unattended Operation

.

Unattended Computer Center Operation: Fifty Questions and Answers

INTRODUCTION

One of the obstacles to the rapid expansion of information technology is a lack of confidence on the part of computer center users, organizational management and even computer center staff that the computer center will be available when it is needed or that response time will be adequate to get work done. Computer center users have been conditioned to expect poor quality through years of conditioning. What has developed is a fundamental lack of confidence on the part of key groups of people that information technology in general and computer centers specifically can meet their expectations. The solution is unattended computer center operation.

In an attempt to overcome some of the misunderstandings about unattended computer center operation and to emphasize that the objective of unattended computer center operation is *quality*, not expense reduction, this chapter answers 50 common questions about unattended computer center operation.

UNDERSTANDING UNATTENDED COMPUTER CENTER OPERATION

1. **What is unattended computer center operation?**
   A computer center is defined in the very broadest sense as a computer processing center without regard to computer size or

computer vendor. Unattended operation is the total automation operation of all data center functions, a dark room environment in which computers run without human intervention. Unattended operation requires the elimination of such traditional and seemingly essential data center operation functions as computer operators, data entry, input/output control and media distribution. Furthermore, it calls for the elimination of such relatively new functions as librarians, production coordinators and help desks. The concept of unattended operation requires looking beyond solutions to today's problems and looking at the future requirements of the data center as capacity expands, availability requirements increase, and on-line processing becomes the only mode of processing.

2.   Has any computer center achieved unattended operation? If not, how do you know it can be achieved?

To the best of my knowledge, no computer center has achieved complete unattended operation. Some dedicated test computers operate unattended; software engineers are given operator capabilities to correct problems. Some major computer centers have isolated the equipment which does not require continuous attention into separate dark rooms, and others are operating a shift or a weekend without human intervention. But no one seems to have achieved total unattended computer center operation.

Some computer centers have made considerable progress, reducing their staff by as much as 75% or more while improving their service levels and improving the quality of life for their users. Those that have achieved this improvement have done so by identifying and removing the obstacles. These early advocates can attest that there is no insurmountable obstacle. Some obstacles cannot be resolved with today's technology, but the receptivity to this movement is so great that it is a certainty that these final obstacles will be quickly resolved.

3.   What is a *dark room* computer operation?

The *dark room* or *lights-out operation* is the process of isolating equipment that does not require intervention and moving it into a dark room or unattended environment. Such equipment includes the central processor, disk drives, communication controllers and like equipment. Very large data centers have done this for a long time.

A second approach to a *dark room* is clustering noncritical computer processing into a *lights-out* period and operate unattended during that period. In this approach, noncritical processing is clustered into periods such as weekends or the graveyard shift. During this period, the computer center is then operated without staff. If the work fails, it is left until morning or Monday, and it is corrected and rerun at that time.

4. **How does a *dark room* differ from unattended computer center operation?**
    Unattended computer center operation is the broader concept of implementing tools and techniques that eliminate or reduce the dependency on human intervention. Its objective is not to black out space or time, but rather to implement tools and techniques to improve quality and to reduce and eliminate the fault points which are the points of human intervention. As the points of human intervention are reduced, the amount of staffing is reduced, and the quality improves. Unattended computer operation and a dark room are addressing the same issue in a different way.

5. **Why do you want to remove all the people from the computer center? Is the benefit worth all the effort?**
    The initial focus of unattended operation is on expense reduction, and the reaction is that staffing does not represent a large portion of the computer center operating expense. Furthermore, the staffing component, as a percent of the total expense of operating a computer center, is becoming smaller, and conversely, the hardware and software components are becoming an increasingly larger percent.

    The computer professionals that ask "Why remove the people?" are asking a valuable question. In most computer centers, the expense of the staff component is in the range of 30%, while the hardware, software and supply components are in the 70%

range. In addition, with the increasing demand for computer capacity and computer center automation software, the hardware and software expense elements are increasing at a faster rate than the need for staff to operate the computer centers.

However, the objective of unattended computer center operation is not expense reduction. The objective is *quality*. One of the significant obstacles to the expansion of information technology as a whole is a lack of confidence on the part of computer center users that the computer center can provide quality services. Automation of the computer center improves quality.

6.   What will happen if I do not move in the direction of unattended computer center operation?

This is a tough question to answer diplomatically. For computer center management, unattended computer center operation is a career decision. If the computer center does not improve quality, the computer center users will go away. Computer center users will justify departmental machines, machines that already operate unattended. Another alternative is that organizational management will recognize the need for unattended computer center operation and bring in someone who will implement unattended computer center operation. I don't think there is a real choice.

7.   What resources are required to implement unattended computer center operation? Will additional staff be required? Will the software or hardware budgets need to be increased?

The resources required to implement unattended computer center operation are already in the computer center. Sell the concept to management up-front. Show them what you are seeking to achieve, and get a commitment to redirect the dollars you save back into the process. As you experience turnover in the computer center, do not replace the positions. Use turnover as an opportunity to eliminate that function, and at every opportunity, consolidate job functions. Target to eliminate key functions, and use the staffing as implementers. This is an opportunity to train and implement at the same time. Make unattended computer center operation a self-funding project.

8. **How can I expect my computer center users to react to unattended computer center operation?**
Computer center users will be suspicious, concerned and unbelieving. They will think you are trying to off-load your work onto them. The users will be concerned that they will be left to flounder about without any assistance, and they will not believe that it can be done. You might be lucky and have computer center users that have a different perspective, but to be on the safe side, assume they will be skeptical, and put together a communication program up-front which specifically addresses these concerns.

9. **How can I effectively approach the computer center users with the unattended computer center direction?**
Address unattended computer center operation from the quality perspective. Remember, these computer users have experienced up to twenty-five years of things not working quite right, of poor response time, of computer failures and incorrect reports. Emphasize that your objective, and your *only* objective, is to improve quality and that improved quality will make their life easier.

10. **What is the single biggest obstacle to achieving unattended computer center operation?**
The human obstacles are the most diabolical. First, most data centers have yet to recognize that unattended operation is achievable, and second, if they have recognized it, they do not consider it possible. The first obstacle is easily overcome through education. The second is more difficult because it becomes a self-fulfilling prophecy. Total unattended operation may not be immediately achievable, but partial accomplishment is immediately achievable. Movement toward the goal will result in immediate gains, and it positions the organization to take advantage of new solutions to traditional obstacles.

Unattended operation can be threatening. By definition, it involves reassigning staff, reeducating and the like. The nature of information technology is such that there is always a greater demand for qualified staff than is available. Attack unattended operation from a positive perspective; emphasize the desire to improve service, to return management control to end users and to develop qualified staff.

11. Can you guarantee that unattended operation will not fail?

Anything that the computer center does to automate itself improves reliability, availability and service. It reduces expense. If the computer center eliminates one error, if it installs one automated tool, if it improves service by one percent point, it has not failed. The improved computer center is better than it would have been if nothing had been done. Anyone can achieve these kinds of improvements. There are, however, no guarantees in computer processing, and unattended computer center operation is no exception.

12. How is success measured? How do I effectively prove that unattended computer center operation is working?

Are your reliability, availability, and service better? Do you have fewer people in the computer center? Does the computer center user have more control over input, processing and output? If you can answer yes to these questions today, and if the answers are still yes this time next month, the month after and so on, then you are successful.

13. How can I assist in making unattended computer center operation happen? What is the single most important action I can take to assist?

Commit to making unattended operation happen. Teach management, computer center staff and computer users alike that it can be done. Systematically identify and remove fault points, design new application systems to accommodate this direction and put pressure on hardware and software vendors (especially IBM) to design for unattended operation. There is no magic, just daily commitment, hard work and a lot of fun.

Computer Center Staffing Issues

14. How can you remove *all* of the staff from the computer center? Will there be some staff in the computer center?

The staff that we are discussing is all of the staff that act as an intermediary between the computer user and the computer. We are discussing data entry, operators, help desks, tape librarians, media handlers, quality control clerks and all the associated layers of management. The objective is to stop inspecting quality into the computer center and to start building quality. The objective is to automate the computer center and to give the computer user the ability to manage its computing requirements.

Yes, there will be staff in the data center, but it will be different. There will be computer operation analysts to analyze and install new hardware and communications as the computer grows, to analyze and replace obsolete hardware and software and to manage the multi-million dollar resource.

15. Are there any disadvantages to removing all the people from the computer center?

There will be the same kind of disadvantages that we had when the phone company eliminated the phone operator to place a call. For some people, it will be difficult to stop working through someone else to get their job done. It is always pleasant to deal with someone nice and helpful. The direction of many industries is self-service whether it is pumping gas, an automatic teller machine, a voice recognition telephone system or a pregnancy test, and the computer center is no exception.

16. What is going to happen to me? Are you going to put me and the other computer center operation staff out on the street?

Under no circumstance. To be successful with unattended operation, the computer center needs to enlist the assistance of the computer center personnel and the computer center user. These are the people that understand the computer center the best. Over the last twenty-five years, there has been a chronic shortage of computing personnel, and there seems to be no solution to this shortage in the near future. No one will throw away good people.

The valuable training that the displaced staff receives will prepare computer center staff for better positions in other areas of computing. I am prepared to make the commitment to training as will all who are successful with unattended computer center operation. The only people who will have any problem in this scenario are those who are not prepared to learn and grow, and that is not a personality trait of computing people.

17. We are a union shop. How do I eliminate a union position without a strike?

There is no doubt that unattended computer center operation is eliminating bargaining unit positions. Unattended computer center operation is committed to improved quality, improved productivity, and improved quality of work life. It offers staff the opportunity to expand their job knowledge, their horizons and their salaries.

The alternative is the same as other industries that fail to automate — no job at all. Unions need to decide whether they are there to protect the interest of their members or their own interest. Unattended operation seems to clearly offer an opportunity to those who support it, and unions can play a vital role in ensuring that the intent is not subverted by the desire for short-term financial gains.

18. What do I do with a computer center employee who feels threatened and is causing other employees to be concerned?

Spend more time communicating. Communicate one on one and in groups with others who see the light. This will not be a frequent occurrence, and if it is frequent, assume you are doing something incorrect. Think through your tactics, and try something else. Remember the response to question number 13. If you remain committed to unattended computer center operation, if you reeducate the computer center staff, and if you are tenacious, you are going to reduce the obstacles to unattended operation.

19. **What does the computer center do with the staff that it displaces?**

The computer center retrains them for better positions in other areas of information technology. Make a commitment to promote all positions from within, and hire from the bottom. Train the displaced staff to fill these positions. Remember, there are still operation analysts in the computer center and other departments that need people such as technical services, database services, application services, the information center and computer user departments. Look around, there are all kinds of people using computers, and they are all looking for staff.

20. **What steps do I take to ensure that the computer center staff is able to be placed in other positions within the organization?**

Put them to work making unattended operation work. When they achieve their objective, they are ready for more responsible positions.

21. **What do I do with people on my staff who do not want to gain new skills, but whose position is slated for elimination?**

Communicate. It is hard to picture someone who does not want to improve. If they do not want a better position, assist them to find something in another computer center. Ultimately, these people will have a problem that only they can solve. This will be an unusual situation.

22. **Our organization is not growing. How do I retrain people into positions when there are no new positions?**

Hang in there. If the organization is contracting the problem is bigger than you can solve. If it is just a question of not growing or growing very slowly, then it may be necessary to carry some extra staff for a while. Most organizations have a minimum of 5% to 10% turnover annually. If you commit to filling positions from within, you should be able to place the displaced people. Remember, you are saving monies. If you carry some people until a position opens, you are only deferring the savings. Talk to your human resources staff at the start, and get their support. Do not surprise them. It is my experience that human resource and management people are supportive if given a chance.

23. As a data center director, why should I voluntarily put myself in a compromising position by reducing my staff? I will lose my power and eventually my job.

The answer to this question is the same as the answer to question six. If you don't, the computer center users will justify a departmental machine, or machine that already operates unattended, or organizational management will recognize the need and bring in someone who will implement unattended computer center operation. This is not a question of choice. We are all in a footrace with professional obsolescence, and if the data center director does not want to lose the race, he or she must move in the direction of unattended operation.

24. How do you introduce the topic of unattended operation to the computer center staff?

Do it as a group. Go through the concepts, and cover as many questions as you can anticipate. Give them materials to go over at their leisure and some time to think about it. Emphasize that it is vital to the success of the computer center and the organization, and ask them for suggestions. Schedule time to get back together and discuss suggestions and questions. It is also very helpful to get the computer center users involved.

25. What can be done to minimize the morale problems within the computer center while moving toward unattended computer center operation?

Communicate. Tell the computer center staff what you are achieving and why it is important. Encourage them to ask questions and to participate in the process. Ensure that everyone has the opportunity for an equal or better position. Use the conversion to unattended operation as an on-the-job training exercise. It gets the staff involved, provides in-service training and actually improves morale.

Computer Center User Issues

26. What is unattended computer center operation going to do for my department?

Computer center users are the benefactors of this process. The early years of data processing were characterized by departments relinquishing some of their management responsibilities to the computer centers. This was the only alternative available for realizing the benefits of the computer. The computer center assumed responsibility for data entry, computer processing, scheduling, report generation and report distribution. Unattended operation returns responsibility for the system to departmental management.

If the computer center users view this process as unloading undesirable tasks on them, they will resist the process. User involvement is essential. Emphasize productivity gains: enormous amounts of time that are expended in meetings and on memos addressing problems caused by human intervention are eliminated. Emphasize morale improvements: errors resulting in disruptions to work schedules, blaming, and a reduction in the quality of work life are eliminated. Promote an awareness that unattended operation resolves these problems and improves morale.

27. How does the computer center expect us users to schedule our own work, key our own data, administer our own report distribution without additional personnel and budget?

The computer user is already doing these functions: they are developing a schedule, writing it down, hand carrying it, following up, attending meetings to discuss why it did not work today when it has for the last twenty days and so on. The computer user is doing the same for data entry and report distribution. What is more, the computer center is doing a similar set of activities. Everything gets done at least twice. If the computer center user does it directly, it takes less time than if they did it manually. It does require some changes in procedures and a little retraining.

28. **Since the computer center is going to save a lot of money by eliminating positions, why can't they transfer the funds to the user department budget?**

The computer center is reducing the effort of the computer user. There is no budget increase for the computer user. In fact in many cases, the user's budget can be reduced. Computer users tend to be skeptical about these budget reductions. Find one prepared to make it happen and demonstrate that it does reduce effort.

29. **Why should the user take on all this new responsibility? Why should I be the one to take the blame when there is a problem since I can now blame the computer center?**

Computer center users are not taking on more work, rather, they are doing things in a more streamlined manner. They are better able to service their mission. Computer center users are being given the opportunity to demonstrate to their management how they can improve quality and improve productivity. There is no blame here; we are discussing praise.

30. **Why eliminate the keypunch department? It can handle peak workloads and it saves us a lot of time.**

Keypunch or batch data entry is an obsolete concept. It is much more effective for computer users to enter data at the source and to edit and correct it immediately. The information is available immediately. There is no transcription and there is no transcription error. There is no lost paperwork. There are no batches that are processed incorrectly, and there are no meetings to determine is to blame and so on. It is a more efficient process. It reduces data entry staff, and it reduces computer user staff. Direct data entry improves quality and saves more time.

31. **Why would you want to have the on-line system available twenty-four hours a day? No one is ever around after six o'clock.**

There is a lot of human intervention involved with managing an on-line network. Bringing the system up and down is an opportunity for error. It requires that the system be purged, resulting in periods of computer under-utilization. The inability to run batch and on-line at the same time and the inability to run multiple systems concurrently are symptoms of rigidity. This lack of flexibility results in human intervention and error. It is amazing what a difference there is in a computer center that can run anything simultaneously with anything else.

Furthermore, we are moving toward self-service. Employees will want to work at home and at off-hours. Think about the implications to your computer center, and you will see why you need twenty-four hour a day on-line systems.

32. How does the nightly batch schedule get defined in an unattended computer center?

The computer users set up their own schedule, and the schedule is modeled to determine if there is sufficient time to complete the schedule. Changes to the daily, weekly or monthly schedule are not frequent, and conflicts are less frequent. When conflicts occur, they will be with systems that cannot be run concurrently with other software systems or on-line processing. Other conflicts arise from ad hoc processing, and if computer users are given the ability to see their schedule modeled, they will make the necessary compromises.

33. Who commits to the workload requests of the computer center user in an unattended computer center?

The information technology group, as part of its capacity planning group, ensures that there are sufficient resources to meet the needs of the organization. This does not change. Automated guidelines and procedures are established for handling ad hoc and abnormal processing. Under normal circumstances, exceptions are rare, and information technology management is still available to mediate.

34. Who informs the computer users of processing problems?

The computer users can inquire about the status of their processing on-line via the scheduling system.

35. Who assists the computer user in an unattended computer center?

The computer center operation analysts who are addressing the source of the remaining problems and applying a permanent correction are available for assistance. These people may be a part of the computer center or of some other group.

36. The computer center staff inspects work requests and finished products for errors before they reach the computer user. With no one in the computer center, won't this lack of inspection result in problems and worse service?

Many errors are created by transcribing data and passing documents to other staff. As the computer user assumes control of such functions, the need for transcription, handling and inspection goes away. The direct input of data requires an intelligent data entry feature: data is edited and corrected on-line. Software is put in place to perform edits and to balance output. The whole objective of unattended computer operation is the identification and permanent correction of errors. Unattended operation results in improved quality, service, reliability and performance.

37. What can be done to minimize computer center user morale problems while moving toward unattended computer center operation?

Communicate. Tell the computer center users what you are achieving and why it is important. Encourage them to ask questions and to participate in the process. Deal with users who are receptive and advertise successes.

38. In an unattended computer center, how are hardware and communications problems identified and resolved on a timely basis?

Security and environmental monitoring devices are available to monitor the vital aspects of the data center in the absence of computer room staff. Such equipment can recognize failing equipment or intrusions and phone designated staff on an exception basis using voice synthesizers. Furthermore, the devices can be queried by cautious or inquisitive management. Some on-call procedures are required, but they may be activated by hardware and communications vendors.

39. Once achieved, what will be the role of the unattended computer center? What services can I expect from the computer center?

The unattended computer center will be a utility available for you at your convenience. The computer center services will be the same except that quality will be much higher.

Technical Obstacles to Unattended Computer Center Operation

40. How do you expect to eliminate tape processing?

Tape processing is a major fault point, and although there are replacement media available, tape is likely to be with computing centers for a long time. The most immediate alternatives to tape are the StorageTek 4400, Automated Cartridge System and the Masstor Systems M860, Storage Management System. Masstor Systems Corporation located in Santa Clara, California does not have a large presence in the United States, but is making a substantial dent in the European market. It appears to be a good potential alternative for tape.

In addition, there are commercially available optical disk systems and the increased density of disk, the reduced expense and the ability to locate the physical devices at considerable distance from the mainframe makes disk to disk backup appear feasible as it was with the IBM 2311 and 2314 disk drive systems (removable disk).

The elimination of tape is difficult, but the dependence on tape can also be mitigated by reducing its use. Computer centers can identify that tape is obsolete and that it is a roadblock to unattended operation and consciously reduce its use. When it is used, it will be a conscious deviation, and the computer center will be cognizant of the consequences. Seek to eliminate this media.

41. How are you going to eliminate the tape library?

Unattended operation requires the elimination of tape since tape is the most rudimentary of manual computer center functions. However, tape will be with us for a long time, and tape management software helps to improve reliability and reduce the direct labor associated with the use of this media. Identify tape as an obsolete media and as a roadblock to unattended computer center operation. Consistently reduce its use.

Tape dataset stacking software should be used in concert with tape management software. Many tapes are backups that are rarely used. Furthermore, many of these backups use only a fraction of the tape volume. By stacking these types of tape datasets, the data center can reduce the physical handling of tapes, reduce the volume of tape inventories, decrease off-site storage cost and improve cost containment. Purchased utilities are available to do tape dataset stacking; an example is TDSU (Tape Data Stacking Utility) from U.S. West in Denver, Colorado.

42. How do you expect to eliminate printing?

Report management and distribution software are available. This software directs reports to a disk device rather than to a printer. Once on disk, it can be retained for a predefined period, viewed and if necessary, printed under the control of an end user. This is not a substitute for on-line queries, but it is an outstanding intermediate step.

43. How are you going to eliminate console operator interaction with the computer?

Identify all computer center procedures which require computer operator intervention. Divide the results of this evaluation into (1) those procedures which are easy to eliminate and (2) those which are difficult to eliminate. Further, divide the difficult into (a) those which can be resolved with installed software and (b) those which require new software.

Establish a plan which defers the difficult changes, and implement the easy changes. The easy changes provide ample opportunities for reducing operator intervention, and once accomplished, establish a presence and foundation for proceeding.

Next, determine the requirements for new software. New software requires a long lead time; get this process started early. Proper utilization of existing software is also a factor. In many cases, software has been purchased and installed but is neither properly nor fully utilized. With these two plans in place, it is much easier to go back and address the more difficult changes.

44. The only automated rerun recovery system on the market today needs to be manually activated to perform the automated rerun. How do we achieve unattended operation with a manual tool?

Nothing is perfect. Implement what you have, and make the most of it. Look for opportunities to extend the features by writing routines that extend the functionality without impacting the integrity of the software. Bring the software supplier into the fold; make sure they understand what you are seeking to achieve, and convince them that it is in their best interest to extend the features. Look for solutions that will solve your problem and assist them to make a profit.

45. How do you handle a physical security problem or a problem with the physical support plant (air conditioning, fire, water chiller, or electrical problems)?

Security and environmental monitoring devices are available to monitor the vital aspects of the computer center in the absence of computer room staff. Furthermore, there is equipment that can recognize failing equipment or intrusions and phone designated staff on an exception basis using voice synthesizers. The devices can be queried for status. In today's world, these may not be one and the same solution, but I am confident that better solutions are on the horizon.

46. What are you going to do when a critical process fails (an application software system or operating software) with no one in attendance at the computer center?

An environmental monitoring system can recognize interruptions to application processing as well as security breaches and failing computer or ancillary equipment. Such equipment recognizes a failing process and phones designated on-call staff.

47. How do you perform routine data library management functions in an unattended computer center?

If they are routine, then automate these functions. If they are not routine, question why you are doing them. There may be a different alternative. If all else fails, there is human intervention from operation analysts, technical services and database services. Remember, these other operations are also overhead functions, and information technology is seeking to automate these functions.

48. How are you going to procedurally accept new jobs into *production status* in an unattended computer center?

Automate the job turnover process, and decentralize it to the computer user and application services. Installing new jobs into production status is a significant source of error in most computer centers. Moving programs into the correct libraries, changing JCL and so on are very labor-intense and error-prone processes. The computer center adds no value to the process and only acts as an inspector.

49. Can a local area network play a role in implementing unattended computer center operation?

A LAN is not an integral part of the unattended scenario, but anything that extends the sphere of influence of the central computer to the computer user and leverages the base of installed equipment is beneficial to the process. The LAN falls into that category.

50. Are there tools that assist in the implementation of unattended computer center operation such as electronic mail and electronic forms authorization?

Definitely install electronic mail and electronic forms authorization. Neither tool is integral to the unattended computer operation process, but they make the transition much easier. Electronic communication makes communications easier and quicker during the transition period. Experiment with electronic conferences: try to get computer users to share hints and experiences via electronic mail.

Twenty Tips For Achieving Unattended Computer Center Operation

INTRODUCTION

Achieving unattended computer center operation is not a black art; it is a marketing exercise. It is achieved by convincing management, staff and end user alike that the true objective of unattended operation is *quality* and by convincing them that it is achievable today.

Computer centers have a fundamental quality problem and the objective of unattended computer center operation is improved *quality*. One of the significant obstacles to the expansion of the computer center and information technology as a whole is a lack of confidence on the part of computer center users, organizational management and even computer center staff that the technology can work. They just do not believe that the computer center will be available when it is needed or that response time will be adequate to get work done.

The problem is that computer centers are so complex that it is not possible to inspect quality into computer center services. The solution is to build quality into the center by systematically identifying the fault points and by permanently eliminating the fault points. Elimination of fault points is the definition of unattended computer center operation.

The obstacles to achieving unattended computer center operation are human and technical. The human obstacles are the most diabolical because they are difficult to detect and harder to correct. Many computer centers do not *recognize* that unattended computer center operation is both possible and desirable. Where the recognition of possibility is absent, so is opportunity. Second, there are those computer center professionals who recognize but who do not *believe* that it is possible or desirable to achieve unattended computer center operation. This, of course, is a self-fulfilling prophecy.

It is the smaller computer centers which do not recognize that unattended computer center operation is possible. These computer centers view automation tools as something that only the *big guys* can afford. On the other hand, the large computer centers are so complex and have so many people that they cannot even visualize an unattended center. It is the computer centers that fall between these extremes that are the prime movers. Computer vendors that offer mid-range or departmental computers provide computers which run unattended. As a result, management realizes that unattended computer operation is possible. It is the mid-range or departmental computers that are the computer center's real competition.

The second obstacle is technical. Although it appears more formidable on the surface, it is actually far less severe. The most significant technical obstacle is tape usage. Although there is no simple, inexpensive replacement alternative to tape, there are ways to significantly reduce the use of tape, to automate the manual handling of tape cartridges and to eliminate its use. A combination of these technologies can be used as a replacement for a significant amount, if not all, of the tape usage. Solutions for other technical obstacles such as computer scheduling, operator interaction with the computer and hard-copy report distribution are available.

Unattended computer center operation is achieved by systematically removing the human and technical obstacles, by designing new application systems to accommodate this direction and by putting pressure on hardware and software vendors to design for unattended operation. This article discusses twenty practical tips for achieving unattended computer center operation.

ACHIEVING UNATTENDED COMPUTER OPERATIONS

1. USER SCHEDULING
Allow computer center users to control the automated computer job scheduler. Insist that vendors make the scheduler *user friendly*. Provide computer users with the ability to add and delete jobs from their schedule. Establish a deadline for changes. Using security software, enforce a moratorium software after the deadline so that computer center staff can analyze any over-scheduling and make corresponding adjustments.

Experience reveals that computer users schedule the computing resources better than the computer center staff. Computer users understand their business cycles and know when their run times are increasing and the impact of requesting additional reports.

Why use change forms when the computer user can make the change from the terminal on his or her desk? Why use forms if the functions of the computer scheduler are on-line? Why use a batch system when an on-line system improves productivity? Give control of the scheduler to the computer user. What better service can a computer center provide than self-service?

2. BATCH WORKLOAD MANAGEMENT
Build or acquire workload balancing tools to determine, within *reasonable* tolerances, that the production batch work can be achieved within the production window. When the tool is in place, provide the computer user the ability to compare the processing request to the available processing window. The automated job scheduler can inhibit the start of a schedule which exceeds the batch window. This provides a self-service environment but prevents computer users from adversely affecting themselves.

Most computer centers have one or more key people who analyze the schedule and *guesstimate* whether the schedule will be complete in the allotted time. Some automated job schedulers have attempted to address this need; however, the number of variables is so large that the reliability level is low. The estimate does not have to be perfect; develop a tool that gives results equal to or better than the expert. Provide the computer user with the tool and resolve the exceptions in a structured way.

3. PARAMETER SUBMISSION

Provide computer users with the facility to submit parameters into their system without knowing JCL. There is no reason why the computer user has to send the computer center a piece of paper. The computer center enters the parameters into the computer using an on-line facility; provide the on-line facility to the user. If the mechanics of the on-line facility are too complicated for a computer center user, create a simple application which edits the parameters and submits them into the JCL ready for job execution.

Avoid job parameters whenever possible. They are points of human intervention and, therefore, are fault points no matter who enters them. Also, remember that no matter how tough the edit controls are, there will be situations when incorrect information is entered. Plan for these situations.

4. ELIMINATION OF COMPUTER CENTER PRINTING

How many millions of instructions does your computer mainframe execute in one second? 10 million? 30 million? 50 million? More? Have you ever thought about how long it takes for the computer user to receive a routine batch report from the computer center? The same day? One day? Two days? A week? In some cases, the reports are lost, and they are never received.

Over the last decade, major computer manufacturers have only designed computers for on-line processing. On-line information retrieval improves productivity, reliability and timeliness, making batch, hard copy reporting an obsolete concept. However, on-line reporting software is not always available, and a good interim step to on-line information retrieval is the electronic report distribution system. With an electronic report distribution system, computer users can view information in report format as soon as the job finishes execution. Computer users are able to extend on-line or hard-copy access to a new report recipient by electronically changing the report distribution.

However, there are many reports and special forms that cannot be eliminated. Examine how long it takes to deliver these reports from the time the batch computer job is completed to the time the computer user receives the report. Now reexamine the same process; this time examine it in terms of where it makes the best business sense to print the report. Computer centers can save valuable time by installing remote batch printers and by installing printers in the mail distribution center. In most cases, printers are no more difficult to operate than copy machines. Personnel who normally perform printing in the computer center or computer user departments can be reassigned to the more strategic distribution areas. Relocating the printers results in operational improvements, and economies of scale can make more people available for other, more productive work.

In many cases, reports go through several different hands after leaving the computer center. They are reviewed, packaged and mailed. Each step is a fault point, a point of potential error and a source of potential delay. Can a step be eliminated and or automated? An automated balance and control system can eliminate the need for manual balancing or integrity checks before it is distributed. Automated review only requires intervention from the computer user when the report is out of balance.

How much is it worth to get computer output into the hands of the computer user in less time, with less cost, while reducing the number of possible points of error and delay?

5. CONSOLE AUTOMATION

How fast does the computer execute when it is waiting for an operator response? Is it reasonable to expect the computer operator to catch important messages, respond to requests on a timely basis and not make any mistakes when millions of messages pass through the console? As computers become faster, the job of the computer operator becomes more complex. At the same time, it is becoming increasingly difficult to find and keep good operators.

The solution to this dilemma is to automate the computer console. Computer systems are too fast and the computer center is too complex for operators to continue to manually interact with the computer. It is essential that computer centers automatically read and respond to messages. Install an automatic console response system to handle all interaction with the computer.

Message response and suppression is the very first step. But why stop there? Use the automated console system to expedite problem resolution by inserting WTO (write to operator) messages into application software to help pinpoint potential application problems before they become a service disruption. Activate corrective action by notifying support personnel or even interfacing with an automated problem notification system.

6. AUTOMATED PROBLEM NOTIFICATION

To achieve unattended computer center operation, it is necessary to identify job failures, to attempt an automated recovery and to escalate the problem to support personnel if that fails. This is achieved by interfacing an automated console response system to an automated rerun/recovery system, an automated job scheduler and an automated notification system. A similar process can be used to identify hardware and data communication failures and automatically notify support personnel and the vendor's hotline.

Integrated systems are not available to address the automated problem notification process. A few vendors appear to be working in the right direction, and within a year or two, there is a high likelihood that at least one supplier will have an integrated problem management system. A real problem management system should automatically attempt to recover failures, automatically call for help and keep a log of who was notified and what happened. This information can be analyzed to isolate recurring problems, and permanent solutions can be developed.

7. TAPE PROCESSING

Many computer centers are being taken over by magnetic tapes. Every time a tape is read, written, cleaned, stored or archived it requires manual handling. As a result of all this manual handling, tape is a major obstacle to achieving unattended operations. However, there are many things that can be done to reduce the labor-intensive nature of this media.

Look at tape retention. Many computer centers have installed IBM 3480 cartridge tape drives. One of the reasons why computer centers installed this new technology was increased reliability. The comparatively poor performance of the 3420's and the associated reel problems caused computer centers to increase the retention periods of their backups. In addition to the technology changes, personnel turnover in user areas adds to increasing the data retention and backup frequencies. Examine backup frequencies and retention and reduce the number of tapes that are retained. The number of tapes stored can be reduced without putting the computer center at risk.

In addition to examining data retention, there are other alternatives to reduce tape handling such as ATL systems (Automated Tape Libraries) These include the StorageTek ATL and the newly announced Memorex-Telex automated library. In addition, Masstor Systems has enhanced the 10 year old IBM mass storage technology providing up to 220 Gbytes of storage in a box the size of a IBM 3380 disk drive.

8.   ELECTRONIC STORAGE BIN SYSTEM

While the computer center is waiting for the effects of new on-line systems and electronic distribution, consider installing an electronic bin system. An electronic bin system significantly reduces report handling. If computer users are coming to the computer center to pick up reports, the electronic bin system eliminates the need for computer center personnel to distribute reports. In addition to using the bin system as an output vehicle, use it as an input device. Assign specific bins to receive input documents until these too are eliminated. This further reduces staffing requirements. Keep in mind, the more the computer center reduces manual handling, the more it improves the quality of service.

9.   LIBRARY MANAGEMENT

Source library management should be performed directly by programming and technical support staff under the protection umbrella of a security package. Programming and technical support staff can move modules into production libraries as part of the application development process. Remember, computer center librarians do not know what a new software module can do; they only know that the proper forms were provided and that they had proper authorization. They are inspecting security.

Using the security system as the substitute for authorization, the computer center can allow programming and technical staff to maintain their own libraries. It is time for computer centers to effectively take advantage of the security system as do the computer center users.

10. OBSOLETE MANUAL PROCEDURES

It is not uncommon to find that computer centers are performing control procedures which are no longer required. In most organizations, it is fair to assume that 20% of the procedures have *no* value. For example, is the computer center filling out control logs/transmittals? Is it really important to know that computer users signed for a report that they never had or subsequently lost? It costs something to track every batch of source documents and every report in and out of the computer center. It requires extensive labor and results in delays for the computer user. Take a close look at these procedures and eliminate everything that is questionable. The computer center stands to gain valuable resources which can be allocated to other computer center automation tasks.

Substitute automation for inspection. Use automation tools such as automated report balancing and control, automatic job scheduling and electronic JCL review to build quality. Build quality into the computer center's product. Do not delay the product or service by manually inspecting it after it has been produced.

11. COMPUTER CENTER PERSONNEL

The computer center staff has a wealth of knowledge that can facilitate the implementation of the automation tools. Give computer center staff an opportunity to get directly involved in the automation process. Furthermore, as the automation tools are implemented, the computer center staff will have increasingly more time to further computer center automation.

Two benefits are derived by involving staff in computer center automation. First, the staff is being provided a career growth path. They are getting hands-on experience in a very exciting process. For the first time, they are being given an opportunity to eliminate the problems that have plagued them. They will love the opportunity to improve their skills while eliminating problems which have been haunting them in their daily routine. Second, and equally important, it accelerates the implementation of computer center automation.

Throughout this process, it is vital that the staff not feel that their livelihood is in jeopardy. If the computer center staff feels threatened, computer center automation will not succeed. Give the computer center staff a firm assurance that they will receive an equal or better position as a result of their participation. Emphasize that the most successful will have the greatest opportunity for promotion and advancement and then follow through. Provide education in those areas of the organization where there is a need and interest.

Do everything possible not to fill vacated positions. Consolidate and eliminate positions through attrition. As positions are vacated, give the staff the chance to learn new aspects of the computer center. The computer center staff will appreciate an opportunity. Remember, every position that is filled is one that will need to be displaced later in the automation process. However, if a position must be filled, move staff around until the position can be filled by casual personnel.

12. MIS EDUCATION

Work closely with the application development staff. Explain the direction of the organization and how they play a vital role in achieving unattended computer center operation. Make them aware that they are one of the benefactors of unattended computer center operation. The less intervention required by computer center staff, the less chance their assistance will be required to recover from an interruption. Point out that computer center intervention is a fault point that needs to be eliminated. If the application software is purchased, identify these fault points to the software vendor and request their elimination.

Many of the computer center automation tools benefit the application development staff. Point out that:

- Automated rerun/recovery can drastically reduce the support requirements from technical service, database and production support staff.
- Automated console operator software can identify and correct repetitive system software problems without causing service interruptions.
- Automatic problem notification software provides support personnel with timely and consistent problem notification, and more importantly it can also communicate the necessary recovery instructions, expediting the recovery process.
- Computer center automation results in more timely and reliable support for their test and ad hoc production.

13. CUSTOMER SERVICE

Computer centers are in the service business. They need to provide consistent, high-quality customer services. As the computer center allows computer users to have more and more direct access to stored information, computer users will need much reinforcing. Be available to answer questions on a timely basis. Computer users must be confident that they will receive support when they experience problems. As computer users become more comfortable with the automated tools, dependency on computer center staff will reduce, and they will become self-supporting.

Without user confidence, unattended computer operation cannot succeed. The computer users must feel that their computing needs are being better served with them in charge than it was with computer center personnel intervening in the process.

14. COMPUTER CENTER USER PERSONNEL

Maintain a strong line of communication with the computer center users. Emphasize that the purpose of unattended operation is to provide consistent, high-quality service. Explain how paper-based documents and associated manual procedures are time-consuming, labor-intense, and error-prone. Give computer users as much control over their computing environment as possible.

Give them user friendly tools that do not require technical knowledge. Provide adequate audit trails and protect data via security software. Computer centers are creating a self-service environment that returns control to the people who can add the most value to information.

15. VENDOR PARTNERSHIP

Work with your vendors. Help make them understand that any technology which requires manual intervention is unacceptable. Assist hardware and software vendors to establish a direction that assures computer center users have the best possible service. High-level, consistent service is only achievable if the computer center eliminates all human intervention between the computer user and the computer. Hardware and software suppliers need to recognize that computer centers have become too complex and demanding to be dependent on human intervention and that computer centers will not accept products that perpetuate intervention.

Most vendors do not understand the concept of unattended operation. The only way to eliminate the technical obstacles to unattended computer center operation is to make vendors aware that it is in their best interest to remove the human element from their products. Learn a lesson from computer center users and clearly identify to suppliers what is needed to achieve unattended computer center operation.

16. DATA ENTRY

Transcribing information to a document for input and processing by the computer center is a time-consuming, expensive and error-prone process. Provide computer users with the facility to enter their data directly into the computer either on-line or in a data collection mode. The overhead involved in the batch data entry process is staggering. In addition, experienced data entry staff are extremely difficult to hire and retain.

Distribute data entry to the source of the information. Do not decentralize data entry. Provide the originator of the information with the ability to communicate with the computer either in on-line or in data collection mode without transcribing the information to an input document. This method of information collection eliminates document logs, coordination meetings, missing batches and peak volume problems. Direct data entry provides the computer users with more time to get data into the system since less intervention is required. It also improves the quality since the person who understands the information best is entering the data into the computer.

17. COMPUTER CENTER OPERATION DOCUMENTATION

How can the computer center ensure that the operational documentation is current? Computer centers can only be assured that documentation is current and accurate if the documentation is part of the automated process. For example, the automated scheduler is the only place where the run frequency of a job is absolutely correct; the electronic report distribution system is the only place where the report distribution is absolutely correct, and the tape management system is the authority on tape retention. The least likely place to find correct information is on a separately maintained document. The more the computer center automates, the less external documentation is required. Unattended computer center operation makes computer center operation documentation, as it is known today, obsolete. The computer center runs better, and the application development staff loves it.

18. DATA SECURITY SOFTWARE

Did you ever stop and think about why the computer industry develops so many manual procedures, and so many sign-off forms? Authorization is required for schedule changes, library moves, report distribution, parameter changes and so on. Have you ever evaluated how much time these procedures take, how many hands the papers go through and how many opportunities there are for error and delay? Computer centers are trying to inspect security. Through inspection procedures, computer centers are trying to ensure that only authorized users and staff have their requests attended.

Inspecting security only accomplishes a false sense of security. Signatures are reviewed, source documents are filed for the annual audit, and security appears to be under control. The odds of a computer center catching an unauthorized person causing accidental or intentional integrity problems are very slim.

Computer centers need to build data security software features into computer center automation. Security software is a positive control over the computer center. It ensures that only authorized users are changing schedules, moving programs into production and reviewing reports. It eliminates the need to maintain files, to look for approved signatures and to maintain paperwork audit trails.

Make sure the automated scheduler, library management system, report management system and all the other computer center automation tools are integrated with the security software. The security software provides a complete audit trail. Computer auditors already have confidence in the security software. This built-in security ensures that the computer center is protected seven days a week twenty-four hours a day.

19. ELECTRONIC VAULTING

Electronic vaulting is the ability to electronically store and retrieve DASD backups and historical information off-site. Most computer center staff are both competent and conscientious. Yet, most computer centers rarely have a perfect audit of their off-site vault. Rarely is everything in the vault that should be there. In most cases, somebody has forgotten to take something off-site, and it remains in the computer room.

Furthermore, conventional vaulting procedures result in delay. Backups are processed and stay in the computer room for hours waiting for someone to pick them up. When they are picked up, a van driver hauls them in an unsecured van to some secured location. There is a real need to move toward electronic vaulting, and this can be achieved with high density storage devices such as the Masstor Systems M960 and M1000 mass storage systems.

20. A SELF-SERVICE COMPUTER CENTER

Eliminate all the procedural steps that do not add value to the data entered into the computer or produced by the computer. Wherever possible, eliminate the bureaucracy or paperwork associated with interfacing to the computer center. In most cases, the people who intervene between the information entered into the computer center and the information produced by the computer center add *no* value to the information. They are actually reducing the quality and timeliness of the information.

This is a self-service mentality. Banks have acclimated computer users to this concept. Not only has the public assumed the duties of a bank teller, but they enjoy it. The public finds it more convenient than conventional banking. It is less costly for the bank and more convenient for the public. This is the mind set that needs to be implemented to achieve unattended computer center operation.

Provide an environment where computer center users can enter their own data, schedule their processing and control the distribution of their output. Provide an environment where the computer center user has complete control over his or her information from start to finish.

CONCLUSION

The objective of unattended computer center operation is to improve computer center quality through simplification and automation. Of all the names for this quality improvement process, *computer center automation, dark room processing, lights-out operation, dark time operation,* the name that best describes this process is *unattended operation.* The word *unattended* in unattended computer center operation refers to the quality improvement process. It is the elimination of fault points, and in the computer center, the fault points are the points of human interface between the computer and the computer user.

The benefits of unattended computer center operation are increased quality, increased user service and decreased labor cost. Both the computer center and the user department experience labor savings. Unattended computer center operation results in increased reliability, and it reestablishes the creditability of the computer center as a viable computer processing option.

The Future of Unattended Computer Center Operation

INTRODUCTION

Information technology evolves in one direction, from the simple to the complex. Computers started out simple. They had no operating system; they processed a single program at a time, and they required much intervention. However, the speed of the CPU increased, high speed tape units were added, operating systems were introduced, direct access storage devices were added, and the operating systems became multi-tasking on-line processing was introduced and the users increased from one to a thousand simultaneous users. Computing became complex very quickly.

Although more complex, computer centers were based on a single image large computer. Large computer centers might have multiple computers that were independent or loosely coupled, but the concept remained the same. In the 1980's, this changed. The mid-range, *departmental* computer became popular; the personal computer was introduced on a large scale, and the multiple processor computer was introduced. The business case for choosing one or the other of these computers was different, and it became economical to do some applications on one type of computer rather than on another.

Applications, such as spreadsheets and word processing, were easy to achieve on a personal computer, and some applications, such as manufacturing systems, became easy to install on a mid-range computer. More than ever, the selection of computers became a software decision rather than a hardware decision.

When viewed in the context of natural evolution, the evolution of information technology from simple to complex, and from single processor to multiple processor, is expected. In nature, organisms (both plant and animal) evolve from the simple to the complex and from single celled to multi-celled. Computer evolution is paralleling this pattern of natural evolution.

As information technology becomes increasingly complex, there is a continuing need to look back and isolate obsolete technologies. There is a need to eliminate technologies that no longer fit into the environment which make it difficult to move forward. On one hand, information technology is becoming increasingly complex, and on the other, there is a need to look back and reduce this complexity by eliminating technologies that no longer fit into the environment.

Furthermore, as the technology moves forward, the opportunities for applying the technology increase. As a result, there are typically four or five opportunities to apply the technology for every one that an organization can economically afford to implement. Under these circumstances, the strategy which seems to work best is to choose the path of least resistance. Implement the technologies that the organization is receptive to or that are the easiest to implement and defer the others to a more opportune time.

A basic understanding of these two concepts, the evolution of information technology from the simple to the complex, and the strategy of implementing technology using the path of least resistance, makes it significantly easier to understand the future direction of unattended computer center operation.

DIRECTION OF COMPUTING

There is a parallel between natural evolution and the evolution of information technology. In natural evolution, life began as a single cell. The cells formed colonies. The cells in the colony eventually formed a symbiotic relationship, and some cells began to perform specialized functions. The cells merged into colonies, and the colonies evolved into a very complex multi-celled structure.

The evolution of computing is paralleling this process. Computers started out as small, single processing units and grew into large complex mainframe computers. In addition, mid-range computers such as the DEC VAX, the IBM System 36 & 38 and the Hewlett Packard 3000 were introduced, and these machines, too, grew in size and complexity. Finally, the personal computer and the workstation were introduced. As mid-range and personal computers became more prevalent, two things began to happen: specialization and networking. Many were dedicated to specialized applications such as office automation, inventory management, manufacturing or scientific research. Furthermore, these computers are networked together into complex computing structures, similar to a network of cells.

To better understand the future direction of unattended computer center operation, it is beneficial to look at the classes of computers, and the communication networks that tie them together.

Mainframe Computers

In the 1960's, the first modern mainframe computers, the IBM 360's, were little more powerful than the personal computers of today. They were relatively slow machines (less than one MIPS) and initially had little main memory (32k to 64K). It was not until the IBM 370 class computer that computers routinely had memories in the range of a million bites or more.

Since the 1960's, mainframe computers have continuously grown in speed and capacity from one generation to the next at a rate of about 100%. Probably the most significant aspect of this evolution is the increasing complexity of the computers. A computer became a network of computers. Specialized computers were used as control units for tape drives, for the disk drives, for the communications and for the I/O devices such as printers and terminals. All these devices are actually small processors in themselves. In fact, as the disk drive series evolved, the control units took on considerable specialization, including channel switching and cache memory. The computers not only became larger and faster, but they became clusters of specialized computers.

Finally, in the 1980's, IBM popularized the concept of a central computer that consisted of multiple processors. Computers had two, three or four processors within the machine. This is obviously the future direction of mainframe computers. Mainframe computers are going to continue to have more and more processors within a single box, and the operating system makes these processors appear as a single image to the computer and to the application program.

The mainframe computer, therefore, started as a simple processing unit that has evolved into an extremely complex machine composed of multiple special purpose processors contained within a single device. This single image device is networked to other computers either directly attached to it or attached through a communications network.

Departmental Computers

The history of small business machines (commonly referred to as minicomputers or, more recently, as departmental computers) is almost as old as the mainframe computer. The difference between the two is that technology has fostered the development of most business systems using large mainframe computers. It is only recently that a wealth of software has become available for the departmental computer. Furthermore, the cost of the small departmental computers has now declined to the point where it is cost effective to use them for applications previously restricted to the mainframe computer.

The high-capacity and relatively low cost of departmental computers seems to imply that this technology is evolving faster than the mainframe computer. In fact, most departmental computers, if not all, are designed exclusively for on-line processing while the common mainframe computers are essentially batch processors converted to on-line processing. As software systems become available for departmental computers, they are typically superior in both cost and performance to comparable software on the mainframe computer. As a result, the departmental computer has experienced a surge in popularity over the last decade.

However, most departmental computers are used essentially the same way as mainframe computers. A whole series of different applications are integrated together into a single general purpose departmental computer. Few organizations have attempted to dedicate departmental computers to single application (payroll, accounts payable, purchasing, and general ledger for example). In almost all cases, the departmental computer is used as a small general purpose computer.

The one notable exception is the manufacturing system. However, even here, a range of application systems run within the manufacturing system shell on the same departmental computer (order entry, inventory, MRP, shop floor control and probably word processing and electronic mail), much the same as they do in mainframe based manufacturing systems.

It is not common for departmental computers to be dedicated to a single application and for multiple departmental computers to be tied together in a network passing information from one system to the next or one computer to the next. Although networking computers could provide distributed or decentralized capabilities for specific departments, very few organizations have attempted to do so. This is probably because of the pervasive mainframe attitude which exists within business computing and the difficulties in managing information which is distributed across multiple sites.

However, as more and more organizations come to recognize that there is a wide variety of software available and that departmental computers are cost effective, they are realizing that it is possible to have mainframe computing without mainframe computers. They are linking together many small departmental computers so that the organization has single image computing composed of many small computers. The intriguing aspect of this tactic is that it is possible to build this network without displacing the mainframe computer. The mainframe computer can be a permanent part of the network, or eventually, it can be phased out.

But most likely, it will become a more or less equal partner in the network.

Personal Computers

In the late 1970's and the early 1980's a whole new class of computers were introduced: the personal computer. Personal computers have the power and capacity of the early mainframe computer, but they are designed as personal computing workstations. The most common applications for the personal computer are word processing, spreadsheets and small database applications. Personal computers are intended to satisfy the needs of individual workers.

Personal computers created a new market. All of a sudden, people who had never thought of using computers were using them. Applications were designed that were not cost effective on mainframe or departmental computers. Furthermore, after their initial introduction, the power and the capacity of the personal computer quickly doubled or tripled and then leveled off at a price/performance ratio that organizations were prepared to pay.

The power and the capacity of the personal computer expanded. As it expanded, the cost increased until the cost of the computer was no longer in synchronization with what a person was prepared to pay for a single work station on their desk. As a result, the capacity of the machine leveled off. Instead, a need developed for the personal computers to talk to one another, to talk to departmental computers and to talk to mainframe computers.

The evolution of the personal computer shifted from increasing in size to adding features onto an existing platform. Boards became available to allow the personal computer to talk to the mainframe; networks were introduced to allow personal computers to talk to one another. Large capacity direct access devices became available, and designated computers became file servers for other machines. A wealth of application software became available. The typical personal computer owner would spend from 20-50% of their initial purchase price every year in order to add software and hardware features to the computer.

Furthermore, personal computers became front-end processors for the larger, more powerful departmental or mainframe computer. This caused organizations to end up with a hierarchy of computers: the personal computers replacing the *dumb* terminal on the desk and the personal computer talking to the departmental computer with pass through capabilities into a mainframe computer.

Workstations

The last class of computers is the workstation. The workstation is very similar in many ways to the personal computer, except for its computing power. In some cases, workstations are in the 1-3 MIPS range (one to three million instructions per second), more powerful than some departmental computers and almost equivalent to the entry level mainframe computer.

The workstation is designed to provide a tremendous amount of computing power to scientific and engineering applications, or any application requiring a tremendous amount of computing but not requiring large amounts of I/O activity. In terms of architecture, the workstation is similar to the personal computer, but in terms of processing capacity, it similar to the mainframe.

Workstations are used primarily in engineering and research where there is a need for large amounts of processing and little application software. They do not have complex, user friendly operating systems, and there is not a wealth of applications software available. What they provide is sheer raw computing power at a reasonable price. Workstations have windowing capabilities similar to the Apple Macintosh. However, because of the complex nature of the computer, they still are not as easy to use. Ease of use is usually a feature of a proprietary operating system and not part of the computer itself.

Workstations can either be stand-alone processors (diskless), or they can be file servers with large capacity disk storage units. In many cases, workstations are purchased without any disk capacity. They are networked together with one machine becoming a file server. The beauty of the workstation is the sheer computing power that is available at a relatively low cost.

Communication Networks

Computers have evolved into four layers: mainframe computers that process work for hundreds to thousands of individual computer users, multi-purpose departmental computers which service from ten to a hundred computer users, personal computers which service a single person but are probably networked to a mainframe computer, and workstations which are the high-powered computers which service an individual and are networked to a file server.

Each has a different price range and each satisfies a different market. Each has a different set of available software, and in many cases, there is much overlap in capabilities between one level of machine and another. Some of the functions that can be done on a personal computer can be done on a mainframe and vice versa. All justification aside, once a computer is installed, there is an almost universal desire to communicate with other computers.

Most organizations have a complex computing environment consisting of multiple computers and multiple computer suppliers. What started out as a single computer has evolved into a network of computers. This network is providing information technology with the ability of having single image computing across multiple computers.

A computer user on the network, whether they are using personal computers, workstations, departmental computers, or mainframes, can access anything on the network. The objective of the network is to provide the computer user with access to an application system irrespective of the location of the hardware platform. What is developing is a community of computers similar to the complex collection of cells with the communications network tying them together in the same way as the nervous system.

COMPUTER CENTER AUTOMATION

Through the early 1980's, mainframe computing was the predominant form of computing. The common computer center had one or more large mainframe computers satisfying the requirements of hundreds or thousands of users. There was an economy of scale associated with this kind of processing. As the mainframe computers increased in speed and capacity in magnitudes of a hundred percent at a time and as the storage capacity increased at a rate of 30-40% per year, it was not reasonable for the computer center to add staffing at the same rate. Furthermore, the computer center operating environment became more complex than it had ever been before.

In order to reduce cost and human intervention and to improve the quality of computer center service, computer centers began to automate. The early automation activities were limited to automating the manual functions of the computer center such as tape management and more recently disk management. It was very difficult to manage thousands of tapes without some sort of assistance. Computer job schedulers were added to control the increasing amount of work that was processed through the mainframe computer. A wealth of other utilities were added to the computer center to improve its operation. However, the computer center was automating itself and not the user of the computer center.

In the early to mid-1980's, this changed with the introduction of the concept of unattended computer center operation. Unattended computer center operation is achieved through the concept of value added data handling, self-service computing and computer center automation. Unattended computer center is extending computer center automation to the computer center user.

Computer center automation is based on installing software that eliminates the human intervention between the computer user and the computer: (1) primary, (2) secondary and (3) support software systems.

The Primary Software Systems

The primary computer center automation software packages are the automation tools that directly interface with the computer. They consist of three software packages: the automated computer job scheduler, the automated console response system and the electronic report distribution system.

1. **Automated Computer Job Scheduler**
    The automated computer job scheduler manages the routine, daily batch computer processing schedule. The objective of the computer job scheduler is to provide computer center users with the ability to change the routine schedule or to process ad hoc work without computer center intervention. Business organizations purchasing a departmental or small business computer or a turnkey system need to make sure this is an integral function of the operating software.

2. **Automated Console Response Systems**
    The automated console response system eliminates all routine interaction between the computer operator and the computer. It is the tie that binds together most of the fifteen software packages that are used to achieve unattended computer operation. The automated console response system is the new quality assurance manager. It improves the quality of the service of the computer center by eliminating the human intervention between the application software systems and the computer and between the computer operation software and the computer.

3. **Electronic Report Distribution System**
    Electronic report distribution software manages and distributes hard-copy reports electronically. This software directs reports to a storage device rather than to a printer. Once on the storage device, it can be retained for a predefined period, viewed

and, if necessary, printed under the control of an end user. This is not a substitute for on-line query, but it is an outstanding intermediate step. It gets the computer user to begin to think in terms of the information they require rather than in terms of reports.

The Secondary Software Systems

The automated computer job scheduler, the automated console response system and the electronic report distribution systems are central to computer center automation. However, at the next level, there are four additional software systems which work closely with the primary software: security software, automated rerun/recovery systems, automated computer monitoring systems and automated problem notification.

1. **Security Systems**
    Security software operates like an umbrella over the top of all the other computer center automation tools. Security software is a prerequisite for a self-service computing environment. It enables users to access their information and software without interfering with the integrity of other users or without relying on central computer center administration. The most common security software is RACF from IBM and Top Secret from Computer Associates.

2. **Automated Rerun/Recovery Systems**
    Rerun/recovery software enables the automatic restart of batch jobs without technical support, database or computer center personnel assistance. Automated batch job restart is crucial to unattended operation. It enables automatic housekeeping so that the only intervention required is to correct the problem and resubmit the job. Batch jobs are within the control of end users; reliance on computer center staff for clean-up and restart is not consistent with the direction of computer center management. Software is available to handle these conditions, and new applications should be designed with this as a requirement.

3. **Automated System Monitors**

Interactive computer system monitors have been available for a long time. This software provides the technical services staff and computer operator with the ability to interactively monitor the performance of the computer system. Within the software, thresholds are set for computer performance and when exceeded, corrective actions can be taken. This software permits the computer operator to manage the operation of the computer. However, when the automated system monitor interacts with an automated console response system, conditions that exceed threshold can be automatically corrected through an automated response. The combination of the automated console response system and the automated system monitor offer the opportunity to automatically correct performance imbalances before they impact the computer user.

4. **Automatic Problem Notification**

Security and environmental monitoring devices are available to monitor the vital aspects of the computer center in the absence of computer room staff. Such equipment can recognize failing equipment or intrusions and phone designated staff on an exception basis using voice synthesizers. Furthermore, the devices can be queried by cautious or inquisitive management.

A similar device is available for computer systems. Messages are passed to a microcomputer based system where they are logged and filtered. Messages that require no action are ignored, and those that are defined to the system initiate a phone call to on-call support personnel. In an unattended computer center, such a device is indispensable for the correction of software failures which are sure to occur in even the best run computer center.

Support Software Systems

Achieving unattended operation requires that the power of the computer be used to manage itself. For at least a couple of decades, information technology experts have been installing automation tools in the computer center to solve independent problems. In addition to the primary and secondary software, there are many other areas where automation can be applied to the computer center. In some cases, these tools will be installed, and in others, they will need to be selected.

1. On-line Data Entry Software

Centralized data entry is an obsolete function. Recent AFCOM studies indicate that only 48% of the computer centers surveyed had a centralized data entry function. In 1984, over 90% of the computer centers had a data entry function, a decrease of almost half (42%). On-line data entry software simulates the functionality of true on-line interactive software. It provides the same opportunity as on-line software to directly enter data. The edit and update facilities are not equal to those of custom on-line update systems, but the software usually provides some logical editing (numerics, date ranges and so on). Furthermore, when on-line data entry software is used in conjunction with a report management system, it eliminates the need for hard-copy error exception reports.

2. Automated Report Balancing and Control

Automate the report balancing process. Frequently, ten or more years of effort are expended on the efficient design of application systems, and little or no effort is spent on automating the balancing process. An entire processing stream will be halted for hours or even days waiting for computer users to review and balance their system. Report balancing software should provide the ability for computer users to define balancing rules and to change them as necessary. It should automatically check and balance reports where required.

3. Library Management

Library management should be performed by the programming and technical support staff under the protection of a security package. Programming and technical support staff should move program modules into production libraries. Remember that computer center librarians do not know what a new software module can do, only that the proper forms were provided and that they had proper authorization. Using the security system as the substitute for authorization, the computer center can allow programming and technical staff to maintain their own libraries. The computer center can effectively take advantage of the security system in the same way as computer center users.

4. Disk Space Management

One of the alternatives that is becoming more and more cost effective as a trade off for tape processing is to substitute disk or direct access storage devices (DASD) for tape as permanent or temporary storage. As a result of these and other uses, the data stored on disk media are growing at a rate of 30% or more a year. This growth pattern has resulted in the increased use of disk management software to ensure that sufficient disk space is available, that it is used efficiently and that its use is not dependent on human intervention.

5. Disk Space ABEND Software

Disk space abend software stops *space-not-available* DASD abends during step initialization. These conditions are associated with disk space availability and management and arise when the IBM MVS operating system is not able to satisfy space allocations for a new dataset. These abends are found in the best run computer centers. Since they are not part of the programming staff's area of responsibility, recovery from these types of abend conditions can place a significant burden on computer center operation, technical service or database staff.

6. JCL Scan Utility

JCL continues to be a very labor-intense and error-prone activity. JCL is the source of a significant portion of the computer center's interruptions and problems. Scanning JCL for syntax errors and/or conformance with computer center standards should be part of building the computer center batch operation schedule, library maintenance and production, and test job submission. Syntax checking is part of the operating system; some automated job schedulers include it as an integral part of their software, and stand-alone software is available for scanning JCL.

7. Tape Management Systems

If the computer center has a large tape inventory, it is almost mandatory that the computer center needs to have a tape management system. Tape management software helps to improve reliability and reduce the direct labor associated with the use of this media. Furthermore, tape management systems are valuable tools for isolating the use and reducing the inventory of tape volumes. They should reduce the labor associated with tape handling, improve the quality of the retention process and assist in identifying ways to reduce tape usage. Tape is a data storage medium that is likely to be with us for a long time. Start reducing the inventory of tapes by no longer designing software systems which require tape as a processing medium.

8. Tape Dataset Stacking Utility

Tape dataset stacking software should be used in concert with tape management software. Statistics indicate that 80% of all tapes use only a few inches or feet of the tape reel. Furthermore, many tapes are backups used only in exception processing, and many of these backups use only a fraction of a tape volume. Install software to stack multiple datasets on a single reel using software. By stacking these types of tape datasets, the computer center can reduce the physical handling of tapes, reduce the volume of tape inventories, decrease off-site storage cost and improve cost containment. Stacking datasets increases the access time to retrieve them, but there is a very good chance that the tape will never be used again or, at worst, that it will be used very infrequently.

DIRECTION OF UNATTENDED COMPUTER OPERATION

Computer center automation is achieved by systematically removing all manual computer center tasks and by replacing them with automation tools. As a result of this direction, software suppliers are beginning to visualize automated computer center operation as a logical unit, and they are attempting to draw these individual software products together into a tightly integrated group of packages. Although integrated, the packages will continue to be marketed separately.

Software vendors are beginning to recognize that a truly unattended computer must operate in a self-service mode. To achieve this, the functions of the automation software packages need to be externalized, allowing the computer center user to enter their own data, to schedule their own jobs, to write their own programs, to electronically distribute their own reports, to administer their own security and to query their own data. Furthermore, all of these functions are accomplished under a security umbrella to insure that staff do not accidentally or intentionally interfere with the information of another computer user.

There is a movement toward a single image computer center automation tool as a result of a tighter integration of the different software systems. Meanwhile, central support organizations are disappearing, and the functionality of the software systems is being extended to the end users of the computer center. However, despite all the progress in both of these areas, the main thrust of all computer center operations continues to be in managing functionality of the large mainframe computers. Departmental computers, workstations, personal computers and networks are being completely ignored. It is assumed that there is no need for automation since there are so relatively few users of these computers.

The problem is very different from what is perceived by computer center management or software vendors. For example, an east coast university has two large mainframe computers and 125 to 150 departmental computers. The total computing capacity of these 125 to 150 computers exceeds the total capacity of the two large mainframe computers. Furthermore, the computing capacity of the personal computers is equal to the total capacity of all the departmental computers and the large mainframe computers.

It is not uncommon for organizations to have far more computing capacity in their network of departmental computers, workstations and personal computers than they do in the computer center. There is a drive to automate the computer center while the departmental computers, workstations and personal computers are being completely ignored. In addition, personal computers, workstations and departmental computers are being introduced with a tremendous amount of enthusiasm. The computer users see a problem that can be solved. They get closely involved with the process and install the computer with little or no additional staffing.

However, after the computer is operational, they go back to their primary job. As a result, the computer user justifies additional staff to operate the computer or oversee the network of personal computers or workstations. The departmental computer is creating a small data processing department. It starts out with one person, then two persons and then a manager. In effect, 125 to 150 departmental computers or networks can lead to the staffing of 250 to 350 people. This is more staff than would be required to manage the same amount of mainframe computing. The answer is not to go back to mainframe computing. The answer is to automate departmental computers and personal computer networks.

What is the new direction for computer center automation? The direction is to externalize the software packages installed on the mainframe onto a stand-alone computer. If it makes good business sense to schedule a single machine, then it makes equally good sense to be able to schedule across multiple computers. If it makes sense to have an automated operator on a central computer center, then it makes equally good sense to have an automated operator on the network managing multiple computers. If it makes sense to have electronic report distribution for the central computer, then the same kind of report distribution should work across the network.

The direction is to externalize the mainframe-based software to a dedicated computer on the network. This computer interacts with the other computers by responding to console messages, scheduling batch jobs, starting the computer in the morning, shutting the computer down at night and doing routine backups. The stand-alone computer eliminates the operator interaction at each of the individual computers and incorporates it into a single central machine tied into the network.

Achieving this objective will require a multi-phased approach. The first step is to externalize the functionality of the computer center operation software packages. Initially, the direction calls for a tighter integration of this software into fewer software packages and then to externalize it onto a single computer. In the first phase, the computer will operate as a peer on a network of like computers. If the network is a network of VAX computers, then the computer will handle all of the interaction with a VAX. If it is a network of Hewlett Packard or UNIX-based computers, the computer will handle all Hewlett Packard or UNIX-based computers.

In the next phase, the computer is able to do precisely the same thing with unlike vendors. Obviously, the differences between dealing with a Unisys, a Digital, an IBM, or a Hewlett Packard computer and their proprietary operating systems is considerable. The level of complexity to manage computers across hardware vendors and software vendors is significantly more complex than dealing with a single vendor.

The future of unattended operations is to eliminate all the manual operation functions from the departmental and low-end computers in the same way that those manual functions are eliminated from the mainframe computing center. Further, the next stage is to tightly integrate all the packages into a single image automation tool that is externalized from the mainframe onto a stand-alone computer. In this way, the same functionality can be provided to all levels of computers: mainframe, departmental, workstation and personal computer. The future of unattended operation is unattended network operation.

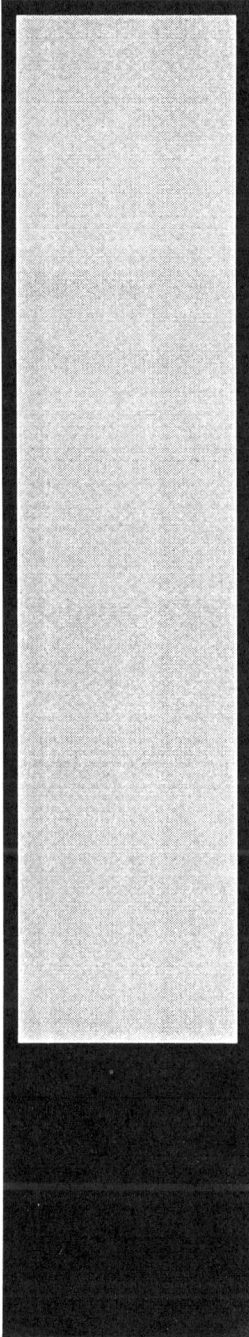

Appendix

Appendix A

Computer Center Automation Suppliers

PRIMARY COMPUTER CENTER AUTOMATION SOFTWARE

VENDOR	PRODUCT NAME
AUTOMATED COMPUTER JOB SCHEDULER	
Altai Software 624 Six Flags Drive Arlington, TX 76011 (800) 227-7774	ZEKE (VSE, VM, MVS)
Chaney Systems 2825 North Maifair Road Wauwatosa, WI 53222 (414) 774-5220	ASF (MVS) (Automated Scheduling Facility)
Computer Associates 711 Stewart Avenue Garden City, NY 11530 (800) 645-3003	CA-ADC2 (MVS) CA-Manager (MVS) CA-7 (MVS) CA-Scheduler (VSE, MVS, VM)
Cybermation 16 Esna Park Drive Markham, Ontario Canada L3R 5X1 (416) 479-4611	ESP (MVS) (Executive Scheduling Processor)

VENDOR	PRODUCT NAME
DataBase Technology Corp. 21 North Skokie Highway Lake Bluff, IL 60044 (312) 295-7590	THE BOSS (MVS)
Goal Systems International Incorporated 7965 North High Street Columbus, OH 43235 (800) 848-4640	JOBTRAC (MVS)
IBM Corporation (See local office)	Operations Planning and Control
Legent, Inc. Two Alleghany Center Pittsburgh, PA 15212 (412) 323-2600	AutoMate/MVS (MVS)
Software AG of North America 11800 Sunrise Valley Drive Reston, VA 22091 (703) 860-5050	Natural Operations Automated Production and Scheduling Control System
Software Engineering of America 2001 Marcus Avenue Lake Success, NY 11042 (516) 328-7000	CSAR (MVS, VSE, VM)
System Center, Inc. (VM Software, Inc.) 1800 Alexander Bell Drive Reston, VA (703) 264-8000	VM SCHEDULE (VM)

VENDOR	PRODUCT NAME
Tone Software Corporation 1735 South Brookhurst Anaheim, CA 92804 (800) 833-8663	CONTROL-M (MVS)

AUTOMATED CONSOLE RESPONSE SYSTEM

Alti Sofware, Inc. 624 Six Flags Drive Arlington, TX 76011 (800) 227-7774	ZACK
Bell Communications Research 290 West Mt. Pleasant Avenue Livingston, NJ 07039 (800) 521-2673	TSSO
Boole & Babbage 510 Oakmead Parkway Sunnyvale, CA 94086 (408) 735-9550	AutoOperator
Candle Corporation 1999 Bundy Drive Los Angeles, CA 90025 (213) 207-1400	AF/OPERATOR (formerly Intercept by Compucept)
CINCOM Systems, Inc. 2300 Montana Road Cincinnati, Ohio 45211 (513) 662-2300	Sys/Master
Computer Associates 711 Stewart Avenue Garden City, NY 11530 (800) 645-3003	CA-OPERA CA-OPERAIDER
Empact Software 1803 Overlake Drive Conyers, GA 30208 (404) 483-8852	WTO-Manager

VENDOR	PRODUCT NAME
Goal Systems International, Inc. 7965 North High Street Columbus, Ohio 43235 (800) 848-4640	FAQS JOBTRAC
IBM Corporation (See local office)	Netview
Infolink Software, Inc. 1400 Fashion Island Blvd. San Mateo, CA 94404 415-574-3305	Automatic Operator
Legent, Inc. Two Alleghany Center Pittsburgh, PA 15212 (412) 323-2600	AutoMate/MVS
NETEC International, Inc. P.O. Box 18538 Dallas, Texas 75218-9990 214-324-2428	Logical Console Operator
On-Line Software International, Inc. P.O. Box 2392 Princeton, NJ 08540	CICS Central
Operation Control Systems, Inc. 560 San Antonio Road Lake Success, NY 11042 (516) 328-7000	OCS/Express (HP3000)

VENDOR	PRODUCT NAME
Software AG of North America 11800 Sunrise Valley Drive Reston, VA 22091 (703) 860-5050	**Natural Console Management**
Software Engineering of America 2001 Marcus Avenue Lake Success, NY 11042 (516) 328-7000	**ODDS**
Systemetrics, Inc. 120 Appleton Street Cambridge, MA 02138 (617) 431-7555	**SENTRY/VMS (DEC VAX/VMS) SENTRY/CONSOLE (DEC VAX/VMS)**
Systems Center, Inc. 1800 Alexander Bell Drive Reston, VA 22091 (800) 562-7100	**VMOPERATOR**
Tone Software Corporation 1735 South Brookhurst Anaheim, CA 92804 (800) 833-8663	**CONTROL-M**
VOTEC Systems, Inc. 2 East Beaver Creek Road Richmond Hills, Ontario CANADA (416) 889-7977	**TIC 1000/2000** (The Intelligent Console)

ELECTRONIC REPORT DISTRIBUTION SYSTEM

Computer Associates 711 Stewart Avenue Garden City, NY 11530 (800) 645-3003	**CA-DISPATCH CA-7/REPORT**
Goal Systems International Incorporated 7965 North High Street Columbus, OH 43235 (800) 848-4640	**SAR/EXPRESS**

VENDOR	PRODUCT NAME
IBM Corporation (See local office)	**RMDS** **Report Management &** **Distribution System**
Legent, Inc. Two Alleghany Center Pittsburgh, PA 15212 (412) 323-2600	**BUNDL**
Mantissa Corporation 244 Goodwin Crest Drive Suite 200 Birmingham, AL 35209 (205) 945-8930	**RMS** Report Management Systems
Mobius Management Systems One Sheron Plaza New Rochelle, NY 10801 (914) 632-7960	**Infopac**
RSD America 100 Merrick Road Suite 500 East Building Rockville Centre, NY 11570 (516) 536-8855	**WSF2**
Software AG of North America 11800 Sunrise Valley Drive Reston, VA 22091 (703) 860-5050	Natural Report Managment
Software Engineering of **America** 2001 Marcus Avenue Lake Success, NY 11042 (516) 328-7000	**$AVRS**(JCL, SYSOUT, SYSLOG) **TRMS**
Startec Software 25-15 50th Street Woodside, NY 11377 (212) 943-9800	**Viewcom**

Systemware Incorporated   JHS-II
12770 Coit Road
Suite 1008
Dallas, Texas 75251-1306
(214) 239-0200

Tone Software   TS-RMDS
1735 South Brookhurst
Anaheim, CA 92804
(714) 991-9460

SECONDARY COMPUTER CENTER AUTOMATION SOFTWARE

VENDOR	PRODUCT NAME

SECURITY SYSTEM

Computer Associates   CA-ACF2
711 Stewart Avenue   CA-TOP SECRET
Garden City, NY 11530
(800) 645-3003

Goal Systems International   ALERT/MVS
7965 North High Street
Columbus, OH 43235
(800) 848-4640

IBM Corporation   RACF
(See local office)

AUTOMATED SYSTEM MONITOR

Candle Corporation   OMEGAMON
1999 Bundy Drive
Los Angeles, CA 90025
(213) 207-1400

AUTOMATED RERUN/RECOVERY SYSTEM

Computer Associates   CA-11
711 Stewart Avenue
Garden City, NY 11530
(800) 645-3003

OTHER COMPUTER CENTER AUTOMATION SOFTWARE

VENDOR	PRODUCT NAME
ON-LINE DATA ENTRY SOFTWARE	
ADREMS Incorporated	**ADDER**
One Hollis Street	
Wellesley, MA 02181	
(617) 235-2223	
H&M System Software, Inc.	**KEYFAST**
25 East Spring Valley Avenue	
Maywood, NJ 07607-9982	
(201) 845-3357	
International Software Technology	**ODEII**
1112 7th Avenue	
Monroe, WI 53566-1347	
(608) 328-8870	
SCS Incorporated	**Key Entry III**
2732 Seventh Avenue	
Birmingham, AL 35233	
(800) 533-6879	
TSI International	**Keymaster**
136 Summit Avenue	
Montvale, NJ 07645	
(201) 307-1580	
TAPE MANAGEMENT SYSTEMS	
Computer Associates	**CA-1**
711 Stewart Avenue	
Garden City, NY 11530	
(800) 645-3003	
TAPE DATASET STACKING UTILITY	
U.S. West	**TDSU**
3350 161st Avenue S.E.	(Tape Dataset Stacking
Belvue, WA 98008	Utility)
(206) 747-4900	

VENDOR	PRODUCT NAME

DISK SPACE ABEND SOFTWARE
Empact Software   STOPEX-37
1803 Overlake Drive
Conyers, GA 30208
(404) 483-8852

AUTOMATED REPORT BALANCING AND CONTROL
UNITEC Systems, Inc.   U/ACR
3030 Warrenville Road
Lisle, IL 60532
(312) 506-1800

COMPUTER CENTER AUTOMATION HARDWARE

VENDOR	PRODUCT NAME

MONITOR/NOTIFICATION SYSTEM
VOTEK   TIC-1000
Two East Beaver Creek Road   TIC-2000
Richmond Hills, Ontario
CANADA L4B 2N3
(416) 889-7977

AUTOMATED TAPE LIBRARY (ATL)
Storage Technology Corp.   StorageTek 4480
Louisville, CO 80028-4385   (Automated Cartridge
(303) 673-5151   System)

Memorex Telex Corporation   Memorex Telex 5400
6422 East 41st Street   (Automated Tape Library)
Tulsa, OK 74135
(918) 627-1111

MASS STORAGE DEVICE
Masstor Systems Corporation   Masstor System
5200 Great America Parkway   M960/M1000
Santa Clara, CA 95052-8017
(408) 988-1008

VENDOR	PRODUCT NAME

OPTICAL DISK

Data/Ware Development, Inc.   DW 34800 Optical Storage
9449 Carroll Park Drive   Subsystem
San Diego, CA 92121
(619) 453-7660

Filenet Corporation   Filenet Optical Library
3565 Harbor Boulevard
Costa Mesa, CA 92626
(714) 966-3400

IBM Corporation   Imageplus
(See local office)

COMPUTER CENTER AUTOMATION SERVICES

VENDOR	PRODUCT NAME

CONSULTING

COMTECH Inc.   George Kurtz
1141 Tamack Lane
Libertyville, IL 60048
(312) 362-6784

Farber/LaChance   Arnold Farber
P.O. Box 26611   Rosemary LaChance
Richmond, VA 23261
(804) 746-9113

KPMG Peat Marwick   Mark Levin
One Boston Place
Boston, MA 02108
(617) 723-7700

SEI   Al Coleman
470 Totten Pond Road
Waltham, MA 02154
(617) 890-2110

VENDOR	PRODUCT NAME
EDUCATION	
ACTS Corporation 101 Highway 281 Suite 301 Marble Falls, TX 78654 (800) 950-ACTS	Bill Carico
The Information Technology Institute 136 Orchard Street Byfield, MA 01922 (617) 353-4648	Howard W. Miller

Suggested Readings

___. *Getting Started In Automating Computer Center Operations:* Sunnyvale: CA, Boole & Babbage, 1988.

Allen, Leilani E. "Data Center Automation: Management Issues." *Boolean World*. (Fall 1988): 7-10.

Bennett, J. W. "A Biased Perspective (Automated Job Scheduling)." *Technical Support Magazine,* (February 1988): 20-21.

Bryce, Milt and Bryce, Tim. "Make or Buy Software." *Journal Of Systems Management*. (August 1987): 6-11.

Cooper, Gary. "The User's View (Automated Job Scheduling)." *Technical Support Magazine*. (February 1988): 50-52.

Coticchia, Greg. "Automation: A Management Discussion." *The Mainframe Journal*. (November/December 1988): 88-93.

Daily, James. "Electronic Vaulting Catches On." *Computerworld:* XXII, no. 51, (December 19, 1988): 21-26.

Hart, Christopher W. L. "The Power Of The Unconditional Service Guarantees." *Harvard Business Review*. (July/August 1988): 54-62.

Hirth, Raymond C. "Job Scheduling and Resource Management." *Technical Support Magazine*. (February 1988): 47-48.

Kador, John. "What's Ahead for Automated Job Scheduling." *Technical Support Magazine*. (February 1988): 16-19.

Kador, John. "Who's On First." *Datacenter Manager*. (March/April 1988): 19-24.

Kador, John, "VMOPERATOR: Putting Muscle Into the VM Operator Console." *The Mainframe Journal*, (November/ December 1988): 100-103.

Kurtz, George. "Operations," *The Computer Operations Manager*. (September/October 1988): 15-21.

Kurtz, George. "The 'Master Plan' — A Conceptual Overview." *The Computer Operations Manager*. (November/December 1988): 10-19.

Lalonde, John. "Execution Scheduling Processor," *Technical Support Magazine*. (February 1988): 60-62.

McClung, John. "The Systems Programmer's View (Automated Job Scheduling)." *Technical Support Magazine*. (February 1988): 60-62.

Miller, Howard W. "20 Tips for Unattended Operations" *Datacenter Manager*. (March/April 1989): 54-59.

Miller, Howard W. "Assessing Your Security Risk Index." *Technical Support Magazine*. (January 1989):35-40.

Miller, Howard W. "Automated Computer Job Scheduling Systems: How to Select and What to Expect." *The Computer Operations Manager*. (March/April 1989): 12-25.

Miller, Howard W. "Automating the Computer Center." *Technical Support Magazine*. (March 1989): 44-49.

Miller, Howard W. "Disaster Recovery Planning." *Journal Of Systems Management*. (March, 1986): 25-30.

Miller, Howard W. "Electronic Report Distribution." *The Mainframe Journal*. (September/October): 74-81.

Miller, Howard W. "End Users Drive Benefit Analysis." *Computerworld*. (August, 10 1987): 59-62.

Miller, Howard W. "The Human Side of Automated Operations." *The Computer Operations Manager*. (January/February 1989): 36-44.

Miller, Howard W. "Implementing Unattended Computer Center Operation" *Technical Support Magazine* (September 1988): 24-31.

Miller, Howard W. "The Information Technology Cost Containment Checklist." *The Mainframe Journal*. (March/April 1988): 75-95.

Miller, Howard W. "Planning for Unattended Data Center Operation." *Mainframe Journal*. (January/February 1988): 10-87.

Miller, Howard W. "The Tie That Binds: Automated Console Response." *Technical Support Magazine*. (September 1988): 24-31.

Miller, Howard W. "The Rationale For Unattended Computer Center Operation." *Computer Associates Dialog*. (June 1989): 1-6.

Miller, Howard W. "Rethinking Computer Center Design," *Technical Support Magazine*. (April 1989): 41-71.

Miller, Howard W. "Unattended Computer Center Operation: 50 Questions and Answers." (*The Mainframe Journal*, April 1989): 58-89.

Miller, Howard W. "Unraveling The Purchased Software Dilema," *Technical Support Magazine*. (June 1989): 50-53.

Stahl, Bob. "Testing for Usability Can Head Off Disaster." *Computerworld*. (December 7, 1988): 83-92.

van Kinsberger, Jack. "Automated Operations Opens The Door To A New Era of Distributed Data Processing." *Boolean World*. (Fall 1988): 3-4.

Williams, James P. "Automated Job Scheduling: Avoiding the Cobbler's Children' Syndrome." The Mainframe Journal, (November/December 1987): 10-15.

Glossary

Glossary of Unattended Computer Center Terminology

ACM: Active Cross reference Module — the impact analysis feature of the PREDICT data dictionary from Software AG. ACM has the ability to perform impact analysis for NATURAL programs stored using ACM.

ADABAS: Mainframe database management system marketed by Software AG. (See IDMS and IMS).

ADABAS SECURITY: This security software package protects ADABAS files, fields and values through the ADABAS file passwords. It is a product of Software AG.

ADC2 (CA-ADC2): ADC2 is the automated batch job scheduling system for IBM mainframe computers to schedule and control batch computer processing, marketed by Computer Associates, Inc.

ADF: Application Development Facility; IBM product, series of programs for developing on-line facilities under IMS/DB.

ADRS: A Departmental Reporting System; a user friendly language designed for direct use by the business professional.

AESTHETICS: One of the eight dimensions of quality. A subjective dimension of information technology quality. Aesthetics is the appearance of the software system. It typically means something different to computer users, management and technicians.

AF/OPERATOR: Automated computer job scheduler marketed by Candle Corporation.

ALPHA TEST: The first phase of software testing by the user.

313

APAS: APAS is a software product that runs transparently inside of ADABAS and provides ADABAS utilization information. APAS is especially useful for identifying performance degradation sources.

APEX: Automated Planning and Execution Control System; used by a computer center to submit jobs to be run for production, supported by Computer Associates, Inc. (no longer actively marketed).

APL: A Programming Language; a user friendly language designed for financial applications.

ARCHIVAL: Storage of inactive database information on a less expensive medium, usually tape.

ARTIFICIAL INTELLIGENCE: A field of computer science that has as its prime focus the modeling of human behavior with computer programs. The field covers the development of theories of brain or mind functioning and advanced computer technology to implement the implications of these theories. In business, it is usually associated with expert systems.

ASF: Automated computer job scheduling system marketed by Chaney Systems, Inc.

AUTO-OPERATOR: Automatic console response system marketed by Boole and Babbage, Inc.

AUTOMATED COMPUTER JOB SCHEDULING SYSTEM: A software system for managing the routine daily batch processing schedule. In an unattended computer center, the functions of this software product are given to the computer user.

AUTOMATED CONSOLE RESPONSE SYSTEM: A software system that eliminates all routine operator responses to the operating system. It is the software that ties together the multiple software packages required to automate the computer center.

AUTOMATED RERUN/RECOVERY SYSTEM: A software system that automates rerun/recovery of batch jobs without technical support, database or computer center personnel support.

AUTOMATED SYSTEM MONITOR: A software system that provides the ability to set thresholds for performance and interactively monitor performance.

AUTOMATE: Automatic console response system marketed by Duquesne Systems, Inc.

AUTOMATIC TAPE LIBRARY: ATL are cartridge tape picking systems that reduce or eliminate the labor required to pick and load tapes. The two most common systems are the StorageTek 4480 and the Memorex Telex 5400.

BACKUP SITE: One or more hardware facilities or computer centers that can successfully process the critical applications of the primary site.

BATCH PROCESSING: A computer processing technique in which data to be processed or programs to be executed are grouped to permit convenient, efficient serial processing.

BATCH JOB SCHEDULE: Manual or automated technique for managing the routine daily batch computer processing schedule. In an unattended computer center, the scheduling functions are returned to the computer user.

BETA TEST: The final phase of software testing by the user before its official release.

BUILT IN QUALITY: The process of identifying errors in the system and systematically isolating the cause and correcting the error at the source.

BUSINESS INTERRUPTION INSURANCE: Business interruption insurance is replacement coverage for income lost as a result of a business interruption. It also covers the incremental cost of activities required to restore full service to the business. Typically, this insurance is relatively inexpensive.

CA-ACF2: Computer data security software package marketed by Computer Associates, Inc.

CA-ADC2: ADC2 is the automated batch job scheduling system for IBM mainframe computers to schedule and control batch computer processing, marketed by Computer Associates, Inc.

CA-DISPATCH: Electronic report distribution system marketed by Computer Associates, Inc.

CA-OPERA: Automatic console response system marketed by Computer Associates, Inc.

CA-SCHEDULER: Automated computer job scheduling system marketed by Computer Associates, Inc.

CA-1: Tape management system marketed by Computer Associates, Inc.

CA-7: An automated scheduler software package marketed by Computer Associates, Inc.

CA-7 REPORT: Electronic report distribution associated with CA-7 system marketed by Computer Associates, Inc.

CA-8: Problem/Change Management software marketed by Computer Associates, Inc.

CA-11: An automated rerun/recovery system marketed by Computer Associates, Inc.

CASE TECHNOLOGY: Computer Assisted Software Engineering: a highly flexible automated software development environment.

CATALOG: A catalog is a special system dataset that contains critical information about all user datasets in the system. There are several catalogs arranged in a hierarchical manner. Information such as the physical location of the data is maintained in the catalog.

CBT: Computer Based Training.

CBX: Central Branch Exchange; telephone switching system.

CHANNEL ATTACHED: Channel attached means that this particular device is connected directly to a mainframe computer channel using high speed channel cables. This is in contrast to an attachment via a telephone line or coax. Channel attachment allows devices to transfer data at extremely fast and efficient rates.

CICS: CICS is an IBM product. It is a teleprocessing or TP monitor. A TP monitor is the program which must be running to allow an on-line function to work. It handles the communication of data from the on-line programs to the database.

CODE GENERATOR: A software system that takes pseudo-code or parameter statements and converts them into a common programming language such as COBOL.

COM-PLETE: The On-line teleprocessing monitor developed, marketed and supported by Software AG.

COMPLIANCE INDEX: A compliance index is determined by the maximum score into the actual score for an item being evaluated. The higher the value, the greater the level of compliance.

CONFIGURATION: Description of the computer hardware components and features and how they are connected.

CONFORMANCE: One of the eight dimensions of quality. This is the most commonly perceived dimension of quality. It is the degree to which the software conforms to the requirements of the computer user.

CONTINGENCY PLAN: The document that contains all the pre- and post-implementation procedures for the recovery from a computer center interruption. Sometimes this document is referred to as disaster recovery plan.

CONTROL-M: Automated computer job scheduling system marketed by Tone Software Corporation.

COOPERATIVE PROCESSING: Cooperative processing is a computing concept that is neither centralized nor distributed processing, but something in between. The concept calls for centralized data storage but processing distributed over multiple machines: centralized data and decentralized computing.

CPU: Central Processing Unit; a term usually equated with a mainframe computer.

DARK ROOM OPERATION: An approach to computer center automation where equipment that does not require human intervention such as the CPU, DASD and communications are clustered into a dark room environment.

DASD (Direct Access Storage Device): DASD is an acronym for the disk drives that are used by data centers to store data.

DATABASE: A collection of interrelated data items processible by one or more application systems. The database permits common data to be integrated and shared between the functional units of a company.

DATA CENTER: The main or central processing site, usually referred to as the computer center or primary site.

DATA ENTRY SOFTWARE: A mainframe based software system that provides the information originator with the opportunity to enter information directly into the computer without transcribing the information onto paper forms.

DATASETS: A dataset is a uniquely named group of data that resides on DASD or on a magnetic tape. The dataset is known by a 44 character dataset name. There can be several different types of datasets, depending on the type of use.

DBA: Database Administration/Administrator(s): database administration has four primary roles: to ensure database integrity, to perform database maintenance, to establish standards, and to process and develop productivity tools.

DEVELOPMENT METHODOLOGY: A structured architecture for developing computer-based software systems.

DISASTER: The inability to operate and maintain critical and secondary systems for one week beyond the original schedule.

DISASTER RECOVERY PLAN: The document that contains all the pre- and postimplementation procedures for the recovery from a computer center disaster. Sometimes this document is referred to as contingency Plan.

DISK SPACE MANAGEMENT: A software system for the management of direct access storage. It automates the decision to migrate or archive information from DASD to a more cost effective device such as tape or mass storage.

DISTRIBUTED COMPUTING: Local computing in one or more end user computing centers. Typically, such centers maintain local data files as well as files that are a subset of master files with the latter being maintained at a central data center. Distributed data centers are usually networked together via a communications network.

DRM: Data Resource Management manages data resources such as business data and related Information systems data and programs in support of business objectives. DRM provides services in three areas — data administration, database administration, and data security administration.

DSA: Data Security Administration: the two primary roles of data security administration are to ensure all users of the computer center have appropriate access to their information to perform business functions and to develop, maintain and ensure adherence to the information protection policy.

DURABILITY: One of the eight dimensions of quality. A measure of the life expectancy of a software system.

80/20 RULE: 80 percent of the improvement comes from 20 percent of the effort.

ELECTRONIC FORMS AUTHORIZATION: A software system to authorize the processing of information through on-line systems without the use of a paper-based document and numerous authorization steps.

ELECTRONIC MAIL: A software system to send electronic messages from one terminal to another or from one computer to another. A paper message replacement.

ELECTRONIC REPORT DISTRIBUTION: A software system to electronically manage and distribute hard-copy reports. The software directs reports to a database that is computer user managed and the reports are viewed electronically at a computer terminal.

ELECTRONIC VAULTING: The ability to electronically store DASD backups and historical information off-site and to retrieve them electronically.

ESP: Automated computer job scheduler marketed by Cybermation.

FEATURES: One of the eight dimensions of quality. Features is similar in nature and closely related to performance. It is the "bells and whistles" of the software system. The features are added to the software system after the basic requirements are satisfied.

FOURTH GENERATION LANGUAGE: An easy to use, non-procedural computer user oriented programming language to improve the productivity of both computer users and computer professionals.

GDS (Generation Dataset): A method of cataloging files.

HARDWARE: The physical computing equipment, that is CPU, Tape Drive, Disk Drive, Terminal, etc.

HELICAL SCAN RECORDING: A high density magnetic tape recording method most frequently used for video recording. Data is store diagonally on a tape versus the longitudinal recording used on on IBM 3420 04 3480 tapes. In helical scanning the read/write head rotates and the tape moves over the head much slower than conventional longitudinal tape.

IBM 3420 TAPE DRIVES: IBM reel to reel tape drive subsystem.

IBM 3480 TAPE DRIVES: IBM cartridge tape drive replacement of the 3420 tape drive subsystem.

IBM 7171: An IBM 7171 is a channel attached control unit that provides protocol conversion for ASCII devices to 3270.

Protocol conversion allows a non-IBM terminal to access applications as if they were real IBM terminals.

IBM 9370: Departmental computer that uses the same architecture as the 3090 AND 4300 computers to leverage software developed for mainframe computers.

IC (Information Center): Under the direction of MIS, this department is used to train personnel in the use of user friendly languages and hardware.

IDMS: Mainframe database management system marketed by Cullinet (See **ADABAS** and **IMS**).

IMS: Information Management System; an IBM program product for IBM that then assists the computer user in implementing teleprocessing and batch type data processing applications that examine and maintain large centralized information files. (See ADABAS and IDMS).

INFO-PAC: Electronic report distribution system marketed by Mobius Management System.

INITIATOR: A logical vehicle which introduces a job to the system and allows a job to begin processing on the computer.

INSPECTED QUALITY: The process of identifying an error in the system, correcting the error in each instance and delivering the product.

IPL (Initial Program Load): The loading of the programs necessary for the running of the computer system.

IPO (Installation Productivity Option): a tape that contains a description of the operating system and all of its options. It also contains the JCL and running instructions for the base system, plus instructions and sample programs/databases to test each feature as it is added to the system.

JCL (Job Control Language): JCL is a set of 80 character records that must be prepared to run a job or program on our system. A job can be the execution of one or more programs arranged in a serial fashion. One uses JCL to describe which programs will be run in what sequence, and what datasets (tape or DASD) will be required as input or output for each program.

JHS-II: Electronic report distribution system marketed by Systemware, Inc.

JOB/JOBSTREAM: A batch program or series of batch programs.

JOBTRAC: Automated computer job scheduler marketed by Bennett Software.

LAN (Local Area Network): A LAN is a very high speed network that connects computers and terminals that are generally in the same geographical area.

LIGHTS-OUT OPERATION: An approach to unattended computer operation that clusters computer processing into a "lights-out" period (usually the third shift or weekends), and the computer center is operated unattended during that period.

LIBRARIAN: Program Management and Security System; the central storage medium for source programs, card image files, JCL, etc., marketed by Computer Associates, Inc.

MASS STORAGE SYSTEMS: High density storage device that stores data using helical scan technology to store data on cartridges that are picked using robotics. The most common device is the Masstor Systems M860, M960 and the M1000.

MASTER CATALOG: A catalog that contains a predefined list of names or prefixes that identify files to the operating system.

MEG (Megabyte): One million characters. A method of measuring the storage capability of a disk or other electronic storage media.

MICROFICHE SYSTEM: A photographic storage medium for printed data that compresses multiple pages of printed output on a single fiche for convenient, compact, long term storage.

MIPS: Millions of Instructions Per Second; a measure of a CPU's power.

MFS (Message Format Services): A series of programs used to define the format of a terminal screen to an application program.

MIS: Management Information Services.

MODEM: A piece of equipment that translates computer language into telephone language.

MVS (Multiple Virtual Storage): MVS is the IBM operating system for 370 type architecture computers (3090, 4300). Most systems use MVS X/A or ESA (the X/A stands for extended architecture and ESA for extended system architecture). The operating system is used to interface user programs with the hardware, and to allow hundreds of programs to run on the computer simultaneously.

NATURAL: A 4th generation user friendly, English type programming language for accessing the data in the ADABAS database. It is developed, marketed, and supported by Software AG.

NATURAL SECURITY: The security software package which protects NATURAL program access to ADABAS data through user, file and application profiles. Users via on-line and batch NATURAL applications are prevented from unauthorized data access. It is developed, marketed, and supported by Software AG.

NCP: Network Control Program.

NETVIEW: An automated network manager and console response system marketed by IBM.

OFF-SITE STORAGE SITE: A secure facility, other than the facility housing the primary computer center, that is close to the backup and which accommodates the backup of critical data and software.

OMEGAMON: A software display monitor for the MVS Operating System; This includes data on jobs, TSO, CPU usage, paging, swapping, etc., marketed by Candle, Inc.

ON-LINE: A computer system that performs transaction processing using its direct-access processing capabilities and on-line input/output and direct access storage devices.

ON-LINE DATA STORAGE: This is information storage: database, VSAM or flat files used to store information.

OPERAIDER: Automated console response system marketed by Computer Associates, Inc.

OPTICAL DISK: A computer storage device that stores information as marks on a recording surface that is sensitive to a given laser light wavelength. The devices are classified as read only, write once/read many times (WORM) and fully erasable.

OPERATING DATA STORAGE: This is storage for the operating software, teleprocessing monitor and all of the support software.

PANVALET: Program Management and Security System; the

central storage medium for source programs, card image files, JCL, etc., marketed by Pansophics, Inc.

PBX (Private Branch Exchange): Private telephone exchanges such as Rolm, AT&T.

PDS (Partitioned Dataset): Dataset on disk, divided into partitions called members, each of which can contain a program or other data.

PERCEIVED QUALITY: One of the eight dimensions of quality. The complexity of software systems acts as a barrier to computer users having an in depth understanding of the features of software systems. Over time, computer users develop a perception of the software system. Unfortunately, in many cases, it is negative.

PEOPLELESS COMPUTER CENTER: Another name for unattended computer center operation or operating the computer center twenty-four hours a day, seven days a week with no human intervention.

PERFORMANCE: One of the eight dimensions of quality. Performance is the primary operating characteristic of a software system. It covers such diverse aspects of software systems such as the expected response time for on-line systems, the turnaround time for batch oriented systems, the ability to operate batch and on-line portions of the system simultaneously and so on.

PERIPHERALS: A device or unit connected to a CPU, such as a tape or disk drive.

PERSONAL COMPUTING: End user computing consisting of such applications as spreadsheets, word processing and fourth generation language programming used on a central processor, distributed computing system or personal computer. This is a largely unregulated activity in most companies.

PORT CHART: A layout of the addresses assigned to a control unit that shows what equipment is attached at each address.

PREDICT: A data dictionary developed, marketed, and supported by Software AG. Predict is used to record information about data and application systems. It is an active controller of standards for both the operational and development database activities with direct user participation.

PROBLEMS-OUT OPERATION: An approach to unattended

computer center operation that reduces dependency on human intervention in the computer center through the installation of automation tools and the elimination of computer center operation problems by isolating the problem and correcting it at the source. It has as its goal the gradual but continuous decrease in the number of people required to operate the computer center.

PRODUCTION: The processing environment for computer jobs and programs that have passed acceptance test. Processing is usually performed under the control of a production scheduler.

PRODUCTION SCHEDULER: The same as automatic job scheduler or batch job scheduler.

PROFESSIONAL OBSOLESCENCE: The concept that technology is making professional jobs obsolete and that professionals need to continue to develop technically and professionally or be bypassed. It is suggested that in the future professionals will make three or more career changes because of professional obsolescence.

PRUDENT MAN RULE: Requires that officers, directors and agents of organizations discharge their duties with the diligence and care that ordinary, prudent men would exercise under similar circumstances.

PSB MAP: A listing of a database(s) physical and/or logical relationships as used by an application program.

PTF: Program Temporary Fix; software modifications from a vendor to temporarily repair a program until the permanent fix (SMP) can be applied. PTF's are submitted by a technical services group.

RACF: Computer data security software package marketed by IBM.

RELIABILITY: One of the eight dimensions of quality. This dimension reflects the probability that the software will work correctly when it is required, that response time will be adequate or that the content of the data is correct.

REPORT BALANCING AND CONTROL: A software system to automatically check and balance reports. It provides computer users with the ability to define balancing rules and change them as necessary.

RESTORE: To bring a database or dataset back to a former state by copying it from a tape or disk file.

RETENTION PERIOD: A specific identified length of time for retaining critical data.

RETRIEVAL: Systematic loading of critical data files from the off-site storage area onto the backup computer.

RJE (Remote Job Entry Facility): Allows batch jobs to be submitted into an IBM computer from a remote sit.

RMDS: Electronic report distribution system marketed by IBM.

SAR/EXPRESS: Electronic report distribution system marketed by JCA Software, Inc.

SECURITY SOFTWARE: A software system that operates as an umbrella over all of the other computer center automation tools. It enables the computer user to access their information without interfering with the integrity of other users' information.

SECURITY AND ENVIRONMENT MONITORING: Hardware and software that recognizes unauthorized intrusions, failing systems or failing hardware and phones designated support staff on an exception basis using a voice synthesizer.

SERVICEABILITY: One of the eight dimensions of quality. Serviceability is the ease with which a software system can be repaired or modified.

SMF (Systems Management Facility): SMF is an IBM supplied facility to produce trace and information records in a standard format. IBM supplies several dozen different types of SMF records that each record different events that occur inside the computer as well as summary information about the machine and software environment. User programs can also use SMF to record information.

SMP (System Modification Program): Maintenance to the system software provided by a vendor to correct errors or add enhancements and applied by Technical Services.

SNA: System Network Architecture.

SOFTWARE: Programs written by the equipment vendor that drive the hardware or user written programs that process and/or generate specific information in either electronic or hard copy paper format.

SPF (System Productivity Facility): A user friendly language working with TSO to provide on-line editing and data entry capabilities, predefined commands and screens for the MIS staff.

SPREADSHEET: Usually refers to an electronic spreadsheet or a software product that supports the addition of numbers across rows and down columns (LOTUS or Excel).

STOPX-37: Disk space abend avoidance software marketed by Empact Software.

SVC (Supervisor Call): An SVC is a special system service routine that is extremely fast and complex. SVC calls generally request services that are machine, device or product dependant.

SYSGEN: A process by which the IMS or MVS user describes items such as databases, application programs, and terminals that make up the IMS or MVS system. Prepared and submitted by Technical Services.

TAPE DATASET STACKING: A software system that stacks multiple datasets on a single tape to increase the utilization of the physical tape and to reduce the number of tapes in a tape library.

TAPE MANAGEMENTA SYSTEM: Series of programs that maintain information about each magnetic tape, such as creation date, label information, expiration date, and so on.

TCP/IP (telecommunication protocol/internetwork protocol): A specific type of protocol (set of communication rules and regulations) that computers can use to communicate over a LAN.

TDSU: Tape dataset stacking utility marketed by U.S. West.

TECHNICAL SERVICES: The programmers responsible for maintaining the operating software on a mainframe computer; the systems programmers.

TELE-COMMUNICATION NETWORK: Communications network linking either terminals to a processing center or linking computer together. They may be Local Area Networks (LAN), Wide Area Networks (WAN) or vendor standards such as IBM's SNA.

TELE-PROCESSING: This is the process of entering transactions from a terminal that examines and/or updates a database.

TELE-PROCESSING MONITOR: Teleprocessing monitors are software packages that allow software to process on-line transactions on a batch-oriented machine. The common TP Monitors are CICS, IMS, COM-PLETE and TSO.

TEST: Environment under which program development and maintenance are performed.

TEXT EDITOR: A software system to facilitate the entry and change management of program code and text into the computer (WYLBUR, ROSCOE, TSO/E).

TIC-2000: An automated console response system that resides on a personal computer It reads and filters filters out console messages and has an auto-call facility to call support staff under pre-specified conditions.

TIME DEPENDENT STORAGE: DASD storage. Storage that needs to be on-line, requires a short response time and has very high utilization.

TIME INDEPENDENT STORAGE: High density storage such as mass storage. Storage that needs to be on-line but where response time requirements do not need to be instantaneous and data volumes are high.

TMS (Tape Management System): A series of programs that maintain information about each magnetic tape, such as creation date, label information, expiration date, etc. The acronym TMS is associated with CA-1, TMS a software product marketed by Computer Associates, Inc.

TOP SECRET: Top Secret is the umbrella security software package that provides authorized access control and protection to facilities and resources. It uses a profile method of authorized access and maintains a comprehensive audit trail of all accesses and violations in both the on-line and batch environment. Top Secret is marketed by Computer Associates, Inc.

TOWER OF BABEL EFFECT: Using multiple programming languages in a computer center and developing dependence on programming efficiency with one language while not knowing how to use another.

TRANSITORY STORAGE: Tape storage. It is a one time medium used to transport information into and out of the computer center, and it is typically used to store high volumes of information.

TS-RMDS: Electronic report distribution system marketed by Tone Software, Inc.

TSO (Time Sharing Option): A user friendly language designed to allow multiple users to use the facilities of the system concurrently and in a conversational manner.

TSO/E (Time Sharing Option/Extended): TSO is an IBM on-line system that is used by some areas in UIS. TSO/E is an enhanced version of TSO that provides interactive assembler debug and full screen shell processing.

U/ACR: Automatic Report balancing and control software to balance and control batch financial reports marketed by Unitech.

UNATTENDED COMPUTER OPERATION: Totally automated operation of all computer center functions, a dark room operation where the computer is operated twenty-four hours a day, seven days a week without human intervention.

UPS (Uninterruptable Power Supply): A machine that provides power protection in the event utility power is lost.

USER FRIENDLY: A computer language designed to be used by personnel who are not data processing professionals.

USER VISCOUS: The opposite of user friendly; a computer hardware or software that requires considerable technical knowledge to use or is very difficult to use.

VALUE ADDED DATA HANDLING: The processing of information in a manner where the information is only handled by those individuals that add value to the information. The concept supports direct data entry by computer users.

VIEWCOM: Electronic report distribution system marketed by Startec Software, Inc.

VOLUME: A volume is the physical unit that contains data. An example is a tape volume, or a DASD volume.

VS: Virtual Storage.

VSAM: An IBM access method that permits direct access to information stored on disk storage by using an index. It is the logical successor to ISAM.

VTAM (Virtual Telecommunications Access Method): VTAM is an IBM product and set of protocols that must be used to write data to and from terminals in the system. Programs typically issue commands such as READ or WRITE which are translated someplace along the line to fairly complex VTAM commands and control areas. The most significant feature of VTAM is the ability for any terminal to use different on-line communication monitors (such as Com-Plete and CICS). VTAM also provides considerable operator control over the terminals in the network.

VTOC (Volume Table Of Contents): A list of all the data on a set of disk drives.

WATS (Wide Area Telephone System): A long distance telephone service offered by AT&T.

WEIGHT: A multiplying factor used to increase the value of an item or requirement under evaluation. The value of the weight depends upon the importance of a requirement. The higher the value the more important (usually 1 to 5 or 1 to 10).

WORKING STORAGE: Reusable storage that is used by the computer to support on-line or batch production performance. It includes such storage as page-swap datasets, spool datasets, temporary datasets and so on.

WORM (Write Once — Read Many): Usually refers to optical disk where data can be read many times but can only be written once.

WSF2 (Writer Scanning Facility 2): An automated Report Management Distribution System marketed by Rogers Software Distribution (RSD) America.

WTO-OPERATOR: Automatic console response system marketed by Impact Software, Inc.

WYLBUR: WYLBUR is an on-line editor that provides full screen text editing, job submission and job retrieval. WYLBUR is used to develop programs and documentation.

ZEKE: Automated computer job scheduling system marketed by Altai Software, Inc.

Index

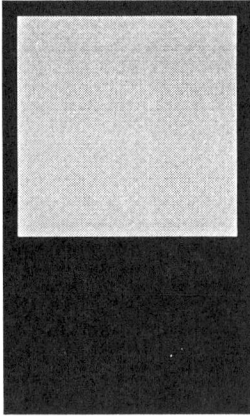

Index

Direct Access Storage Devices
(DASD), 13, 134, 155, 186
direct input, 254
disaster recovery contingency
plan, 94, 140
disk space ABEND, 50
disk space ABEND software,
187, 288
disk space management, 13,
186, 288
documentation storage 95
Duquesne, 162
durability, 30
DW 34800 optical storage subsystem, 130

E

Eight Dimensions of Quality,
27
80-20 rule, 31
elapsed time, 48
electrical power, 152
electrical problems, 257
electronic cash registers, 9
electronic data processing
(EDP) auditor, 107
electronic forms authorization,
44, 258
electronic mail, 14, 44, 228, 258
electronic report, 98
electronic report distribution,
xv, 46
electronic report distribution
system, 180, 284
electronic storage bin system,
72

electronic vault, 94
electronic vaulting, xiii, 78, 139,
155
eliminate print, 70
empty shell, 90
encryption, 85
encryption policy, 84
environmental monitoring, 6
equipment vendor agreement,
90
evaluation, 86
Excel, 111, 213
extended outage, 87

F

Faber/LaChance Consultants,
8
fault point, ix, 7, 44, 67
filenet corporation, 130
fire, 257
fire protection, 151
features, 28
4GL's, 163

G

Gartner Group, 5

H

halo effects, 167
hang condition, 207
hardware, 6
help desks, 5, 48, 76